Glory and Terror

SEVEN DEATHS UNDER THE FRENCH REVOLUTION

Glory and Terror

SEVEN DEATHS UNDER THE FRENCH REVOLUTION

BY ANTOINE DE BAECQUE

TRANSLATED BY CHARLOTTE MANDELL

ROUTLEDGE

NEW YORK • LONDON

Published in 2001 by
Routledge
29 West 35th Street
New York, NY 10001

Published in Great Britain by
Routledge
11 New Fetter Lane
London EC4P 4EE

Routledge is an imprint of the Taylor & Francis Group.

Glory and Terror: Seven Deaths under the French Revolution was originally published in French in 1997 under the title *La gloire et l'effroi: Sept morts sous la Terreur*. Copyright © 1997 Éditions Grasset & Fasquelle

Assistance for the translation was provided by the French Ministry of Culture.

Library of Congress Cataloging-in-Publication Data
Baecque, Antoine de
[Gloire et l'effroi. English]
Glory and terror : seven deaths under the French Revolution / by Antoine de Baecque ; translated by Charlotte Mandell.
p. cm.
Includes bibliographical references and index.
ISBN 0-415-92616-5 (hardbound)
1. France—History—Reign of Terror, 1793–1794—Psychological aspects. 2. Death—Psychological aspects—History—18th century. 3. Martyrs—France—Bibliography. 4. Body, human— Symbolic aspects—France—History—18th century. I. Title.

DC183.5.B2713 2001
944.04'4'0922—dc21 00-064030

Printed in the United States of America on acid-free paper.

10 9 8 7 6 5 4 3 2 1

Contents

Introduction
Sublime Abjection: The Ascendancy of Corpses 1

Mirabeau; or, The Spectacle of a Public Corpse........15

Voltaire; or, The Body of the Philosopher King........37

The Princesse de Lamballe; or, Sex Slaughtered........61

Louis XVI; or, The Sacred Remains........87

Geffroy; or, The Fear of Others........121

Robespierre; or, The Terrible Tableau........145

Madame Necker; or, The Poetry of the Corpse........175

Author's Acknowledgments........205

Notes........207

Index........235

Pierre-Narcisse Guérin, *The Death of Brutus.* Oil on canvas. Musée de la Révolution Française, Vizille, France. Courtesy of the Musée de la Révolution Française, Vizille.

Introduction

SUBLIME ABJECTION: THE ASCENDANCY OF CORPSES

> From ten half-overturned carriages there fell slowly, and with a muffled sound, into a wide, deep ditch, naked corpses, bleeding, still steaming, headless. I thought I was having one of those visions that tormented Orestes. Ten or twelve children, the oldest of whom did not seem to me to have reached his fourteenth year, were pointing out to each other, among all these bloody torsos, the ones that bore some deformities, the ones that, sliding from the carriages into the ditch, took an attitude that recalled to their already corrupt imagination lewd ideas. . . . They laughed, they made loud jokes, without shame and without fear.
>
> —Amaury Duval, *Des sépultures*

On April 3, 1793, the (formerly Royal) Academy of Painting chose the death of Brutus as the subject for the competition for its Grand Prize.[1] The subject is surprising. For if certain events in the life of Lucius Junius Brutus, a tutelary figure thanks to his virtue and his austerity, are famous in the eighteenth century, his death, on the other hand, remains an obscure episode in the Roman histories.[2] The men of the Enlightenment—Voltaire with his drama, Jacques-Louis David with his painting—admired Brutus as the avenger of Lucretia, expelling from Rome the Tarquins, that criminal family installed on the throne. Brutus too was the man who placed law above everything, the consul of the Roman Republic sacrificing his own sons and handing them over to the executioner because they had conspired against the general interest. "What struck peoples' minds above all else," writes Livy, "is that his function of consul imposed on the father the task of punishing his sons, and that his unbendingness compelled him personally to order an execution, the very sight of which was not spared him." The tragedy written by Voltaire in 1730 is based on this sacrifice dictated by the letter of the law, just as is the painting exhibited by

David at the Salon of 1789, which sets its action in Brutus's home at the instant that "they are bringing back the bodies of the two sons on stretchers to give them burial." In the foreground, slightly in shadow, the hero turns away his gaze but does not tremble, attaining the sublime by his fierce virtue.

The French revolutionaries, and then the Republicans even more, chose Brutus as tutelary figure for their patriotic movements. David's painting was celebrated as a prophecy of the revolutionary ideal. Voltaire's play won a new triumph that the performance of November 19, 1790, symbolized: before an enthusiastic audience, the curtain fell on a final tableau whose staging imitated the painter's composition. And the white marble bust of Junius Brutus, sculpted by Philippe Boiston, was placed by the deputies in their meeting hall in September 1792, in front of the rostrum of the orators, who did not fail, time and again, to call on the Republican hero to witness their commitment to the cause of the public good. However, it is not this life that the Academy of Painting proposes for the contest in 1793, but the death of Brutus, "the moment when his body, carried by Roman knights, is received by the Consuls and the Senate, outside the gates of Rome."

The committee of experts, including David, drew this little-known episode from Charles Rollin's *Histoire romaine* [Roman History] and from Pierre Baillot's *Récit de la Révolution de Rome* [Tale of the Roman Revolution], mentioning Brutus's mortal combat with Aruns, son of Tarquin, far from the city and in front of the assembled armies: "The public mourning gave his funeral the brilliance of a triumph. The most distinguished personages lifted the hero's body from the battlefield, and carried it back to Rome covered with palm fronds and flowers. The army followed, giving voice to the most heartfelt sorrows. . . . The Romans were in mourning for a year, as for a father. All these honors rendered to the memory of the foremost citizen, who died for his country, increasingly inculcated love of country, a noble emulation to serve it, and a public spirit, strongest weapon of a free people."[3]

The subject of the competition, the first of the very young French Republic,[4] thus places a corpse at the center of representation. This choice relies on some examples, and was fueled by certain obligatory references: a few from books, few and unusual in view of the multitude of stories about the rape of Lucretia, the expulsion of the Tarquins, or the sacrifice of his sons by Brutus; then the example of the Roman funeral ceremonies that historians—but also physicians—sometimes took as the model of an "art of death" that was simple, severe, stripped bare[5]; and finally, the interest roused by neoclassical artists in the "beautiful heroic deaths," illustrated by a recrudescence of paintings showing dying warriors or their funerals. So we can speak of a veritable genre, especially among the numerous young students of David, at the end of the eighteenth century: that of the "dying athlete," a male beauty confronted with his ultimate ordeal, and most often sublimated by it.[6] Nonetheless the fact remains that even though explanations can be found for it, the choice of the Academy of Painting is surprising, even paradoxical: it makes a corpse rise up in the heart of the first Republican competition, as if only this morbid presence had the power to seal the fate of the new community, revive the founding oath, engender the fable of origins.

The French Republic, like that of Rome, was born from an oath taken over a corpse. The body of Lucretia gave a morbid impetus to the ancient republic, the corpse of Louis XVI to the French Republic. In both cases, the oath was taken over the blood of a corpse, almost comforted by it. And the Republic then strengthened itself from corpse to corpse, the dead bodies of its martyred children or of its execrated enemies. The painting competition of Year II seeks, then, to make an image of this tragic feeling, to bring into view this necessary and cumbersome corpse. Brutus is the martyr of all republics; he is their corpse, at once original and final. Brutus is Lepeletier, [Louis-Michel Lepeletier de St. Fargeau, 1760–1793, president of the Constituent Assembly in 1790, was killed by a Royalist for voting for the King's execution.—TRANS.] put to death by a Royalist a few weeks before the committee's choice, and soon he will be Jean-Paul Marat, assassinated a few months later. It is as if Brutus most closely defined the characteristics of a morbid drive indissociable from Republican political passion.

Seven young painters were accepted to compete for the prize, each working on their composition during the summer of 1793. In the course of this same summer, the Academy of Painting was dissolved, replaced by a jury of fifty members charged with awarding the prizes in the name of a "principle that must regenerate taste for the arts."[7] From then on, the former judgment, that "the arts served only to satisfy the pride and caprice of a few sybarites gorged with gold," had to give way to a taste in which "the qualities of heroism, of civic virtues, offered to the gaze of the people, will electrify the soul, and will cause all the passions of glory, of devotion to the salvation of the country, to germinate in it." The canvases of the entrants were exhibited to the public gaze for five days. Then the jurors met for a day to deliberate, under the obligation to justify their decision in writing, with the publication of a report in view. In January 1794 the contest finally took place. All the jurors were in agreement about rejecting all but two of the paintings submitted, then by a very large majority (forty-four votes against three) chose to reward the work of the young Harriet, a student of Jacques-Louis David, rather than that of Pierre-Narcisse Guérin, student of Jean-Baptiste Regnault. In this choice, it seems that the influence of David was the determining factor, and that the jurors were rallying around a disciple of the great painter as much as around a painting, which was in any case quite conventional and straightforward in its presentation. The painting has disappeared today, but we can imagine it as being rather scholarly, according to the opinions that were preserved in the form of minutes of the jury's deliberations.[8]

The second painting, recently exhibited in the Museum of the French Revolution in Vizille, was the occasion of a much more lively debate.[9] All the jurors recognized in it a well-mastered skill, a more virtuoso style, a more confident maturity, but cried out in indignation at the appearance of Brutus's corpse. If Harriet, the prizewinner, treated the body of the hero that died in combat like "a caricature of the antique," taking into account all the stereotypes of the representation of *la belle mort,* "vigorous and vast" corpse, "very colorful," "voluminous," even endowed with "too much freshness" and thus "not dead enough," Guérin chose the opposite side: he painted a corpse where the marks of decomposition are already advanced, dislocated in parts (notably the left shoulder), fixed in a contorted rigidity (the right hand), with an almost repulsive facial expression, and with an absolutely deathly complexion of a greenish hue. Guérin's canvas, in its composition, disposition, and play of colors, and in the appearance of most of the bodies, nonetheless conforms thoroughly to the canons of the classical revival. But to paint the central corpse, Guérin seems to have departed radically from the concept of ideal beauty,[10] choosing grotesque expression rather than serenity, repulsive death as opposed to harmony, morbid realism against the ideal of virile flesh. "Thin and almost livid," "dislocated corpse," "unrecognizable hero": these are some of the verdicts that motivated the rejection of the painting, summarized by Lesueur's expression, "This was not the image I had formed of a free man who has just died for his country." For the jurors had this heroic image before their eyes, perfect, inspired, in the months that preceded their meeting and their vote: the

Marat offered by David to the Convention[11] in October 1793. In this representation, nothing recalled the putrefaction of Marat's body; the ideal body of the martyr corresponded to the watchword of the time: "Marat is not dead." According to this model, the painting of Brutus's corpse should have denied its disappearance, thus resuscitating "the heroic body of the martyr"[12] in respect for Republican principles.

Why is there such a difference in the codes of representation? Why does this corpse acquire such a morbid power, in a way inverting the qualities of David's *Marat* or *Lepeletier*?[13] During the competition of Year II, the few defenders of Guérin, notably Athanase Détournelle in his *Journal de la société républicaine des arts* [Journal of the Republican Society of the Arts], advance the argument of realism: "All the members of the jury were in agreement in finding Brutus' body represented as being dead for too long a time; I did indeed note this fault, but nonetheless I think that a corpse that has spent a day in a hot country does not entirely have the tone of the prize-winning painting.... I pondered this question on the day after August 10th, and I noticed at the end of eighteen hours, both among the Swiss, and among our comrades, much more pallor than color.... Thus I believe that the natural tone of a swarthy Roman must, a day after his death, be quite different from those drawn. May my readers pardon this lugubrious digression! Painters, too, must live in the catacombs and in the night of tombs to be able to affect our souls with more truth."

For the young Guérin, this "truth" showed through in the "horror" of Brutus's corpse—no doubt effectively, since it was associated with the realism of a body treated poorly by a long exposure to the sun on its way back to Rome; also, and especially, since it mirrored the revolutionary event. Guérin's corpse is the direct, absolutely contemporary echo of the actual body of Marat (before it was idealized by David), assassinated on July 13, 1793, and exhibited to the public in the days that followed during a ceremony of contemplation in the Eglise des Cordeliers and then in the course of the funeral ceremony that traversed Paris.[14] Each time, during these public spectacles organized by David, the body of Marat is visible, arranged in its semi-nudity, speaking to everyone thanks to a composition based on the "pedagogy of wounds."[15] David has a precise idea about this subject when he is in charge of the ceremonies, an idea that he expresses before his colleagues at the Convention on July 15, 1793: "The day before his death, I found Marat in an attitude that struck me. He was writing his last thoughts for the salvation of the people. It doesn't do to uncover some parts of his body, for you know he had a leprosy, and his blood was fevered; but I thought it would be interesting to offer him to you in the attitude in which I found him, writing in his bath for the happiness of the people."

David makes it clear: Marat was afflicted with a grave malady of the skin, and was no doubt soon going to die, exhausted and eaten away, even if Charlotte Corday had spared him.[16] That quickly makes the first tableau thought out by David for the exhibition of the martyr's corpse unusable, and constrains him to fall back on another dramatic representation: "I assured myself with my own eyes," he says the next day, July 16, at the Convention, "of the impossibility of putting my first ideas relative to Citizen Marat into execution. Putrefaction prohibits placing him standing up, or even sitting. Because of that, we decided to place him on a bed, like Lepeletier, half-covered with a simple sheet, which will give the idea of the bath quite well."

Thus Marat, at the Cordeliers, rests stretched out on a "bed of pain covered with flowers," his head surrounded by a crown of oak, his torso bare, the wound visible, "a large wound colored with blood" offered to the gazes of the Republicans. His corpse is paraded in the same attitude during the funeral ceremony on July 17, an eight-hour-long procession during which the people of Paris communed one last time with their "friend." The whole produced an "impression of awe," the arrangement of the corpse accentuating it even more, recalling as it did the ritual that had presided over the funeral ceremony of Lepeletier on January 24, 1793, as Louis-Sébastien Mercier described it: "This ceremony had an excessively remarkable character. They placed the corpse on the ruined base of the equestrian statue of Louis XIV in the middle of the Place Vendôme. There, his funeral oration was uttered by a voice that made itself heard over all the roofs. It was very cold. Lepeletier's body, naked, livid, and bloody, showing the large wound that had been inflicted on it, was carried on a kind of procession bed and paraded slowly in a very long route accompanied by the Convention as well as the Society of Jacobins. The latter had its banner, and just beside it we could see another of its invention: it had as its pennant the shirt, the waistcoat, and especially the trousers of Lepeletier still dripping with blood."[17]

There again, David had organized the ceremony, composing a kind of preliminary *macabre tableau* before idealizing it, a few weeks later, when painting the martyred corpse. Each time, David offers two compositions (*tableaux*) to the Republicans: that of the actual exhibition of the corpse, a direct confrontation of the community with the body of the martyr, and that of the idealized painting, an aesthetic emotion faced with the work of art, the corpse rendered glorious. These two morbid feelings, horrified compassion and aesthetic emotion, are complementary in the eyes of the painter. Guérin seems to have set down on his canvas the "first" of the two paintings composed by David, that of the direct exhibition of the corpse. And it is this that neither the master nor his contemporaries are able to accept.

But it is this singular presence of the corpse that we have to explain, this sudden shock confronting death in the work, this rising up of the decomposed, disfigured body, its skin livid, putrefied, contrary to all the codes of representation, to all the rules of decorum. The only satisfactory explanation is political. Yet Pierre-Narcisse Guérin was not a militant painter, nor even an ally of Jacobin radicalism. He would even be considered as one of the artistic heralds of conservatism and of the relenting at the end of the Directory.[18] But in 1793 he is young, scarcely twenty years old, and that summer is unusual, experienced by all the Republicans as anguish and tragedy, punctuated by fears of invasion, of conspiracy, of public misery, animated by the calls to vengeance and the trust placed in the Terror as an absolute system of defense of the threatened community. All Republicans are afraid, and it behooves them to be terrifying in turn. An actual corpse embodies all that by itself: the murdered body of Marat. He is the besieged, mistreated Republic, and all citizens rally round him, recognizing themselves in him. At the same time, Marat's corpse very quickly comes to embody the execrated figure of the enemy, of the other, through its repulsive ugliness, its signs of horror. Doesn't it show the formidable green color, a rallying emblem of the Royalists since the beginning of the Revolution (the color of the livery of the Comte d'Artois), a symbol associated with the criminal woman herself, Charlotte Corday, of whom Henriot could write on the day after the murder in the *Courrier universel:* "Beware of green hats, the woman who assassinated Marat had a green hat."

Marat's corpse thus takes on all the trappings of a political ghost. It haunts the political scene, at once an adulated apparition and a symbol of horror, martyr of the Republic and decomposed body, corrupted by the very signs of the enemy. All the descriptions of Marat's funeral make paradoxical feelings coincide, juxtaposing glory and terror upon this corpse. "The mortal remains were ceremonially conveyed into the garden of the Cordeliers, but the ceremony was nothing but simple and patriotic. The people took part peacefully and in a touching disorder, whence resulted the most picturesque scene."[19] This patriotic tableau in no way prevents the macabre and terrible scene, worthy of an anxious pastoral: "The excessive heat of the day, the species of illness with which Marat was afflicted, hastened the putrefaction of his body. Despite embalming, putrid exhalations made themselves strongly smelt; they even had to bleach the skin of his face and the part of the body that was left uncovered, so that the sight of them would be bearable in the funeral ceremony accorded him."[20] The sublime, here, is born from horror. For the corpse is rotting to provoke the feeling of the sublime, which alone is capable of causing it to rise up again from the repulsive horror in which it steeps, "passing from the depths of abjection to what is truly sublime."

Guérin's ambition too was to compose this nightmare painting, and his Brutus almost naturally reveals the disfigured and sublime traits of Marat's corpse. For the men present in his painting are living a nightmare: the Republic is dying beneath their eyes in the person of Brutus, and the body of the hero must convey this terror, this fear, while at the same time transport them. The death of the father of the Roman Republic, like that of the friend of the people, is a bad dream: his orphans can only imagine visions of horror in which the murdered corpse is the centerpiece, a fearful vision that must still fuel and inflame the spirit of the people, and lead the senses imperiously to demand a Terror that reason rejects.[21]

In the manner of Guérin's *Brutus* or Marat's funeral, the corpse is at the heart of rituals, representations, and visions during the most critical moments of the French Revolution, between the summer of 1791 and the summer of Thermidor, Year II. In the course of these three years, the corpse is the conceptual object that allows revolutionary politics to be thought out, a sublime abjection that defines the aesthetic and philosophical category proper to this moment of history.[22] Death, then, is omnipresent in the thoughts of a country that sees itself as besieged, attacked, assassinated, that defends itself by a language of the terrible; the government of the Terror installs itself little by little and a repressive politics takes hold for which "Sainte Guillotine" very quickly becomes the symbol.[23] The French Revolution in its central episode represented itself as a tragedy, in the profound, ancient sense of the word: on dead bodies is conferred the power to discourse about the city. The corpse is the sign of the death of the enemy, the mutilated and scorned remains of "guilty victims" whose wounds are the bloody signature of the Terror; it reveals the "cruelty" of the conspirators and counterrevolutionaries, it falls under the blade of the guillotine. It also testifies to the suffering and sacrifice of the Republicans, engendering the language of emotion, hate or compassion. It is present, given over to view, exhibited in the course of funeral celebrations and processions, taken in charge by the rites and precise actions of execution. The sight of it must be endured, since it symbolizes the test of truth of a political system.

This test binds the political community together. Thus as a starting point, the community provided itself with corpses that it learned how to see and how to read (Mirabeau, the first "Great Man" of the Revolution to die publicly, whose body was examined by thousands of witnesses), to venerate (Voltaire, paraded naked to the Panthéon, stretched out on a triumphal chariot, disinterred thirteen years after his death) or to hate (Louis XVI: his "impure blood" drenches the brothers of the Republic, freed from the tutelage of a "despotic" father whose remains are scattered into a communal ditch) and dismember and outrage (the corpse of the Princesse de Lamballe, a lady at the court massacred in September 1792). Similarly, martyrs played a large role in Republican identity, their wounds reviving emotion, calling for vengeance, mobilizing energies (Geffroy, his eloquent wound presented to the Convention during the summer of 1794). As for the victims of the guillotine, they symbolized the tragedy that citizens had to surmount to accede to Republicanism or the scapegoats whose sacrifice could purge the political scene (Robespierre, the tyrant turned corpse, expiating the Terror all by himself while still allowing the French to overcome it and forget it). The corpse, then, is the measure of everything, to the point of obsession, to the point of madness of a universe wholly ruled by the constraints that the corpse imposes, the precautions it demands, the visions and thoughts to which it gives birth (Madame Necker, whose life was haunted by the assurance of signs of death and the morbid fear of being buried prematurely, and whose death was occupied by the desire to make her corpse presentable, to safeguard and adorn it, to make it beautiful, almost "alive").

This book outlines seven *portraits of corpses* famous during the French Revolution: Mirabeau, Voltaire, Lamballe, Louis XVI, Geffroy, Robespierre, and Madame Necker. Through them, it tries to understand the morbid passions that pervaded the society at that moment. These portraits of corpses thus offer an interpretation of the Terror, formulating hypotheses that, in the style of historical and literary investigation, of psychopathological inquiry, give an account of the motivations of a political life that was suddenly abandoning calm reason, intangible principles, and ordinary methods of public action. Each political decision at that instant enters a dialogue with death, with the corpse that legitimizes it, the corpse that it engenders, or the actual body, constantly threatened, of the one that makes the decision. It is through this *discourse of corpses* that a period like the Terror can be contemplated.

Still, this ordeal is new, thus terrible; all the ideas on death, all the funeral practices fashioned by the Enlightenment, tended to distance corpses from the living, sought to protect the gaze from the spectacle of dead bodies.[24] During the funeral, for instance, more and more systematically the corpse was enclosed in a closed coffin. Similarly, the practices of visiting the dying and keeping vigil with corpses became rare. It was as if the link between the living and the dead had to be cut that had existed daily till then, thanks to the customary juxtaposition of bodies. If the corpse became less present to the gazes of people of the time, it returned in stories and representations in imaginary form.[25] Novels about the living dead, a taste for the morbid, macabre eroticism, funereal anecdote—all these modes of reading the world are important in the second half of the eighteenth century and offer to the collective imagination a configuration of the gothic novel (*roman noir*). It is with such stories in mind that the French would live and survive during the Terror, at a time that produced real corpses on top of real corpses to be witnessed by sensibilities that multiplied them in imagination. Poetry of night and tomb, novels of the dead, gothic melodramas all project their visions upon a political scene in which the protagonists have taken on the traits of funereal figures, in which the heroes "from the beginning understood 'to act' (*agir*) on the model of 'to suffer (*pâtir*).'"[26] The Revolution thus knows a tragic fate, and shows affinities with the political experimentation of macabre situations that infected the fictional constructs toward the end of Enlightenment. The revolutionary scene is thus the passage from a thought-out socialization (no doubt long dreamt of) as optimistic, to a socialization experienced as painful, incorporating exclusion, surveillance, and punishment into the traditional methods of promoting virtue. Revolutionary culture, in putting into practice the illuminated fiction of the corpse, corresponds to the moment of the loss of innocence in the evolution of modern democracies.

But this corpse that startlingly appears on the revolutionary public scene, to the point of taking the exact measure of politics, is later rejected with all the more vehemence, banished with all the more rigor. From the Directory onward, the corpse once again becomes taboo in the public sphere, relegated to the background in the name of hygiene and good manners. The competition organized by the National Institute of Arts and Sciences in Year VIII "on questions relative to funeral ceremonies and places of burial" is explicit on this point: it is a matter of denying the spectacular and morbid ceremonies of the Terror, of forgetting those "funereal and hideous processions," and almost of atoning for them by rediscovering and resuming the Enlightenment's culture of death.[27] The ritual exhibition of corpses is from then on regarded as a monstrosity typical of a government that is itself monstrous. So in the Paris of the beginnings of the nineteenth century an institution comes to play this role of protection, of ramparts drawn up against haunting presence and faced with the invading metaphorization of the morbid: the morgue.[28] This becomes the place specifically assigned to corpses, charged with receiving them, classifying them, observing them, as well as rigorously confining them and circumventing their power over the senses and imaginations. The public hygiene proclaimed by Alexandre Parent-Duchâtelet tries to rationalize the "body of Paris" (*corps de Paris*),[29] controlling its impulses, whether morbid or sexual, political or social. Corpses are put in their place—in the bosom of the family or in the morgue—and escape the public gaze that had given them a role and a meaning at the time of the Terror. They are no longer a metaphor for the world but an absence, a taboo, a mystery that can only be cleared up by stories of crime, detective novels, or historical melodramas.[30] Corpses take their leave from the public scene and find their place in fiction, and it is no longer their presence that makes sense but their absence, their way of being held at a distance. The terrible measure of the Revolution has become the shameful secret of the bourgeois century that is beginning to assert itself.

To plunge into the tragic heart of the Revolution is on the contrary to run the risk of a "history of paroxysm and horror," to use Alain Corbin's phrase.[31] Why, for instance, do the "visions of corpses" multiply under the Revolution? Chroniclers vie with each other to note their effect—one woman "bringing into the world a male child who has dark eyes, a broken nose, an excrescence of flesh around his neck" after she had seen the day before the bloated and mangled corpse of a massacred man; another woman becoming "mad, almost dead" after a morbid spectacle; a third "petrified, as if she had seen the head of Medusa." Why do funereal anecdotes and curiosities—the alleged glass of blood drunk by Mlle de Sombreuil to save her father from massacre, the dismembering of the body of the Princesse de Lamballe, the tanning of human skin by Meudon to make culottes for members of the Committee of Public Safety—invade histories and memoirs?

All of a sudden, on the occasion of a phenomenal crisis of public conscience, the corpse rises up again at the end of the eighteenth century as a sensitive weak point in society's discourse about itself. Suddenly people need the presence and image of the corpse to understand themselves, to take the (im)measure ([*dé*]*mesure*) of the upheavals they are instigating. Though defenses against nature (and their own nature) are enforced little by little and made stronger and more stringent, the people's inner life has *been made savage*. And it is this secret part of the people's psyche that imposes itself on the manner of violence and death when the Terror seems the only way to survive in politics, and that monopolizes fantasies of power and reveals the heroism of powerlessness. The corpse is precisely the form that relates both the mastery of man *and* his increasing savagery. It is the cause both of a possible rationalization—dissected, anatomized, classified, ordered—and of a probable excess, a madness, image of a world prey to fear and agitation. As Philippe Ariès explained, it is still the time "when doctors lose their sang-froid when faced with the corpse."[32] This morbid presence, even though shaped and a priori contained by science, is free to offer itself for the interpretations of a moment of history. Thought about, the corpse suddenly escapes, temporarily, to become a thinking form.

Gauvre de P. L'Elu, *Les Amis de la Constitution Aux Mânes de Mirabeau.* Cliché Bibliothèque Nationale de France, Paris.

Mirabeau

OR, THE SPECTACLE OF A PUBLIC CORPSE

On Wednesday, March 30, 1791, the Rue de la Chaussée-d'Antin is invaded by a restless crowd, "a prodigious and continual concourse of citizens of all ranks and all parties," reports a privileged witness, Cabanis, Mirabeau's doctor.[1] The people are all hurrying there because Honoré-Gabriel-Victor Riquetti de Mirabeau is dying. Their rallying together consecrates one last time the decisive role played by the orator in leading France from the old to the new regime. In fact it is this Provençal count, excluded from his order, then finding refuge with the delegates of the commoners after the elections to the Estates General who in May 1789 most swiftly abandons, along with Abbé Sieyès, the weighty uniform of representative of the old estates to don the suit of the political man of the new National Assembly. We can thus define Mirabeau as the first great political man of the Revolution.[2]

He is first of all the most charismatic personality, the one people notice. The description is famous, but it is worth lingering on: "He carried his head high and tilted back. His thick head of hair, raised up and crimped on his wide forehead, ended in part on top of his ears, in thick curls. His ugliness, in short, had something imposing about it," Jean Étienne Marie Portalis grudgingly admits, jealous and admiring.[3] And then Mirabeau is the man who is heard the most. His talents as orator are immense, the one who seems to be the most vigorous handler of words at the beginning of the Revolution. As orator he has the hardly negligible talent of knowing how to fill the Assembly with enthusiasm, and then lead it forward. From June 23, 1789, when he replies to the speaker of the assembly, Dreux-Brézé, and sends him back to his Ancien Régime etiquette, to March 27, 1791, when he utters his last speech before the Constituent Assembly, Mirabeau remains the "Shakespeare of eloquence," to use a phrase of his only rival in this domain, the young Antoine Barnave [a leading member of the Feuillants–TRANS.].

As imposing as he is as a political man, Mirabeau reveals himself to be an expert politician. A faculty—quickness of intervention—and an *idée fixe*—defense of a monarchy, defense adapted to the revolutionary moment—preside over this strategy. In fact Mirabeau has the quality of a skillful politician. He thinks quickly, if not necessarily always correctly. His interventions at the Assembly steadily demonstrate a keen sense of repartee and an impromptu and decisive ability to orate, to "chain the movements of representatives to his words." But Mirabeau is still defending the same political system: a constitutional monarchy that has integrated new ideas. It is in this equilibrium between the executive power of the king and the legislative power of the representatives of the nation that Mirabeau sees his ideal constitution. He will not live long enough to see the king take his oath on it. But the supreme determinant of Mirabeau's political career, this ability that makes him the most powerful man of the Constituent Assembly, is the knack of always calling on public opinion, calling it to witness. Continuously, countering the attacks of innumerable rivals and insinuations on the scandal of his private life, he recovers his popularity. Then, despite accusations and suspicions, he ends up carrying the day. That is why his power is fascinating: before anyone else, he knew how make an absolute value of politics, and not just of the virtuous aspect of politics.

Nonetheless, the path followed by Mirabeau to this political glory was quite tortuous, his itinerary very somber—that of the scandalous life in the Ancien Régime, from escapes to lawsuits, from adulteries to mistresses, from prisons to dungeons, from the Ile de Ré to the Château d'If, from the fort of Joux to that of Vincennes, where this young libertine rebel of the French nobility, depraved, rebellious, a philosopher and a pornographer, spent a total of three years of his life between 1777 and 1782. Using these "lives" and these reputations, the counterrevolutionary press knows how to play with a certain virtuosity in trying to discredit one of the heroes of the Revolution. The death of Mirabeau revives these accusations as well as resuscitates the tale of his political triumph. Around his corpse, the paper war rages. Is it the edifying story of a life dedicated to the public good, that of the orator of the nation, that will triumph thanks to the moderate press in favor of the balanced constitution Mirabeau defended? Or is it the other side—the politician, haunted by a scandalous private life—that will rise up again under the insistence of the Royalist press?

And a last political current, no less present, with a third variant on the subject of the body of Mirabeau: the radical press, which from the spring of 1791 openly praises the Republic. This press tries to profit from the death of Mirabeau to deploy its discourse of anguish, accusation, and universal call to vigilance. The orator might even have been assassinated, poisoned, and "they" are trying to hush up the affair—a good way for the patriot press to denounce the counterrevolution while at the same time to deplore the inaction of the moderate power of the National Assembly or of the Parisian municipality. The radicals, seeing "nefarious conspiracies" in all the mysteries of revolutionary Paris, want suddenly to accelerate the movement of the Revolution, demanding systematic surveillance, exacting just punishments, and calling the people to militant action.

The "death of Mirabeau," from March 29, 1791, when news of the orator's illness is spread in Paris, till April 4, when they celebrate his funeral ceremony, thus provides a corpse for the spectacle. And on this body, politics is legible, decipherable: the politics of Mirabeau as well as those of the rival parties, groups, factions. These divergent readings of one single corpse make the disappearance of the great orator the first "public death" of a political scene now emancipated from monarchical ritual.

"WHAT WAS MIRABEAU?"

The Rue de la Chaussée-d'Antin is soon closed to traffic, as much to "spare the sick man the annoyance of the passage of fiacres [carriages]"[4] as to make space for the public to assemble for a look at him. Many witnesses stress, beyond the familiar phrase, the public character of this "public gathering":[5] "From the first day on, Mirabeau's illness had become of public interest. On Tuesday evening [March 29] people were already hurrying over from everywhere to hear news of him. The idea that he had run the greatest danger began to make people feel how precious this head was.... His door was continuously besieged by a succession of many visitors. The street filled with people, and in all the public places, groups spoke only of this illness that was regarded as so great an event. Bulletins were issued many times throughout the day, but did not satisfy universal unrest. In the intervals between them, oral reports also had to be posted; and as soon as they appeared, they were taken away in such a great number, that [those responsible for them] finally took it upon themselves to have them printed [for distribution]. Relatives, friends, acquaintances filled the house, the courtyard and the garden, where the number was renewed from hour to hour; deputations followed each other: on Wednesday evening the Society of Friends of the Constitution sent a delegation led by M. Barnave. Outside, the crowd swelled, impatient for news of the sick man, sometimes resigned, sometimes agitated."[6]

The space of the patriot's death is thus very precisely arranged, almost choreographed, according to successive concentric circles: the "assembly of friends"[7]—Cheralies de Lamarck, Charles-Maurice de Talleyrand, Pierre Jean George Cabanis, Nicolas Frochot; the stream of delegations (club, *section,* Assembly, municipality, *département*); the presence of the crowd; then the distribution of the medical bulletin. Mirabeau himself wanted to make a spectacle of it: "While he lived, or rather when he felt death, he wanted to see all his friends endlessly next to him, and all the public ceaselessly around his home,"[8] a spectacle to which he gives replies, which are then reported by the press: "I [Cabanis] spoke to him of the extraordinary interest that they were taking in his illness, of the urgency with which the people asked everywhere for news of him and came to his door to hear of it. 'Ah . . . Yes,' he answered, 'without a doubt, such a good people is indeed worthy of one devoting oneself to their service. It was glorious for me to consecrate my whole life to them; I feel that it is sweet to me to die in their midst.' "[9]

This spectacle of public death is reinforced by the very attitude of those close to him, releasing medical bulletins, taking care to keep the entire crowd's attention: "On the day of April 1st, Cabanis, the physician, let the public know that he expected, by the evening or the night, a crisis that would decide the life or death of the sick man. The crisis announced by the doctor was awaited with the greatest impatience by the assembled people, whose concourse did not cease all night long."[10] So much that Cabanis himself can evoke a "death full of life": "On Thursday morning, [Mirabeau's] physiognomy took on an aspect that it never lost. It was that of death, but of a death full of life, if one can express oneself thus, in the sense that the sick man did not stop receiving, conversing, listening to the public that surrounded his bed and his abode."[11] Here is a "dead man," but one who "speaks to the public": in this encounter, carefully organized, remains the gaze of transparency, borne by comings and goings, by bulletins, by the doctor's regular announcements, by the words of the sick man that are quickly relayed in the press.

But what transparency? For this crowd is inclined to let tales of the great man's death oppose each other; it makes his contradictory lives rise again, and it mixes two possible transparencies. This duality confers its interest on the spectacle of Mirabeau's death. What was Mirabeau? The question is posed as soon as his illness is announced, by a pamphlet that promises, "It is a completely naked Riquetti [Mirabeau] that you will see."[12] Some of the orator's "private lives," not at all unheard of at the time of his death, quickly appear or appear again, a *Confession générale* [General confession] as well as *Mémoires secrets sur la vie civile, morale et politique du ci-devant souverain des Français* [Secret memoirs on the civil, moral, and political life of the former sovereign of the French]. This game of unveiling is not to the dying man's advantage: all the works insist on the debauchery of his youth, the lure of gain, repeated scandals. No one in the crowd that peoples the rue de la Chaussée-d'Antin is foiled by that. Mirabeau is not a model of virtue, to the point that Brissot, in his *Patriote français,* can violently reprimand a colleague who referred to the orator as being "eloquent and virtuous": "Mirabeau himself—I knew him well enough to affirm it—would have crossed out that second word. It is not at all suitable for free men to tell a lie over the grave, and one does no honor, to oneself or to him, by a lie."[13]

Mirabeau thus sets a delicate trap for revolutionary transparency: how to put a patriot soul into a depraved body? In the urgency of the hours of a brutal demise, the answer forms: *talent* resolves the contradiction. It alone permits the paradoxical coupling that engenders a strange monster, a political chimera: the virtue of the eloquent and the depravation of the senses. Mirabeau is sacred, then, for the moment—"the most talented man of all," which Brissot, still in shock and yet austere, sums up in a phrase: "Mirabeau is no more.... We must cast away from his tomb any reproaches that can be made of him. Let us cover his faults with a veil and let us throw only flowers on his corpse."[14] Thus a first possible transparency is defined: that of talent, which in Mirabeau's case leads from the spectacle of death to be beheld over the public corpse to political glory.

In this sense Mirabeau, thanks to his talent and to the suddenness of his death—as Brissot says, "a corpse with praises" rather than "branded with vices"—temporarily escapes being denounced, the supreme test of revolutionary transparency. But he himself contributed to forming the practice of denunciation, praising it in many texts in the name of the higher interest of the nation. A little after his death, and even more so later, the nation turns against Mirabeau's way of living; that is to say, against his corpse, since it is over his remains that the press will pronounce the perversity of his life. On the first occasion, though, the orator was caught during his lifetime in the mesh of this tightened net. As rumors and suspicions multiplied in the wake of October 4 and 5, 1789, lampoons ranking him at the head of the "regicide plot of the Orléans faction," he himself replied through a well-argued letter addressed to the Comité des Recherches de l'Assemblée [Investigative Committee of the Assembly], a letter published by his bookseller, Lejay.[15] In his "Letter on public denunciation" Mirabeau, taking the initiative, defined himself as a "vigilant sentinel" and, justifying the practice of denunciation historically as well as politically, attacked the Comte de Saint-Priest, minister of the king, who had "insidiously" incited the women of Paris to go to Versailles to provoke the sovereign and the Assembly. The orator justified his move by an enthusiastic eulogy of surveillance, calling his adversary before the "tribunal of public opinion": "May it please heaven, since the enemies of the State threaten the Assembly, that each of its members faithfully deposit in his breast all his fears! Beside the good citizens cited at the tribunal of public opinion, who could easily be justified, how many actual guilty ones might not have been unmasked beneath this surveillance! Believe me, only at this price are the people free. When it is exercised by a despot, public accusation causes horror. But in the National Assembly, in the midst of the dangers that surround us, I regard it as the most important of our new virtues; it is a purely defensive weapon, or rather it is the *palladium* of our nascent liberty." To place liberty under the protection of denunciation: the argument is perfectly fitted into the praise of public denunciation promoted by the Patriot press at that time. But, ranked thus in a space of absolute transparency, Mirabeau is not spared the penetrating gaze.

From the autumn of 1789 on, Mirabeau's career is in the center of the political debate. Already, certain people take up his defense in the name of his "talent," wishing to dissociate private behavior and public life: "We must believe that one can remain a good patriot and be useful and necessary to our present revolution while forgetting one's own dissolute practices; similarly, certain examples of virtue will always be bad politics,"[16] notes one of the writers of Mirabeau's "workshop," charged with hurrying to his aid.[17] But most of the pamphlets, on the contrary, seize on the "denouncer denounced" to insist on the perverse effects of public denunciation, as well as on the defects in Mirabeau's private life. "Today, famous pens dedicated first to defending liberty dirty themselves without shame,"[18] writes one, an accusation relayed after his exile in Switzerland by the Marquis de Lally-Tollendal, addressing

Mirabeau: "How many uncontrollable hatreds you inflame! How many passions you arm! How many victims you will make! You desire the greatest latitude to make accusations.... Be content: your system makes all of France, and all the horrors it brings with it, into a vast field of calumny. But take care: denunciation, taken in its absolute sense, always carries an idea of shame and crime that falls back on the behavior of the one that exploits it."[19] Lally is not wrong: the accuser is the first to be targeted by his act; he must be irreproachable. Mirabeau, with his public notoriety, is not.

The *Lettre aux commettants* [Letter to supporters], attributed to Servan, and then the *Trahison découverte* [Treason discovered], attributed to Charles de Lameth, offer in addition a detailed portrayal of Mirabeau's habits, as they aim to break the public career of the Provençal deputy. The former tries to destroy the argument of "talent useful to the nation": "He has great talents, you say.... A courtesan, the vilest of prostitutes, may have the greatest beauty, but do you despise her less? Would you give her the clothing, the finery of your wife, telling her: 'Go represent my wife in a public festival'?"[20] As for Lameth, in a similar logic, he recognizes the necessity of transparency, which condemns Mirabeau to censure. The virtue of private life, he explains in May 1790, is the very condition of a useful public life. The body leads politics, and the dissolute senses of the former cause suspicion to fall on the rigor of the latter: "We took pleasure in seeing two people in you, the private man and the public man," writes Lameth about Mirabeau. "As a private man, we threw a veil on your strayings; as a public man, we exalted your genius.... Today we are forced to regard you as our cruelest enemy. Today we are forced to recognize your private strayings, for they are the reason that you will never have morality, principles, honor, good faith; we are forced to say that you have violated the home of your host, by taking away his wife; that you were sent as a spy to Prussia; that you were always sold to the highest and latest bidder."[21]

Under pressure of political rivalries, scandalous life breaks through the surface of usefulness. Can the talent Mirabeau offers the nation seal these breaches and bypass the transparency between private and public life extolled by Lameth as well as by most Patriots? Can talent provide Mirabeau, *despite everything,* with a path toward public recognition? These are the stakes that the spectacle of his death take on, a spectacle that the crowd can see played, in various ways, over his dying body, and then over his corpse. In an obvious way, then, Mirabeau's body is the first sign of a public reading of political space. It is only by the proofs that his corpse will bring that the orator can free himself from the trap of denunciation, by erasing the absolute transparency between private and public life in order to substitute a second kind: the one that leads from his suffering body, given over to the public gaze, toward the glory of his political talent sacrificed to the nation.[22]

Three tales of Mirabeau's death circulate in the newspapers and pamphlets, and thus among the "people assembled" around his bed. The first is a story of scandal of the flesh; the second is a conspiracy affair; the third aims to calm the tumult and presents itself as a "succinct story of the physiological life" of the sick man, an entirely natural, clinical story of a body that gave itself too much to the Revolution, of a body that has become a sublime corpse, a body that will henceforth bear witness to an untouchable reputation. The first two retrace a *shameful transparency*: Mirabeau, libertine, hypocrite, ends his career as a corpse eaten away by venereal disease or poisoned by political plots. The third tries to construct a *dreamed transparency*: Mirabeau, talented, accedes to the role of Patriot martyr thanks to a body full of pain, exhausted by work, and watched over by the crowd of his friends. Three different tales, but each one told from the open corpse (*à cadavre ouvert*).

"On Sunday, 26 March, M. Mirabeau had treated all his senses to such an excess of pleasure, of which he had always taken advantage, that he felt extremely weary," begins the tale of scandal. It is an "orgy" that kills Mirabeau, who throughout his entire life has undermined his body, "exhausted his machine by venereal illness."[23] The *Actes des apôtres,*[24] then above all the *Orgie et testament de Mirabeau,* give more details, situating the action in the course of a pleasure party made up of six guests: Talleyrand and Charles de la Villette at the sides of the Patriot orator, accompanied by three "opera girls." The *Actes* explains that the great man, "too confident in his strength," "in the embraces of an Opera dancer drew the germs of death."[25] The "dancer" herself describes the meeting, in the *Orgie de Mirabeau,* using the first person that the satire of scandal so likes: "M. de Mirabeau passionately loved my music. He was not, like many others, a passive lover of the fine arts; he often played his part in my concert, and a number of people attest that he would play marvelously on his horn [*cor,* punning on *corps* "body"—TRANS.]. . . . That night, then, he favored me with his choice. I was the door that welcomed his vessel, excessively mutilated by the shock of storms, and leaking everywhere. . . . The night was scarcely brilliant; Mirabeau's spendings were very mediocre, and the thermometer of his pleasures rose only two degrees."[26] In the virtuoso and insidious language of licentious satire, Mirabeau, "rotten body"[27] though vigorous till then, falls toward death following a final "lascivula-constitutional celebration," a last "legislativo-gallant orgy."[28] Diseased, abusing his sexual powers: the reading is clearly about a scandalous death for a body made dissolute by pleasure, a body soon to become a shameful corpse.

The second register of reading this corpse concerns the great fear of conspiracy. In fact rumors had been circulating since March 30, 1791: Mirabeau might have been poisoned; such a sudden decline could be explained only by a malicious hand. Such rumors are not new. The Provençal count, himself suspected of intrigue, lives surrounded by jealous men and by dangers. Cabanis, his doctor, reports an edifying story: "In the final days of October 1790, a very painful colic, caused by many glasses of iced water, entrained a terrible pain. This colic seized him between midnight and one o'clock. His entire household thought he was poisoned, and cried conspiracy."[29] Less circumspect than Cabanis, some pamphlets at the very beginning of April 1791 have already found a guilty man: Mirabeau's young secretary, de Comps, who was found three hours before the master's death, covered with blood, superficially wounded by the "strokes of a pocket knife," a failed suicide. Immediately suspected, "treated and guarded in order to learn from him if it is because of suffering or some other secret motive that he was forced to such desperation,"[30] the secretary is questioned soon afterward. While his deposition seems to exonerate him, it does not dismiss rumors of conspiracy—quite the contrary: "He said he was delirious. He had heard rumor of poison, conspiracy, betrayal. He thought he was poisoned by a broth, taken by him, which might have contained death, and had preferred, in an access of madness, to give himself death without waiting."[31]

This pathology of conspiracy is favorable to all interpretations. One zealous commentator even discovers a powerful organizer, the "great fomenter of the assassination of Mirabeau": Alexandre de Lameth, rival of the orator and brother of Charles, the denigrator (mentioned above) of the private habits of the Provençal deputy. Lameth even refused to participate in the delegation of the Société des Amis de la Constitution [Society of Friends of the Constitution] that came to visit the great man as he lay dying on the evening of March 30, an infallible sign, according to the journalist, of his presence behind the machination. The accuser thus tries to establish the whole transparency around

Mirabeau's corpse, describes the "secret forces of intrigue," and tells of the "hidden, but hardy" characteristics: "I know that just a few days before his death, he was threatened with assassination; I know that when he went to the countryside, several of his friends were obliged to accompany him armed. I know that he spoke of it to the heads of the Parisian police. I know that he had said before his death that he knew his Alexandre, that he was capable of everything; that all methods were good to him, but especially the shortest."[32] Despite the numerous refutations of the press and the municipality of Paris, then, and despite those close to the orator as well as the National Assembly, Mirabeau's corpse is caught in the mechanism of denunciation of conspiracy, and becomes an emblem of poisoning. The corpse bears a secret that all the informers of the Patriot periodicals dream of revealing.

The final tale of the great man's death intends to refute the accusations of orgies and dismiss the specter of conspiracy. It is a story of the natural exhaustion of a body that has expended too much of itself on the "defense of the Revolution," tired by the "insalubrious air in the meeting-rooms of the National Assembly," used up by "the disorder of concentration, sleepless nights, his efforts at the rostrum and in discussion," the "sensitive fibers" eaten away by "the continual state of profound emotion in which public affairs kept him."[33] Cabanis writes scrupulously of this pathology of political engagement in his *Journal de la maladie et de la mort d'Honoré-Gabriel-Victor Riquetti de Mirabeau* [Journal of the illness and death of . . .], an account of his most famous patient. The journal, published immediately after the death, "enters into the most intimate medical details," clinical considerations necessary to the establishment of the absolute truth of the story. Cabanis recalls the chronic illnesses of his patient—jaundice, then persistent ophthalmia, frequent colic and digestive troubles, and finally rheumatic pains: "We clearly saw that there existed a humour without a well-determined nature, which the action of political life tended to chase from his mind but that struck at different doors of the body more and more violently, to such an extent that he was never without one of these morbid incommodities."[34]

Day by day, and then hour by hour, the doctor reports the decisive crisis of this long illness that, very suddenly, overcame his patient despite his own vigorous efforts. The "most insupportable sufferings" and "the most terrifying physiognomy" do not prevent Mirabeau from thinking or commenting on his death, planning a public spectacle around his body. The final scene[35] takes place on the morning of April 2 when, after a night of delirium mixed with "a language of energy, precision and brilliance," the dying man orders the windows to be opened, "to listen one last time to the murmur of the crowd," then has himself washed, shaved, and perfumed, bringing his close ones together: "My friends, I will die today," he tells them. Cabanis describes these final hours before death, which occurred at 8:30 in the morning, when Mirabeau speaks and then, exhausted, writes on a piece of paper, remaining for a long time "hand in hand with us assembled around him," before being overcome by a "terrifying pain." The *Journal* closes with this, after the autopsy of the corpse, both clinical *and* patriotic, political *because* it is medical: "The stomach, the duodenum, a large part of the liver, the right kidney, the diaphragm, and the pericardium showed signs of inflammation, or rather, in my opinion, congestion of the blood. The pericardium contained a considerable quantity of a thick, yellowish, opaque matter; lymphatic coagulations covered the entire outer surface of the heart with the exception of the tip. The state of the heart, of the pericardium, and of the diaphragm can be regarded with certainty as fatal. I will say only one word to conclude; but this word includes everything: it is that Mirabeau died irreproachable before his country, his friends, and the public that surrounded him."[36] The anatomical precision of the account is necessary for the final political affirmation: Mirabeau died "naturally," without orgy or conspiracy. The medical gaze brought to the corpse is the best proof of the orator's political glory, for it offers to Mirabeau an honorable, fatal spectacle, all the while legitimizing the homage given an exhausted man, but a man washed clean of final suspicions. Mirabeau's truth could stem from his corpse: excesses certainly were his downfall, but these excesses were above all those of patriotism, of political involvement, even more than those of sensual pleasures.

THE EXAMINATION OF THE CORPSE

Even this medical narrative does not serve to establish all the desired transparency around the corpse. Very quickly, the crowd requires, even more than the doctors' report, a series of medical bulletins culminating with a diagnosis of death by natural causes. The public, urged on, actively demands supplementary proof that this corpse is washed clean of all suspicions of debauchery and conspiracy: "Due to some fear of poisoning, due to some rumors, the people haughtily request that the body be opened; in its suffering, the people are not prepared to believe that this supernatural being was taken away suddenly, at forty-five years of age, by a natural death."[37] The doctors and political authorities decide, under pressure, to offer the public a final "visit," that of a public autopsy. That is how, for the first time, and over an opened body, the accession of the corpse as public space of the revolutionary political scene takes place.

The state prosecutor of the tribunal of the first arrondissement of the *département* of Paris takes it upon himself to give the ceremony all the solemnity and publicity required. Thus on the afternoon of Saturday, April 2, a few hours after Mirabeau's death, the magistrate calls for the assembly, on the next day at ten o'clock, of a representative sample suitable for guaranteeing the legitimacy of the operation. There is indeed a massive presence of medical authorities, but there is also a political delegation, a representation of the neighborhood and deputation of the crowd that, still just as numerous, waits before the door of the great man: "The violence of the illness, its rapid progress, the quickness of death, perhaps also the fears that Mirabeau's celebrity, the services he devoted to the public cause, and the misfortune of the circumstances, seem to justify up to a certain point, have caused suspicion that the death could not be natural. To verify the fact, or to destroy suspicions, perhaps poorly founded, it is necessary to proceed to the opening and examination of the corpse, and to locate all publicity and all possible authenticity in this inspection. To these ends, I request that it be ordered that tomorrow, Sunday, the third of the present month, those Gentlemen whom it would please you to name, should come, at ten o'clock in the morning, to the house where the above-mentioned *sieur* Mirabeau passed away, along with the public prosecutor, two adjunct notables, the head surgeon of the National Cavalry, the surgeon of the municipality, the two surgeons attached to the tribunal, whatever number of doctors that the *sections* of Paris would like to delegate, the closest relatives, six neighbors of the deceased, all to be present at the opening and inspection of the corpse," state the minutes signed by the state prosecutor.[38]

On Sunday, a large tent is erected in Mirabeau's garden, and, "placed beneath the aforementioned," a large table covered with a sheet, "surrounded by basins and utensils necessary for the opening of the body," to allow the surgeons to effect the examination of the corpse.[39] Polverel, the public prosecutor of the first arrondissement, and Fourcroy, the doctor chosen by the family to do the autopsy, are surrounded, guided, and watched over by an imposing presence—four municipal and eight departmental agents, five members of the Mirabeau clan, five doctors who came with the prosecutor, thirteen doctors delegated by the *sections* (particularly that of the Grange-Batelière, the orator's *section*), eight doctors close to the great man's entourage, six neighbors, and seven people "delegated by the people, which was out in force on the Rue de la Chaussée-d'Antin."[40] In total, fifty-six witnesses were present at the autopsy of the corpse, all named and accounted for. ("Apart from family, all the witnesses had to justify their presence, indicating whether they were relatives or related as far as the fourth degree."[41]) Each witness is cited with title, function, and address. Each one had to take a double oath before the operation, of "fidelity to the constitution" and of "examining the corpse and reporting its condition in good faith and conscience for the public good." Indeed, "a few people, indisposed, withdrew," but the defections were offset by "a great number of national guards who found themselves in front of said house and in the garden to maintain order there and to watch over public safety."[42] The examination of the corpse, meticulous, lasts over two hours, "reported and dictated word by word to the clerk by the acting surgeons, always in the presence of the above-mentioned persons." The autopsy report is thus devoted to the "opening of the lower stomach" (one page of description), the "opening of the chest" (half a page), and the "opening of the head" (six lines), to conclude in full clarity: "In accord with the facts reported above, said doctors and surgeons deem that the opening of the corpse reveals no cause that could be regarded as fatal other than the state in which the pericardium, heart and diaphragm were found; what they have declared being sincere and truthful."[43]

The conclusions add to Cabanis's narrative: Mirabeau died without poison or debauchery, and fifty-six witnesses judged it so. This macabre testimony, guaranteeing a dignified spectacle of death and acting as prelude to a civic apotheosis, is then widely reported, relayed in press accounts and taken up by some pamphlets. The report itself, in its entirety, its raw form, its "scientificness," is printed: "It was decreed, unanimously, that a sufficient number of copies should be printed to be distributed to the presidents and members of the National Assembly, to the *sections* of Paris, and in the county towns of the surrounding cantons. At the suggestion of a witness, that it was of essential import once to give the greatest publicity to these reports throughout the extent of the French Empire, it was also decreed that a copy should be addressed to each of the Directories of the *départements* and the districts, with the request, by way of a special letter signed by the members of the departmental committee of Paris, to spread knowledge of the report to all the good citizens of their arrondissement."[44] Moreover, as a final precaution, a final guarantee of transparency, each copy is "marked by hand" with the stamp of the authority distributing it, "to avoid any counterfeiting or clandestine publication."[45] In Paris, it is the *sections* that bring this report to the attention of the citizens. The eight *sections* surrounding Mirabeau's domicile take charge of the task, from the Grange-Batelière to the Rue Poissonnière, from the Place Vendôme to the Luxembourg and to Saint-André-des-Arts: a good quarter of Parisian space is thus directly concerned by the investigation of the great man's corpse.

Once the body has been opened, examined, and the observations distributed to Paris and the *départements,* the funeral ceremony begins, swift but imposing, playing the spectacle of public death one last time. After the autopsy the corpse is embalmed, then placed under seal in a lead coffin; the heart, "prepared separately," is "enclosed in a lead box." The two macabre objects, in the course of the day of April 3, are exhibited in the garden, where relatives, politicians, and official deputations file by. However, between Barère's announcement of the deceased the day before and the opening of the meeting of the National Assembly, an unprecedented ceremony has taken place: the Revolution has decided to incorporate the illustrious corpse into the political community. The "universal regrets" decreed by the Assembly on the morning of April 2 little by little construct a new funeral ceremony, that of the "great man with the grateful homeland." Here again, the reading of the corpse offers an ideal transparency. Not only will the deputies be in the final procession—"We will all go!"[46] exclaims Edmond Dubois-Crancé to avoid any "ridiculous discussion" on the suitable number of members delegated to the ceremony—but they try to place Mirabeau at the center of every gaze and all attention. Desmeuniers thus proposed to hear the final discourse written by the orator, transmitted to Talleyrand from the deathbed. On April 2, then, the latter came to read it: "I was, yesterday evening, at the side of M. Mirabeau; death was everywhere in this abode, except in the soul of my friend; he was still, in this fatal instant, a public man. He was informed of what the Assembly's occupation was, and he confided to me, on this subject [the right of succession and the freedom to make a will], the work that you are going to hear. There is not one commendation that you will give him that will not recall to you what an immense prey death has just seized. The author of this writing is no more; but in hearing him, you will almost be present at his last sighs."[47]

When Talleyrand reads this long discourse "in which Mirabeau still breathes,"[48] it is indeed the spectacle of public death that, infinitely multiplying the patriot's image, takes possession of the political space. The corpse was given over to public view by tales, rumors, periodicals, medical bulletins, and the autopsy report, while the speech of the orator is reconstituted by Talleyrand's simulacrum before the Assembly. Everyone, from the onlookers at the Rue de la Chaussée-d'Antin to the newspaper reader, the citizen informed by the report read by the departmental administration, to the member of the Assembly listening to the final discourse—all can, must, "be present at the last sighs" and then "examine the corpse."

THE POLITICS OF TEARS

The revolutionary community reserves an apotheosis for its first public corpse: the funeral ceremony ends at the "temple of great men," at the "patriotic catacombs."[49] On the morning of April 3, 1791, the National Assembly receives a deputation of forty-eight *sections* of Paris, demanding a "public mourning" and a "burial at the Champ de la Fédération" for Mirabeau.[50] This request troubles the deputies— "a profound silence . . . lasted five or six minutes," states Brissot.[51] The deputies, expecting another ceremony, are disconcerted by the request: the Champ-de-Mars was visited nine months earlier by Louis XVI during the Festival of the Federation, and the arrival of Mirabeau's corpse on the scene might be susceptible to bad interpretations—the "king of opinion" succeeding the king of the constitution or, even worse, the corrupt man succeeding his corrupter. Soon Goupil "breaks the silence" of the deputies and offers a solution: "When England lost Newton, it placed his sad remains in Westminster; the Parliament of England took on mourning. I leave it, Gentlemen, to your prudence to decide, according to the example of that free nation, what circumstances and our political and religious customs allow us at this time."[52] This discourse is interrupted by a deputation from the *département* of Paris, led by La Rochefoucauld and the general prosecutor, Pastoret, who carries the day by listing five measures: "That the new building of Sainte-Geneviève be destined to receive the ashes of great men, dating from the epoch of our liberty"; "That the National Assembly can alone judge on which men this honor will be conferred"; "That Mirabeau be judged worthy of it"; "That the exceptions that might take place, for some great men who died before the revolution, such as Descartes, Voltaire, Rousseau, be made only by the National Assembly"; "That the Directory of the *département* of Paris be charged with promptly readying the building of Sainte-Geneviève to fulfill its new destiny, and with having engraved below the pediment, these words: 'In recognition of the great men of the Country.' "[53] Fermont, Robespierre, and Barnave support Pastoret's address, while Jean-Jacques Despréménil and Montlausier contest it: the Constitutional Committee is charged with the file. Whatever the case, the administration of the *département* of Paris, much more than the municipality or the Assembly, is at the origin of the spectacle of Mirabeau's death: the public autopsy of the corpse, as well as the suggestion of the Panthéon, came from its ranks.

On the morning of April 4, the National Assembly follows the advice of the *département* of Paris. Le Chapelier reports in the name of the Constitutional Committee on the honors for great men, and requests that its colleagues adopt Pastoret's suggestions, to which it adds a clause for the future: the Assembly will not be able to rule on one of its own members; only the subsequent legislature can provide for that. Mirabeau, right away, is presented as the only exception, the only corpse whose glory is immediately taken charge of by his contemporaries. No doubt that is because he was also the only one unable to wait: left in a "closet," this corpse would very quickly be "corrupted." A picture from the summer of 1792 will moreover emphasize this with much irony, showing Mirabeau's skeleton in the iron wardrobe of Louis XVI. Mirabeau's secret correspondence with the king, a morbid sign of his treason and corruption, is here symbolized by his decomposed corpse. On the contrary, placed immediately in the Panthéon, he seems untouchable—though we know that in November 1793 Mireabeau's corpse will shamefully leave the Panthéon by the side door, never to return, shortly after that of Marat is admitted by the main entrance.

Be that as it may, the authorities of the *départements* in the spring of 1791 have already made their arrangements: Mirabeau's funeral takes place on the very afternoon of the decree of pantheonization, leading the body from the Rue de la Chaussée-d'Antin to the old church of Sainte-Geneviève (the new one, henceforth to be the Panthéon, has not yet been consecrated to receive the remains of great men), passing by Saint-Eustache, where the religious and civic funeral service is planned. The illness, death, and funeral of Mirabeau thus unfold over six days, a surprising rapidity that outstrips both rumor and the Assembly but imposes the desired transparency: the speedy consecration of Mirabeau's corpse takes his rivals unawares and annihilates all hesitations, attracting civic honors at the very instant of the great man's death without delving into memory or opening a compromising private life to the public gaze.

The procession on Monday, April 4, speaks of this transparency, based on the lively affection renewed by a corpse and not on "cold reason": "The sudden death makes all enmities silent, and envy is mute before the imposing spectacle of public suffering. All the misdeeds of the private man vanish in the rumbling of the funeral drums and in the mournfulness of the ceremony. His corpse saved Mirabeau,"[54] shrewdly writes an anonymous author. The procession's impression is immense, and emphasizes the dramatization of mourning. Nicolas Ruault describes the ceremony thus to his brother: "The cortege left the dead man's house, on Rue de la Chaussée-d'Antin, at around six o'clock in the evening, almost at night, to go to Sainte-Geneviève. It was preceded, accompanied, and followed by more than six thousand men from the army and from the national guards, who marched with torches, arms lowered. Half the troop was on foot, half on horseback. The cortege was formed by the National Assembly in a body, by the Municipality, the *Département*, the deputies of the *sections,* and by the entire society of Jacobins. The lead casket was carried by sixteen voluntary grenadiers and fusiliers. A funeral band preceded and followed the corpse, but it was so sad and funereal that it made tears fall, especially when the music was mixed with the tolling of the belfry. Sizeable groups of musicians, filling the gaps between the drums, played mournful and most sensitive airs that moved all hearts to sadness. It seemed as if we were about to go down with the coffin to the land of the dead. The cortege stopped at Saint-Eustache and didn't arrive at Sainte-Geneviève until eleven o'clock in the evening. The ceremony lasted five hours. More than 300,000 spectators were witnesses to it; there were even some on the rooftops which the procession passed."[55]

The pause at Saint-Eustache itself entered into this process of dramatization, till then so insistent through the music and the torchlights of the cortege. The stop was marked by a tragic accident: "Mirabeau's corpse was placed in the chancel of the church. The National Guard shot a salvo of farewell. The noise was terrible, the church shook from it; we even thought it might collapse. A stone that had come loose from the vault by the commotion of this repeated and noisy salvo smashed the head of a grenadier, spurting blood onto the bier where the coffin was. This accident, which would have troubled joyful celebrations, added one more dark note to this lugubrious solemnity."[56] Wounded body, public corpse, lugubrious feelings, and spurts of blood: Mirabeau's pantheonization, generally presented as the result of a plan of the Age of Enlightenment, keeps the imprint of a spectacle of tragic feelings. This imprint is the very condition of transparency: the public must look at the corpse, the public must lament at the drum rolls, the public must see by torchlight: it descends to the land of the dead and forgets the all-too-alive Mirabeau of sensual pleasures.

Brissot, Marat, and Camille Desmoulins—Mirabeau's most radical adversaries—were the first to regret this precipitation of tragic affections. Marat would keep bringing up the medical account of Mirabeau's death, giving this physiological journal a lost opacity, hunting for conspiracy and signs of poison. On April 4, *L'Ami du peuple,* Marat's periodical, offered its explanation. Mirabeau, "the man of all the conspiracies against the people," might nonetheless have refused to participate in the "Day of Swords" at the end of February 1791, which was supposed to eliminate "the majority of good Patriots": "He refused to take part in a new conspiracy, and this refusal become his death sentence."[57] The orator's secretary was indeed the one who carried out this revenge of the "French poisoners." Although the report on the opening of the corpse had revealed no trace of a conspiracy, Marat was convinced of it, recalling that on April 5, all the doctors at the autopsy were "henchmen of the Ancien Régime."[58] A "correspondent" to the periodical confirmed this four days later: "Yes, Mirabeau was indeed poisoned. Two of the surgeons confessed to me that they saw the stomach covered with livid spots, inevitable signs of irritant poisons."[59] The affair was "hushed up," and Mirabeau's corpse here takes on a singular mystery.[60]

Brissot too wants to break the fictitious transparency constructed around the great man's corpse, that "virtue made of a veil."[61] But it is not by setting up a scene of conspiracy that Brissot calls Mirabeau's death into question; it is by rediscovering the space of denunciation, the other transparency, that of the gaze into the private life of the public man. The *Patriote français,* Brissot's paper, thus alerts its readers: "You must mistrust exaggerations of pain and calumnies of hate alike,"[62] then rails against the over-hasty pantheonization:

"Why was this deliberation not put off to another day? One deliberates poorly in the presence of enthusiasm or of grief, and a great man has nothing to fear from cool discussion."[63] Brissot misses "cool discussion," otherwise called the main initiatory rite imposed on true great men: public denunciation and the ordeal of truth. "By a law of the Egyptians," the journalist recalls, "the character and actions of the dead were submitted to a solemn examination; the judges committed to this task pronounced the punishments and rewards due to the memory of the deceased. Nothing was hidden from this impartial test and this *final judgment.* The Kings themselves were subjected to it. I demand that, in accordance with this institution, and with the principles of the friends of truth, who should give in only to reason and not to enthusiasm, we establish in the Assembly a means to open public discussion about the judgment that I solicit for an impartial report on the talents and imperfections, greater or lesser, of Honoré Gabriel Mirabeau."[64]

The "final judgment" desired by Brissot defined an intransigent transparency between private and public in which Mirabeau's virtue, and then that of Brissot himself, would soon founder: an impossible space of private *and* public perfection. As for Mirabeau's corpse, it offered to its admirers of 1791 another logic, that of a "veiled transparency"—transparency owed to the public body, this corpse offered to all eyes—a warping in the play of correspondences arranged by Mirabeau, his doctors, and the *département* of Paris. The great man's corpse offers a "political pathology" that bears witness to his talent and his heroic, superhuman, fatal involvement in the affairs of the city, not an illustration of his private life. Mirabeau "died well politically"—that is what Cabanis's clinical account, as well as the autopsy on the corpse and the tragic procession, meant to demonstrate. Mirabeau must be judged by his vices—Brissot, Marat, and Desmoulins demand it. Mirabeau's corpse, then—opened to the eyes of all, but hiding its secrets, according to some—offers two transparencies to the public, and is established on two steps in the ladder of omnivision, which Emmanuel Sieyès, after the experience of the Terror, will designate under the names of *ré-publique* and *ré-totale,* contrasting the tight but tolerant constraints of the former with the "bad plans" of the latter, choosing, in a way, veiled transparency against the exorbitant sacrifices of absolute transparency.[65]

The Revolution tried to effect a decisive enlargement of the restrained sphere of "public opinion" into the space of a political transparency proper to the "French people."[66] The journalists had this ambition, and imposed it on the body politic, which soon integrated it into its rituals, its judgments, and its discourses. But how far should this transparency that establishes the new political space be stretched? Should it be limited to the strict public domain, or stretched into private life? Should it be erected as a tribunal of talent, or made into a palladium of virtue? These two readings of transparency stand in opposition to each other. Yet from now on, in a distinct sway toward a quasi-"mediatized" modernity, the politician must devote himself to the public gaze, relayed by the press, whether this gaze delves into his private habits, using denunciation, or remains fixed on actions in the city, comparing the various "talents" proposed for election. Mirabeau's death marks the first time that, starting from and thanks to the spectacular visibility of a corpse, this mechanism of gazes that forms the structure of the political scene typical of modern democracies is introduced.

Louis Lagrenée (the younger), *The Transfer of Voltaire's Remains to the Panthéon.* Engraving highlighted with a watercolor wash. Musée Carnavalet, Paris. Copyright © Photothèque des Musées de la ville de Paris. Photo: Jean-Yves Trocaz

Voltaire

OR, THE BODY OF THE PHILOSOPHER KING

On April 14, 1791, one might have read in the *Chronique de Paris,* from the pen of one of its regular contributors, the Marquis Charles de Villette, a letter calling the citizens of the capital to witness:

> Brothers and Friends,
>
> I have taken the liberty to erase, on the corner of my house, this inscription: *Quai des Théatins;* and I have just substituted for it: *Quai de Voltaire.* It is at my house that this great man has died. His memory is as immortal as his works. We will always have a Voltaire, and we will never again have the Theatine priests. I do not know if the Municipals [*Municipaux*], the Supervisors [*Voyers*], the Representatives [*Commissaires*] of the neighborhood will find this new denomination illegal, since they did not order it; but I thought that the decree of the National Assembly, which is preparing public honors for Mirabeau, Jean-Jacques and Voltaire, was, for this legitimate innovation, a sufficient authority.[1]

Soon congratulated by Camille Desmoulins and certain "regulars of the Café Procope,"[2] Villette comments on his action with witty eloquence:[3] on the night of April 13–14, by the light of a torch held by "two robust citizens," he scratched out the name of the religious convent, already abandoned for some months, to replace it with that of the philosopher, who stayed for a few months, and then died in 1778, on the second floor of the town house the Marquis bought in 1766. Under Villette's pen, then, the toponymical transfer, from "Théatins" to "Voltaire," takes on a unique character. It is first inscribed in a precise commemorative context: Mirabeau died on April 2 and has just been promised the "Temple of great men." Voltaire, Rousseau, and Descartes are under consideration to follow him there, and Villette takes advantage of this circumstance to revive the campaign he has been leading on behalf of a public homage to the philosopher from Ferney, his master and friend—rumor has it that he might even be his father.[4] Moreover, this ceremony is part of a very lively anticlerical agitation in Paris that spring, in which sometimes violent rituals (the persecution of monks and priests who had not yet taken the oath; the "burning" of the effigy of the pope at the Palais-Royal; a wave of anticlerical pamphlets) are the responses to the publication of the papal brief condemning the civil constitution of the clergy.

Villette's deed was not a real surprise for the Parisians. Since Voltaire's death on May 30, 1778, the marquis had been demanding honors due the philosopher, namely a tomb in Paris or even, in imitation of Westminster Abbey, whose example was being made known through the writings of Louis-Sébastien Mercier or Villette himself,[5] a building reserved by the country for the ashes of its great men. Thanks to the Revolution, the idea of a public homage to Voltaire took on more insistence, and successively Villette, Mérard de Saint-Just, the Marquis de Ximènes, and Anarchasis Cloots[6] formulated the request for it in different periodicals or petitions between December 1789 and spring 1791. The "creation" of the Quai de Voltaire is thus presented as a stage on the way to a homage to the philosopher, a stage suggested to the Marquis de Villette by a letter dated on January 14, 1791, published in the *Chronique de Paris:* "The monks will disappear," insists the author, Gabriel Brizard (one of the fervent readers of the anticlerical philosopher), "and soon we also won't have Jacobins [the Parisian Dominicans, whose former friar became the meeting place for the revolutionary "Jacobins"—TRANS.], or Récollets [a French congregation of priests called the "Récollets"—TRANS.], or Capucins, or Capucines [Capuchin friars or nuns—TRANS.], or Carmelites with or without shoes [Carmelites and Discalced Carmelties—TRANS.], or Feuillants [one group of the Cistercians, whose former convent became the meeting place for the revolutionary "Feuillants"—TRANS.], or Cordeliers [Franciscans—TRANS.], or Picpus [Congregation of the Sacred Hearts of Jesus and Mary and of the Perpetual Adoration of the Blessed Sacrament of the Altar, called the Congregation of Picpus—TRANS.], and so forth. Why should we conserve the names when the things have ceased to exist? It is clear that we should change the nomenclature of the streets and monuments that still bear these bizarre names. It is time to replace them with those of great men or great events that have made the homeland illustrious."[7] In this new patriotic topography, one of the privileged forms of symbolic regeneration unique to the Revolutionaries,[8] Voltaire thus finds his place: "I will go from my house to the Champs-Elysées passing by the magnificent *Quai de Voltaire,* and I will say: it is here that the author of the *Henriade,* of *Brutus* and of *Mahomet,* the destroyer of prejudices and of fanaticism, ended his career," Brizard dreams.[9] In mid-April 1791 this dream has become reality, for the municipality of Paris does not oppose Villette's deed. On the contrary, it is consecrated twice: symbolically by the citizen Palloy, the businessman charged in July 1789 with the demolition of the Bastille, who offers Villette four stones from the fortress, engraved with the philosopher's name, to be placed on the four corners of the quay;[10] then by an official dedication, thanks to the pause opposite Villette's house made by the cortege conveying Voltaire's remains on July 11, 1791.

TALES OF MORTAL AGONY

The purpose of this pause is to recall the final days of the great man. On February 5, 1778, Voltaire left Ferney for Paris for a triumphant reunion with the capital.[11] Having taken up residence with Villette—his closest disciple, married the preceding year to Mlle de Varicourt, the "beautiful and good" protégée of the philosopher, in the very chapel of Ferney—the great man receives visitors. Villette, perhaps a little too proud of having such a guest, devotes himself, say the satires, with much vanity to the pleasure of showing him to all Paris:

Wee Villette, it's all in vain,	Petit Villette, c'est en vain,
That you aspire to win fame;	Que vous prétendez à la gloire;
You'll never be bigger than a dwarf	Vous ne serez jamais qu'un nain
Showing a carnival giant off.[12]	Qui montre un géant de foire.

Voltaire has a personal triumph over the sixth performance of his tragedy *Irène,* played "by the usual actors of the King." On March 30, 1778, present in the theater's box of honor, he is crowned "venerable old man," "sage among sages." Onstage, before the presentation, the actors address this quatrain to him:

In the eyes of enchanted *tout Paris*	Aux yeux de Paris enchanté
Please accept our homage	Reçois en ce jour un hommage
That will be confirmed from age to age	Que confirmera d'âge en âge
By replace posterity.	La severe postérité.

The triumph is continued after the presentation, when Voltaire returns to Villette's town house, on an illuminated quay where the crowd jostles each other to see the master pass by.[13]

Two months later, the crowd is again present, but this time, anxious. Since May 20, the rumor has been circulating that the philosopher is dying. His agony lasts ten days and is almost public, so much are the comings and goings of the doctors and those close to Voltaire echoed and commented on by observers. Rumors, often distorted, fly so quickly that the Parisian press cannot welcome them without risk. The government, fearing trouble, forbids theaters from presenting Voltaire's plays until further notice, and periodicals from mentioning his illness, and later his death.[14] But very quickly, beginning at the end of May, news of the philosopher's alarming health, and then of his death, spreads, mainly in letters, literary pamphlets, or French-language newspapers printed abroad.[15] In this logic of the impossibility of holding back information, the year 1779 is a second triumph for Voltaire, a posthumous triumph corresponding to his arrival in Paris, greeted by a multitude of eulogies and poems, the preceding year. The French Academy, for instance, proposes a poem in honor of Voltaire as subject of that year's competition, and almost eighty versifiers respond.[16] Complementing the poetry, reports of Voltaire's illness and death appear, their recurrent theme the serenity of the dying man, passing away calmly in agreement with that wisdom so many eulogies unstintingly lavish on him. Condorcet, d'Alembert, Grimm, La Harpe, and Villette see in him the figure of the fulfilled old man, recognized by the "kindness of the Parisians"[17] and received at the Champs-Élysées by those great men, his brothers, particularly by Henri IV, as an engraving of the time shows.[18]

The cortege of July 1791, remembering both Voltaire's triumph at the Théâtre-Français and his peaceful death, wants to copy them geographically and symbolically. The pause on the Quai de Voltaire, opposite Villette's house, and the actual presence of the philosopher's body, "asleep on a triumphal chariot," will be the transcription of those events. Yet if this mimetic dimension, with a gap of thirteen years, is undeniable, the expiation is equally impressive, if not more so. It is a matter, according to Villette's own words, of "revenging" Voltaire,[19] or of "repairing the outrage done to that great man,"[20] to use the words of the report proposing his conveyance to Paris, presented by Gossin to the Constituent Assembly on May 30, 1791.

This injury to Voltaire that the conveyance to the Panthéon, and particularly the pause on the quay, must erase, was "the ultimate work of fanaticism."[21]

Not only did the priest of Saint-Sulpice refuse to bury Voltaire, but the writer's nephew, Abbé Mignot, had to transfer the body outside the capital in a disguised coach to the abbey of Sellières in Champagne, where he was the representative, and where Voltaire was buried shortly afterward, with a Catholic ritual.[22] The shame of this concealed burial still hangs over the Parisians. It is also what the transferal of July 1791 must expiate: "Voltaire's body, refused by the priest of Saint-Sulpice, was shamefully paraded from the city to the country, from the country to the city; and a little community of Bernardines [a Cistercian group—TRANS.] alone escapes the general delusion, since it had the good fortune to be directed by the nephew of the great man, and had the courage to scorn public opinion by gathering his ashes and giving him burial. The philosophy which today plays a great role, and flourishes over the debris of Gothic ideas, wanted to revenge the insult that had been offered him in the person of one of his most faithful disciples. The light that it spread on this occasion opened all eyes; arrogance fell away and the Constitutional Committee said: 'Gentlemen, the slave-nation has persecuted its hero; the free nation will declare him great. Today is the anniversary of his death: time presses, let us decide on his transferal back to Paris,' "[23] an admirer of the philosopher writes on May 30, 1791, following the decree of the pantheonization of the great man.

The corpse cast out of Paris: there are the "French slaves" led by fanaticism; the body led back to the capital and transferred to Saint-Geneviève: there is the "regenerated nation" taking up again with its "philosopher heroes." The philosopher's body becomes the physical sign of a temporal rupture between the Ancien Régime and the new one. It is an apotheosis. In this sense, the transfer of Voltaire's body, the commemoration of his fine death and expiation of the error committed over his corpse, must be a glorious celebration, greater than any other, of the body. The intact corpse of the old man will be at the center of all symbolism, all eulogies, and thanks to it the philosophical virtues of the great man will be celebrated. At the heart of this apotheosis nonetheless exists a paradox: the body is the prime element of a celebration meant to do homage to a fine intelligence, to the "conscience of the century." To understand this paradox, we must return once more to the circumstances of Voltaire's death.

A "fine death" is what Voltaire's followers assert, insisting on the tranquillity that surrounded the final moments of the philosopher, an episode imitated by the ceremony on July 11, 1791 during the pause before the Villette house. A horrible death, insists on the contrary the enemies of Voltaire, starting in June

1778. Eaten away by the sin of pride, the philosopher supposedly "died in infamy" in the face of God and his officiating priests. Relying on the testimony of Dr. Tronchin, one of Voltaire's doctors, the scandalous versions of the philosopher's death circulate very quickly and in profusion, disseminated by certain clerical circles or by the Jansenist group, rival to the Voltairean salons.[24] But 1778 is not the first time that his enemies make Voltaire die in horrible conditions. As with Don Juan's defiant death, the myth of the dying philosopher defying God was illustrated many times in purely fictional pamphlets. Already in 1762 Voltaire is tormented, then carried away, by the devil, and the "testament" published on that occasion instances "all his faults and sacrileges."[25] Fiction operates again in 1773 in a pamphlet entitled *Voltaire aux Champs-Elysiens, oraison funèbre, histoire, satyre, le tout à volonté* [Voltaire at the Elysian Fields: funeral oration, history, satire, all as you like it],[26] and then in 1776: *Voltaire de retour des Ombres, et sur le point d'y retourner pour n'en plus revenir* [Voltaire back from the Shades, and on the point of returning there never to come back again].[27] All these tales of anticipated death are constructed on the same basic framework: the descent to hell of the Antichrist, a schema that can be derived from the most famous of all of them, *La Relation de la maladie, confession et mort de M. de Voltaire* [Description of the illness, confession, and death of M. de Voltaire],[28] by Nicolas Sélis, published for the first time in 1761. After a long confession in which Voltaire confesses all his faults, punishment comes, reported by the philosopher's "valet": "At eleven o'clock in the evening, the sufferings of my master ceased, and he dozed off. I began to bless Heaven for such a happy resolution, when we heard in the chimney a muffled sound like that of people talking together and pushing each other. Almost immediately they were in our room and we saw a numerous legion of devils armed with burning torches. They separated: some approached us to keep us at bay, and the others surrounded M. de Voltaire's bed. Their leader came forward, and said to him, thrusting one of his claws in his face, 'Dost thou sleep, Brutus?' 'Leave me alone,' answered M. de Voltaire. 'Dost thou remember,' continued the Devil, 'a letter that I wrote to you a little while ago? I announced to you the place that I am saving for you in Hell. You will not die at all, and you will descend, completely alive, to roast in my kingdoms.' At that instant, he made a sign to his escort: they picked up the body of my master and disappeared in a terrifying roar. Such was the tragic end of M. de Voltaire."

On the actual death of the philosopher, on May 30, 1778, diabolic machinery is reintroduced according to two different registers: on the one hand, the satirical fiction of Voltairean tone turned against its initiator, and on the other, the realistic, pseudoscientific narrative of scandalous death, much more disturbing. Taking advantage of circumstances to republish a number of old "testaments" and other "visits to hell" of Voltaire, the authors sometimes add to them a description of the recent death agony, just as fictive a description as those that came before: "His face was alternately pale and burning; his hair was on end; his eyes seemed at every instant ready to pop out of their sockets, the eyeballs bleeding; the skin on his limbs, torn and livid, revealed rotten muscles: a black, infected blood spurted out of his veins; you could hear a buzzing in his intestines like that of fire roaring in furnaces; he was suffering a thousand deaths; he was grinding his teeth, crying, praying to God, swearing, making the sign of the cross, and declaiming the 'Epistle to Urania.' "[29]

All these descriptions of the final but too late conversion of Voltaire, set by the act of dying against his own degenerate body possessed by the demon, nonetheless hark back to a precise, "realistic," almost clinical testimony reported by the *Gazette de Cologne* on July 7, 1778—that of Dr. Tronchin, former doctor to the philosopher: "This death was not a peaceful death. M. de Voltaire entered into frightful agitations, crying furiously, 'I am abandoned by God and men.' He bit his fingers, and bringing his hands into his chamber pot, seizing what was in it, he ate it. I would like all those who were seduced by his books to have been witnesses to this death. It is not possible to be unswayed by such a spectacle."[30]

Voltaire, man of sacrilege and pleasure, was like Don Juan punished by his body. A dirty, painful, rotting, stinking body, responding to the final fury of a sacrilegious spirit decrying God while at the same time calling on his aid—that is the vision of shameful death, worthy of a prophecy of Ezekiel, exact counterpart of the serene death of a philosopher calm up to his final breath, propagated by the narrative of those close to him. This scandal of a bad death constitutes exactly the outrage that the reburial of 1791 must, in the eyes of the Marquis de Villette and other Voltaireans, rectify.

THE PHILOSOPHER'S REMAINS

The definitive occasion to wash away the injury done to Voltaire's body was first seized by his disciple Villette on November 10, 1790, in a speech at the Club des Jacobins, of which he was one of the active members: "According to the decrees of the National Assembly, the abbey of Sellières has been sold.

Voltaire's body rests there; it belongs to the Nation. Will you suffer it that this precious relic become the property of an individual? Will you suffer it that it be sold like national or ecclesiastic property? The name of Voltaire is so imposing that his praise becomes superfluous. Our glorious revolution is the fruit of his works. It is the philosophers that have made the decrees; it is the philosophers that propagate them and defend them. The Society of Friends of the Constitution is the proof of that. It is up to them to demand Voltaire's body; it is up to them to go console his shade and gather together his mortal remains at Sellières, the remains of a simple citizen, who was greater than all the kings of the earth. The homages that we owe him are prepared, are demanded by the public honors given Jean-Jacques and Franklin. You will no doubt approve, Gentlemen, the transferal of Voltaire to Paris; it is a question of determining the place where he should be laid down. Voltaire distributed glory, and received it from no one. If the English have gathered their great men in Westminster, why should we hesitate to place Voltaire's coffin in the finest of our temples, in the new Sainte-Geneviève, opposite the mausoleum of Descartes? That is where I offer to raise a monument to him at my expense. Voltaire, in this religious ceremony, will have his faithful friends as a cortege; they are among us in a great number; I would name them by fixing my gaze here on the best friends of the Constitution, on its most intrepid defenders."[31]

The disciple's devotion was appreciated, and his speech printed. The campaign of opinion orchestrated by Villette and the paper he wrote for, the *Chronique de Paris,* took advantage of a favorable context: on November 17, 1790, the Théâtre de la Nation played Voltaire's *Brutus* again, to a triumphal welcome. On November 23, Villette, before raising the curtain, took the stand and won support: "Gentlemen, I demand in the name of the motherland that Voltaire's coffin be transported to Paris; this transferal will mark the last gasp of fanaticism. The charlatans of the Church and of the cassock did not forgive him for having unmasked them; they persecuted him until his last sigh. The day before his death, the court sent him a *lettre de cachet;* the parliament a decree for seizure of the body, and the priests condemned him to be thrown into the ditch. It is up to Romans, to Frenchmen like you, to expiate so many outrages; it is up to you to demand that the ashes of Voltaire be laid down in the Basilica of Sainte-Geneviève, opposite Descartes. If this petition for the pilgrimage from the abbey of Sellières and the monument to Voltaire suffers from the least difficulty, I offer that everything be done at my expense."[32]

Villette's determination soon met cooperation from the municipality of Paris: M. Charron wrote to him on March 9, 1791 that he had been charged with conducting the affair of Voltaire's transferal. On April 3, on the occasion of Mirabeau's death, the National Assembly decided to place the "remains of its great men" in the church of Sainte-Geneviève, transformed into a "Temple of French Genius" or "Patriotic Catacombs."[33] The Assembly reserved for itself the right to place there the bodies of certain "prophets" who died before 1789, including Descartes, Rousseau, and Voltaire. The way was clear for a ceremony of public homage to the doyen of Ferney, and Villette rushed in, taking advantage of the sale of the abbey of Sellières, where the body rested, as national property. Voltaire now sought a burial. The deputies offered it to him on May 30, 1791, the thirteenth anniversary of his death: "The National Assembly, after having heard the report of its Constitutional Committee, decrees that Marie-François Arouet Voltaire is worthy to receive the honors awarded to great men: that consequently his remains will be transferred from the abbey of Sellières to the church of Romilly, and then to that of Sainte-Geneviève, in Paris. It charges the *département* of Paris with the execution of the present decree."[34] Although not unanimous, the Constituent Assembly did not hesitate for long in taking this decision: only Lanjuinais and Chabroud voiced reservations, while Brugnon tried to drown Voltaire between Montesquieu and Mably. The philosopher's body would thus find an environment worthy of the spirit that animated it. Nothing remained but to define the circumstances and organize the ceremony of his glorious corpse.

The first act of this "ascent" to Paris, this civic apotheosis, was the exhumation of the philosopher's body from its place in the Sellières abbey. Considering the rumors that had been spread thirteen years before about the shameful death and the state of the body, all precautions were taken by the mayor of Romilly (a parish that includes the abbey), who was in charge of the operation. The municipal officer made a detailed description of it in a letter addressed to the Marquis de Villette, published in the *Chronique de Paris* on May 14, 1791: "On 9 May last, we had two surgeons accompany us, along with four witnesses. They signed the report on the state of the body. We found it whole and very well preserved, thanks to the care you had taken to have it embalmed."[35] The report extracted from the register of proceedings kept in the office of Romilly in fact states that "the flesh was desiccated but preserved by embalming," but indicates nonetheless the absence of one foot.[36] Little by little, moreover, other "relics"[37] will disappear, distributed to those close to Voltaire or to the organizers of the transferal, a veritable cult of the martyr of philosophy: first the heart, embalmed by Villette in 1778, is preserved in a room of his town house; then the first metatarsal bone, taken at the time of exhumation by one of the two surgeons present; two teeth, one kept by Charron, the Parisian organizer of the transferal, the other by A. F. Lemaire, editor of the *Citoyen français,* who for a long time carried it in a locket on which was engraved,

Priests have caused such evil on the earth— I wield against them Voltaire's tooth[38]	Les prêtres ont causé tant de mal à la terre Que je garde contre eux une dent de Voltaire

and finally the calcaneum, also detached at the time of the exhumation and kept by one of the witnesses. Voltaire's body providing relics: beyond fetishism, we find here a concrete phenomenon of sanctification answering point by point the diabolization constructed by the philosopher's adversaries at the time of his death. Whatever the case may be, even beyond this cult of the relics of the philosopher-martyr, the report of the mayor of Romilly brings a precious element to the public ceremonial: the actual corpse of Voltaire, which, thirteen years after his decease, is in a state to be displayed. "It will be a beautiful ceremony. The arrangements are already made and the body of this great man is perfectly preserved; the features are recognizable after thirteen years in the tomb, thanks to M. de Villette, who had taken care to have it embalmed,"[39] writes Nicolas Ruault in his newspaper on May 17, 1791. The face, in particular, remains perfectly preserved, the features immediately recognizable; and this, as we will see, is indispensable to the successful unfolding of the ritual, as if a miraculous "Veronica's Veil" had allowed the philosopher's image to be saved at the instant of his death, in the course of the crucifixion imposed on his body by religious intolerance.

This identification with the victim of the Passion will go even further: the mayor of Romilly describes the procession that leads Voltaire's body from Sellières to his church as a veritable resurrection of the philosopher. "After the exhumation, and with unanimous consent, we exposed the body to public view so that everyone could see it. An oak-leaf crown was placed on his head. We carried him thus, exposed to the view of all, up to Romilly. On the path, flowers were strewn by the handful onto the linen cloths of his resurrection. Women held up their children, and made them kiss the sheet, presenting crowns of roses. A crowd of young people, interrupting the march, offered this note: 'Our fathers, enlightened by Voltaire, today revenge the outrages of fanaticism.' At eight o'clock in the evening, in the church at Romilly, Voltaire was exhibited in the chancel and exposed to view. At midnight, we closed the coffin and put seals on the four corners. A mausoleum was erected, guarded by two thousand arms."[40]

The good state of preservation of Voltaire's remains is continually brought up in reports and commentaries, along with the healthy look of the corpse, which, far from repulsing women and children, attracted their homage. It was as if, thirteen years after his death, Voltaire's body directly signified by its state of preservation the victory of the philosopher's values (at the forefront of which were generally placed justice, tolerance, and liberty) over "fanaticism" and "despotism." This bodily proof of the glory of Voltaire's mind is at the center of all attention. It is this body that the mayor of Romilly must protect, on one hand against attack and profanation (he relates that "two individuals loitering around the church and seeming to be of bad intentions" were arrested and questioned), and on the other hand against rumors that, in a persistent tone, continue to be fed by the anti-Voltaire papers.[41]

Echoing earlier accounts of the shameful death of the philosopher, now stories concerning the "evil remains" were not, in fact, lacking. If the embalmed and preserved body announces Voltaire's glory, his rapid putrefaction and foul smell are, *a contrario,* synonymous with his moral decrepitude.[42] Thus the state of Voltaire's remains provokes vigorous polemics. To the intact "resurrection" of the philosopher as reported by the mayor of Romilly, the miraculous figure publicized by Villette, there is counterposed its complete decomposition: "Voltaire's body, embalmed in haste, was transferred, during exceedingly hot weather, to the abbey of his nephew at Sellières. The carriage that brought him, and the room of the abbey where they first placed him, were for a long time poisoned by the virtue of the saint; for many months, one could not endure the infection. Quickly they dug a ditch in the church, threw lime into it, covered the body with a little earth, and re-tiled the floor over it; and with these slight precautions, Voltaire made not so horrid a smell. One might have said that the evil one had made Voltaire stink so much to make a niche for him with the Bernardine Fathers who were welcoming him,"[43] writes an ill-intentioned journalist in July 1791. Even more widespread, a second rumor offers another scandal to the imagination: after the degeneration and putrefaction comes the theft and substitution of the corpse. Voltaire's corpse is supposedly lost or stolen and replaced by a crude substitute. Thus the *Journal de la cour et de la ville,* edited by the Royalist pamphleteer Gautier, publishes a false letter from Villette revealing that the philosopher's remains, having decomposed, were scattered by the storm that blew up on the day of his exhumation.[44] Others speak of a mysterious transfer in a trunk to London,[45] or of the replacement of Voltaire's body by that of the old gardener of the abbey,[46] or by that of a "centenarian peasant from the Jura"[47] (no doubt Jean Jacob, the 120-year-old man who had come to greet the National Assembly in October 1789).

The most detailed story is reported by the *Feuille du jour* of the monarchist Parisau: "The whole district is talking about how a few months after his death, a tall stranger, thought to be Russian, came to Sellières to visit the grave, informing himself of everything with much assiduity; they showed him the place. He had the position of the head and feet shown to him. This man seemed insatiable for details on this subject, which no doubt seemed sacred to him. One fine night, the deceased was raised up from his resting-place, and the Russian no longer appeared. In the good old days, one would have said that the Devil had come to carry off his friend.... At four o'clock in the morning they woke up the prior of the abbey, a man of spirit, well brought up, who had once served. They recognized the fresh traces of the crime. Earth had been moved, tiles poorly replaced, and a strong odor stank up the church. They searched the place, the body was no longer there. That is what they are generally saying in the country, on the faith of these very believable witnesses; one of them told this story recently to twenty people. This singular theft could only have an honorable intention. The Russian perhaps wanted to give Voltaire the same honor that was given to the love-struck and guilty Escombat, whose body, preserved by art and anatomical injections, ornamented a garden pavilion at the house of the actor Rich in Glocester-Shire [*sic*]*:* but the frail and stinking frame of Voltaire, consumed by old age, by ills, and then even more by putrefaction and quicklime, was not able to serve such a brilliant experiment. Whatever the case may be, the czarina, as we know, had constructed in one of her gardens a house alike in every way to the Ferney château; the arrangement and furnishings were absolutely the same. Voltaire's library occupied the same place as at Ferney; only Voltaire was missing from these touching arrangements in his honor. At one time, they printed that the remains of his fabric, concealed at Sellières and recomposed by a true miracle of art, had served to give this presentation the only degree of likeness that it could still acquire.... We, though, we have nothing else, in every sense, but a false relic."[48]

The mayor, then the priest of Romilly, then Villette, were all able to refute these strange rumors and stories; the important thing is that they were written and peddled, forcing the reinterment ceremony to center on the appearance itself of the philosopher.[49] The editor of the *Feuille du jour* goes so far as to wonder, "Was the actual presence of Voltaire necessary for his triumph? It is to his name, to his immortal spirit that honors have been given, and yet the celebration of his genius could not do without his corpse."[50] In fact, the actual presence of the corpse was one of the major concerns for the organizers of the celebration, just as it was for his adversaries. Charron thus insists on personally watching over the transfer of the body from Romilly to the gates of Paris, between July 6 and 10, while at each stop (Provins, Nangis, Grignes, Brie-Comte-Robert) flowers are thrown on the coffin, guards are organized, and masses are said.[51] Until the end, they fear an act of violence against the body of the writer, and take extensive precautions against corpse robbers, be they enemies or admirers. Even the final night, from July 10 to 11, seems quite agitated: "An expedition of the philosopher's enemies again revealed itself, trying to remove the remains of the great man; but the battalions of the neighboring *sections* were called, and the bands of fanatics were repulsed," proudly states the *Chronique de Paris;* we do not really know if it was a matter of known fact, or the bulletin of a victory thought up in order better to emphasize the precious presence of the great man's actual body.[52] On the following day, the day of the transfer, again some desperate attempts are mentioned, like the "fanatical action of a rowdy priest who tried to sully the philosopher's body during its exhibition on the ruins of the Bastille."[53]

THE TRIUMPH OF A CORPSE

For greater security, and even more so for greater readability, the procession carrying the philosopher's remains to Sainte-Geneviève is composed around the simplification of Voltaire's presence. Attention and emotion are first centered on the corpse, presented majestically on an antique bed, covered for the most part with a sheet so as to hide the mutilations undergone in the course of thirteen years spent in the abbey of Sellières, but allowing "the recognizable traits of his face to be admired": "The monumental chariot was twenty feet tall and rose to the height of the second floor of people's houses, causing the streets to vibrate in its progress with a noise like some phenomenon of nature. Twelve white horses, grouped in fours, almost unadorned, and caparisoned with a simple drapery decorated with the national colors, pulled the chariot supported on four bronze wheels of antique pattern. A sarcophagus of porphyry raised on three steps enclosed the casket. On this sarcophagus, Voltaire appeared stretched out, in the attitude of sleep, on an antique bed. At his sides, one could see a broken lyre and, behind the headboard, a figure symbolizing Eternity, bearing the crown of stars over Voltaire's head. Four genii holding reversed torches and in the attitude of grief adorned the lateral edges of the sarcophagus, and four theatrical masks decorated its four angles. All these ornaments were in bronze and linked by garlands of laurels. On the front were these words: 'To the shades of Voltaire.' On the opposite side, one could read this great innovative thought of the French Constitution: 'Mortals are equal; it is not birth, but virtue alone that makes the difference.' On one of the sides: 'You must love laws, you must be a slave to them, bear all their weight; whoever wants to violate them does not love his motherland.' On the other side: 'God, give us death rather than slavery.' These lines are taken from *Brutus*."[54]

The body is present, but fragile, put on display like a "precious relic," distanced from the gaze of Parisians by its elevation of over eighteen feet. In addition, the organizers of the ceremony—Charron, Villette, Jacques Cellerier, and David (for the decoration of the chariot)—wanted to multiply likenesses of Voltaire in the cortege, imposing his image by bodily and symbolic representations as much by the expressiveness of the corpse.[55] Not only was the philosopher's body present, high in the air of Paris, but also a statue by Jean-Antoine Houdon was integrated into the center of the procession, representing the philosopher smiling, sitting in his armchair, one of the best-known images of Voltaire. The object was "carried by men dressed in old-fashioned costume, surrounded by young students of the Academies dressed in Roman costume, holding up trophies to his glory."[56] The procession featured such "trophies," like the "edition of the Works of Voltaire, forming a library corps, carried by men in old-fashioned outfits," or again a number of quotations from the philosopher scattered throughout all the groups.[57]

Finally, each stop along the route (the site of the Bastille, where Voltaire was twice imprisoned; the Opéra, where he is represented in a bust; Villette's house, where he died; the theater of the Ancienne Comédie, "where he triumphed") was chosen so that the different stages of the philosopher's life could be presented. The organizers, reconstituting the tale of Voltaire through his body (or bodies), in the end rejected only one register: a living likeness. Not that some of them didn't seriously contemplate it; Antoine Joseph Gorsas told his friend Villette about an "extraordinary idea": "There lives in Villiers-la-Garenne, near Paris, a man of about eighty years, whose resemblance to Voltaire is more than striking: same face, same size; tall, spindly legs; a philosopher's thinness of body. Add to that a lot of gaiety in his character; finally, for this individual to resemble completely the immortal author of the *Henriade,* all that is lacking is the divine fire with which the poet was animated. This living portrait of Voltaire made the idea dawn in M. de Villette's head of using him as a living likeness on the day of the transfer, in addition to the actual remains and Houdon's statue, and through this representation to let those who did not have the good fortune to see him alive get to know the *grand homme* in some way. To make the portrayal perfect, it would be necessary to dress the character in clothes that Voltaire would have worn. We know that M. de Villette possesses all the effects of this famous man. This idea may be unusual, but we submit it to the prudence of M. de Villette."[58]

That prudent gentleman dismissed the idea: the actual body of the philosopher would squelch any rumors of shameful death and substitution of the corpse, whereas a simulacrum could revive them at any time. There was only one Voltaire, even if his body could be regarded in many ways. The procession was rather long (around two thousand people), and organized around two well-defined poles of attention. On one hand, bringing up the rear of the procession, the monumental chariot carried the corpse, preceded by family and close friends; on the other hand, at the center of the cortege, was Houdon's statue, the bust of which was later cast in considerable quantity for distribution to the *sections* and clubs. These two halves joined to form an apotheosis conceived according to a studied ritual of corporeal appearance. Voltaire's "sleep," a serene sleep lasting thirteen years, crowned by an allegory of eternity, was in fact an explicit reply to the old rumors concerning his wretched death. The misadventures of his corpse propagated by the clerical press are invalidated by the actual presence of the body. As for Houdon's statue, it was a rather direct response to Jean-Baptiste Pigalle's sculpture completed in 1770, representing the aged and naked body of the philosopher in a hyperrealistic attitude that had shocked a number of Voltaire's friends and relatives, in the first rank of whom was d'Alembert, who spoke of it at the time as "a kind of skeleton."[59] Houdon's work stemmed more from Voltarean imagery, allying wisdom and kindness, dressing the philosopher's body and placing a smile on his lips. Pigalle's statue joined together in one disturbing whole the mind of the philosopher, that face symbolic of genius, and his old man's body, a state of his decrepitude; the writings about his shameful death invented a degenerated body to make of it the symbol of a failing, atheistic and depraved soul. As for the apotheosis of July 1791, it sought to "spiritualize" the philosopher's body, or to give bodily proof of spiritual genius, by presenting the corpse to the public gaze, preserved by "sleep," and by multiplying it by means of substitutions symbolic of eternity—porphyry sarcophagus, sculptures, literary trophies, antique costumes, and so on. Without any possible doubt, this was a doubling of the philosopher's body, juxtaposing actual corpse with symbolic body. Around Voltaire's corpse, not repulsive but with a "sweet presence," this "philosophical corpse,"[60] everything is in readiness to imprint "majestic emotions"[61] on the minds of Parisians. As Nicolas Ruault wrote, "The celebration of Voltaire, or rather his triumph, was magnificent. It would have been even more beautiful if the fine weather had lasted throughout the day. The procession was very long, and varied with all kinds of antique outfits of men and women, who walked in front, alongside, and behind the triumphal chariot, raised twenty-five feet high, surmounted by the statue of immortality under which was placed the body of the great man. After stopping at the square in front of the former Bastille, it stopped next at the portals of the Opéra, where actors and actresses sang a hymn. It then passed over the Pont-Royal and rested for three-quarters of an hour opposite the Pavillon de Flore, under the eyes of the king, who saw this entire ceremony from his window. He was sitting in an armchair, his legs crossed on a footstool. Antoinette came into his room and had the drapes drawn. The cortege continued on its route and made a long pause opposite the house of M. de Villette."[62]

THE REBIRTH OF VOLTAIRE

The long pause opposite the house on the Quai Voltaire was carefully planned. The most precise description of it was given, as might be expected, in Villette's own paper, the *Chronique de Paris,* an organ of pro-Voltairean and anticlerical militancy.[63] This stop played on the register of sublimation of the philosopher's body by profiting from a particular emotional context: after thirteen years, Voltaire has returned to the place of his death, the town house where he knew his last worldly triumph, crowned by literary Paris, and where he began his eternal "sleep" despite malicious rumors and clerical fury. The pause was effectively organized as a spectacle of triumph at once classical and theatrical: an amphitheater was built opposite the house, and the scenery recalled the evening of March 30, 1778, the crowning of *Irène*. The *Chronique de Paris* says clearly, "Opposite the house, they had erected scaffolding on which a multitude of people was placed. It was a unique spectacle to see, this crowd that covered the Quai Voltaire, the Pont-Royal, the Pont-Neuf, and all without disorder, without tumult, with an air of joy and fraternity that it is difficult to convey. Another sight, no less imposing, was presented by all the windows of this magnificent quay, filled with animated spectators, who were no doubt of varied sentiments, but who contributed just as much to the grandeur of the celebration. As soon as the first flags were seen from afar, the earth was strewn with flowers and greenery. The air resounded with applause and cries of joy. All watched the ceremony unfold in the greatest order. Each of the groups was greeted fraternally by the spectators, and each group returned fraternal greetings to them."[64]

It was a matter, then, of replaying the philosopher's triumph, erasing the outrage that the Church had inflicted on Voltaire on this same site, as much by the denial of burial as by the slanders about his wretched death. This outrage was overcome thanks to the introduction of the ancient cult of heroes, and then by a specific homage made to the great man's involvement in the century's struggles for tolerance; a few characters were chosen to bear witness to these virtuous actions. The scenery and the costumes were those of antiquity: "Charles Villette's house was ornamented in a very pleasant manner: in front of the façade was a canopy of greenery, beneath which hung a crown. An outdoor amphitheater was covered with women and young people clothed in white, garlands of roses on their heads, civic crowns in hand."[65] As for the personages and bodies, they were "Voltairean": Mme de Villette, adopted daughter of the philosopher, "in a costume of old-fashioned mourning, a garland of white roses, and a belt on which the dear departed was represented in black, with her daughter [five years old] beside her, wearing the same garland," was accompanied by "the two daughters of [Jean] Calas," symbols of Voltaire's antidespotic activity. Moreover, on the façade of the town house was inscribed, in large letters, "His spirit is everywhere and his heart is here," an allusion to the precious relic that Villette kept. Into this carefully prepared setting, then, the procession can enter. "Finally, the statue made by M. Houdon appeared. It stops in front of the amphitheater, and is placed under the leafy arbor and beneath the crown; at that moment, Mme de Villette descended and was carried to the statue of her adoptive father, her eyes bathed in delicious tears of sentiment, her face animated by the sweet emotions of filial piety. She approaches, civic crown in hand, bows down religiously before the great man, lets her head rest for an instant on his breast, and puts the crown on his head, to the applause of an immense crowd of people, touched by her grace and her respect for the memory of the bard of *Zaïre*. At the same time, she carried her daughter, brought her close to the great man and dedicated her, through a kind of consecration, to reason, to philosophy, and to liberty."[66] Antiquity and Voltairean surroundings: that is the ultimate triumph of the remembered philosopher, as he knew it in the course of his last Parisian stay.

This triumph is succeeded by death and then eternal rebirth, thanks to a dramatic enactment of bodily doubling. The double body of Voltaire is spatially integrated into the unfolding of the procession. All during this first part of the pause at the Quai Voltaire, when the statue of Voltaire conveys the philosopher's triumph to the people and his intimates, the chariot carrying the actual corpse, due to the length of the cortege, remains on the Pont-Royal. Thus, the "sleeping" body must impress the king, seated before the window of the Flore pavilion, and can simultaneously "see" the triumph of his likeness crowned by Mme de Villette and Calas's daughters from the other side of the bridge. Afterward, when the procession starts up again "to the sound of a lugubrious music expressing mourning and grief," the corpse approaches the abode where it fell asleep thirteen years before. The moment of transition, ritual of death, recalls the last moments of May 30, 1778. But this death is no longer sad, or shameful, or tortured: "Soon the sadness of funereal regrets gave way to the joy of immortality, and lines from a hymn by Marie-Joseph Chénier, set to music by François-Joseph Gossec, performed upon ancient instruments copied from Trajan's column—and which produced the most beautiful effect—celebrated the beneficial deeds of Voltaire and the influence of his genius."[67] Chénier's hymn in fact describes the happy return of the philosopher to the scene of his unhappy death:

These ashes once by tyrants banished	Jadis par les tyrans cette cendre exilée
Long from grieving friends had vanished;	Au milieu des sanglots fuyait loin de nos yeux;

A free people calls them home	Mais par un peuple libre aujourd'hui rappelée
To consecrate the site today.	Elle vient en consacrer les lieux.
Now is no time to pour out tears,	Ce ne sont plus des pleurs qu'il est temps de répandre,
Today's for triumph, not for fears.	C'est le jour du triomphe et non pas des regrets
Greet his ashes with song and dance,	Que nos chants d'allégresse accompagnent la cendre
Honor the brightest light of France.[68]	Du plus illustre des Français.

Just as the exhumation at Sellières and the transport of the corpse to Romilly had been presented by followers of Voltaire as a symbolic resurrection to counter the rumors concerning the putrefaction or even the disappearance, pure and simple, of the philosopher's body, so now the organization of the pause at the Quai Voltaire is marked by a tale of resurrection. The stations of the two bodies stress this regeneration imposed on the king's gaze: Voltaire's corpse is present successively at the triumph of his statue, his likeness crowned by public opinion, then at his death, and finally at his resurrection. These three stages are very simply rendered by Gossec's music and sung in Chénier's hymn: at first a first lugubrious transition recalling death, then a joyous air summoning regeneration. Chénier writes of it better than anyone, and the choruses present in the amphitheater of the Quai Voltaire echo it:

Our walls, deprived of you, will regain you.	Nos murs privés de toi vont te reconquérir.
Citizens, all of you, march before Voltaire	Citoyens, courez tous au-devant de Voltaire:
Reborn among us, cherished, great, and glorified.[69]	Il renaît parmi nous, grand, chéri, respecté.

This rebirth of Voltaire seemed at the time like the sign of the collective regeneration of the French people. The resumption of the procession, after the pause and Chénier's hymn, in fact resembles a double regeneration—the philosopher's regeneration entraining the people's: "When the chariot started up again, Mme de Villette, with her daughter and the two Calas women, descended from the amphitheater; the ladies followed them, and this admirable cortege made a touching contrast to the brave National Guard and the robust citizens, conquerors of the Bastille, who make more than one Bouillé grow pale."[70] Dressed in white, symbolizing the beneficent action of the philosopher, Mme de Villette and the Calas women, surrounded by women, are like the reborn spirit of Voltaire, finding their place, in harmony with, and in "touching contrast" to, the regenerated body of the French people, soldiers and virile conquerors of the Bastille. The "great citizen body" is formed. The organization of this pause is an elaborate ritual of emotion: it doubles the bodies (the two appearances of Voltaire, the double presence of those close to Voltaire and of the anonymous people, the existence side by side of Voltaire's corpse and the living king) in order better to unite them through the process of regeneration: Voltaire's corpse *becomes* an immortal sleeping body, and the people are prompted to action by this recognition.

How can Voltaire's wretched death be expiated? Or, in other words, how can the Ancien Régime be expiated? The organization of the transferal of the philosopher's remains turns around this question. To answer it, revolutionaries seem to have turned to their profit, the narrative, ceremonial, and sacred schema of their adversaries, those same adversaries who had trumpeted the shameful death of Voltaire. The schema they borrowed—apotheosis, triumph founded on the suffering/death/resurrection triptych—is quite obviously Christ-like, played out at each stage of the ceremony, from the exhumation in Romilly to the pause at the Quai Voltaire. To the tales of Voltaire's descent to hell, his stinking, rotten body carried away by the Evil One (whether he takes the form of a Russian giant or little devils) is counterposed this public ascension. The context was eminently favorable to this transfer of ritual values, for Voltaire's reburial takes place in a climate of frenzied anticlerical agitation in Paris. Since the spring, "anti-church" expeditions have multiplied. In this combat of representations, the pastiche, or the transfer's subversion of the rites and beliefs of the adversary, is a powerful argument, either because the traditionalist papers ape revolutionary practices and discourses in order the better to mock them, or because the anticlerical Patriots organize *auto-da-fés* against religious works, burn effigies of the pope, or set up apotheoses for their heroes—first Mirabeau, then Voltaire. Just as Pope Pius VI is sent down to hell, in the pamphlets and caricatures Mirabeau and Voltaire are raised to paradise, or to the "Temple of the Great," all the while taking on the forms and stages of the traditional mystic itinerary.

Moreover, the ceremony of July 11, 1791, comes at a time when the body of the king has just come undone. Patriot pamphlets and cartoons used violent and ironic attacks against the physical body of Louis XVI, generalizing his representation into that of a pig, a hog, dirty, impotent, at the time of the Varennes episode. It is at the end of June that Voltaire's transfer takes place, at a time when journals and pamphlets are filled with the tale of the abortive flight, or of the "abduction," of the king to Varennes. There again, the shift of focus of narrative and ceremonial schemas from one sovereign to another plays with all its effects. Voltaire borrows the schema of *royal continuity* from the Bourbons. Thus, as was already being sung in Beaumarchais,

Death demolishes the shrine	De vingt rois que l'on encense
Of twenty kings you thought divine.	Le trépas brise l'autel.
But Voltaire is immortal[71]	Et Voltaire est immortel

The ceremony of the transfer of the great man's remains shows him to the eyes of Parisians through the presence of bodies. The corpse is present, before being hidden from view, at the ritual of its symbolic substitutes: his statue is crowned, his books are honored, and his memory is venerated through a multiform imagery. The corpse observes, "from life," the *gift of immortality* that the public lavishes on its various representations.

This process takes place precisely at the moment when the figure of the king loses once and for all the forms of its symbolic glory, in the affair of Varennes. A print engraved in mid-July 1791 communicates this transferal of representations of corporeal sovereignty. Fame sings the praises of the "immortal man" in front of the glorious double body of Voltaire—his smiling, crowned bust presented with the chariot bearing his preserved corpse in the background—while the same goddess, to discredit the "faux pas" king, "horror of the human race," trumpets into . . . the grotesquely discredited king's anus. Chroniclers of the time noted this subversion of royal ceremony: "Never did the funeral of a sovereign present such a majestic ensemble. The triumphal march, begun at three o'clock in the afternoon, lasted till ten o'clock in the evening, as if four Voltaires had been led to the tomb, so much did each of the stops gratify the wishes of the public," writes Prudhomme.[72] Four Voltaires—never had a king thus doubled his corporeal doubling. For the philosopher and his champions, it was a way better to assure the continuity of his function and his glory, that of "king of public opinion."[73]

The transfer of Voltaire's remains, like the transfers of the representations practiced in conjunction with it, is thus inseparable from the agitated context of the spring, then the summer, of 1791. The ceremony had the aim of suspending revolutionary time by devoting it, for a day, to the glory of one of its prophets. But, caught between anticlerical actuality, the flight of the king, and Republican mobilization, it cannot reach this aim. Opponents of the philosopher, in fact, are not lacking, and never laid down their arms. First, Jansenist circles petitioned in May 1791 against the reburial of a writer supposed to have advocated the "corruption of public morals";[74] thus Lajuinais rose up on May 8 in the Assembly to oppose the eternal courtier, the "man of pleasure" to whom certain "acknowledgments"—but no "esteem"—are due for some of his stands.[75] Secondly, the Catholics faithful to the pope shouted abuse at the corpse during the passage of transferal to the Bastille—"God, you will be revenged"[76]—trying at every opportunity to make off with or scatter his remains, or spreading rumors and tales about divine punishment of the miscreant, and about the disappearance of his corpse. For the struggle leaves profound corporeal traces.

Always, in discrediting Voltaire, it is through the body that attacks must be conveyed: man of luxury and pleasure, the philosopher sinned by the body and will be punished by it—degenerate, suffering, putrefied, scattered, stolen. Voltaire's intimates are associated with these attacks, and the organizers of the transfer, particularly Villette, are included in this degeneracy. The fantastic account that *L'Apothéose de Voltaire,* a satiric Royalist lampoon of July 1791, offers of the pause at Quai Voltaire allows this register of insulting and degrading allusion to be grasped: "Voltaire's family, lined up opposite the quai, will be presided over by the posterior (*ci-derrière*) Marquis de Villette, retroactive citizen of Paris, turning his back to everyone to show the heart of immortal genius that he carries at the place where the author of *La Pucelle* placed the second trumpet of renown. From time to time, he regales Beautiful and Good [his wife] with praise for the 'Headless,' and with the interesting tale of the heroic expedition of October 6, 1789 [Mme de Villette's brother, bodyguard of the king, was murdered in October, and his head brought back to Paris on a stake]."[77] Voltaire's adversaries make deliberate use of sodomy and murder in their satires and attacks, with this register of a dissolute, monstrous, degenerate body. To the burning of an effigy of the pope, and later to the prolonged Patriot carnival around the body of the king after Varennes, are counterposed the outrages directed at the corpses of Mirabeau and Voltaire, ridiculed and demonized by the Royalist press. The organizers of Voltaire's ceremony of reinterment, as before with the apotheosis of Mirabeau, must position themselves on this terrain, led into these games of subversion of representations, games exacerbated by the symbolic war of the long spring of 1791. The reply of the Voltaireans is thus inscribed in terms of an apotheosis as grandiloquent as it is philosophical. Subverting the royal funeral rites of old, and the Catholic ceremonies, the revolutionaries integrate the bodies they have in their charge into a logic that is as much their own as that of the adversary, as much enlightened as monarchical and baroque. For if the appearances of the transfer of Voltaire's remains conforms (from costumes to quotations) to the spirit of the philosopher, the ceremonial schema—in the stages toward announced resurrection and the obsession with a corpse that is described, exhibited and copied—belongs to another narrative and aesthetic system. Thus, in these battles of representations—that is, these ways of showing oneself or naming the other—important transformations of beliefs and rituals are observed. The revolutionaries can and must struggle with ancient, traditional weapons, while the Royalists know how to use the words of their enemies ("Voltairean" irony not the least of these).

Leon-Maxime Faivre, *The Corpse of the Princesse de Lamballe*. Oil on canvas. Chateaux de Versailles et de Trianon, Versailles, France. Courtesy of the Réunion des Musées Nationaux/Art Resource, New York. Photo: Gerard Blot

The Princesse de Lamballe

OR, SEX SLAUGHTERED

"This poor mystery of a woman, paraded all over Paris, all the way to the Temple . . ."[1] Thus Michelet reminds his readers of the outrage done to the corpse of Mme de Lamballe, whose sex, mutilated and torn out, was carried like a trophy next to her head, heart, and disemboweled body by a joyous procession headed for the prison of the Temple, where the queen, Marie-Antoinette, dear friend of the murdered princess, was incarcerated. Earlier, the historian had told the story of the execution: "They seize her, they want her to take an oath over a heap of corpses. They strike her on the forehead. The blood streams down; it is the signal for the murder, she falls pierced with blows. They tear off everything, her dress, her slip; and naked as God had made her, she is spread out on the corner of a boundary-stone, at the entrance to the Rue Saint-Antoine. They leave her exposed there from eight o'clock in the morning till noon, then they cut away her head and the sacred parts of the body."[2]

A PHANTASMAGORIC PROJECTION

Around eight o'clock in the morning, on September 3, 1792, the princess was presented to the fearful Tribunal of the People, hurriedly improvised, in session at the office of the Prison de la Force. Since the day before, it had been pronouncing swift, often hasty judgments, handing prisoners over to a few slaughterers officiating in front of the prison, in the street, surrounded by a large crowd, with sabers, lances, and bludgeons. In four days 1,300 people were thus massacred in Paris, at the Abbaye, La Force, and the Conciergerie, including nonjuring priests, aristocrats, and common prisoners.[3] Gasping for breath, held at arm's length, almost unconscious, Mme de Lamballe, one of the highest dignitaries of the Ancien Régime, daughter of the prince of Savoie, daughter-in-law of the fabulously wealthy Duc de Penthièvre, majordomo of the queen's house, was sentenced, after a summary questioning, to be "sent away (*élargie*)," or put to death, in the coded language of the slaughterers. Then her torture began,[4] when two men carried her into the street: "She received a saber blow behind her head which took off her cap. Her long hair fell onto her shoulders. Another saber blow hit her eye; blood gushed forth; her dress was stained with it. She tried to fall down, to let herself die, but they forced her to get up again, to walk over corpses, and the crowd, silent, watched the slaughter. She fell again. A certain Charlat knocked her senseless with a log, and as she seemed lifeless, they attacked her perhaps still-living body relentlessly. Pierced through by saber and lance blows, she was no more than a shapeless thing, red with blood, unrecognizable. There were no longer any limits to hatred, to violence; it was up to whoever could invent the most terrible torture. A butcher boy, named Grison, cut off her head with his butcher's knife."[5]

A procession set off, brandishing the macabre trophies, dragging the body from the end of two ropes tied to the princess's feet. It visited Toulouse's house, Parisian residence of the Lamballes, then the tower of the Temple, place of imprisonment for the royal family. There, a municipal officer on duty takes up the narration of the terrible spectacle: "We heard tell of the massacre of some people of the court; at thirteen o'clock, they announced to us the death of the Princesse de Lamballe whose head, they said, they brought, to make it bow to Marie-Antoinette, and then to drag them both through the streets of Paris. . . . We heard tumultuous and prolonged shouts: they were here! . . . Two individuals dragged a naked body by its legs, headless, its back on the ground and its abdomen laid open up to the chest. The cortege halts. On a shaky platform, the corpse is ceremoniously spread out, and the limbs arranged with a kind of art, and above all a sang-froid, which leaves a vast field to the meditations of the wise. To my right, at the end of a lance, was a head that often brushed against my face because of the movements the bearer made when he gesticulated. To my left, another one, more horrible, held in one hand the intestines of the victim against his chest, and in the other a large knife. Behind them, a large collier held hung from a lance, above my forehead, a scrap of camisole soaked with blood and mire."[6]

The crowd demanded the appearance of the royal family at the window of the tower of the Temple; a young officer passed the request on to the king. Marie-Antoinette fainted while the cortege outside demanded her head. "It was a diabolic scene that would have required Milton to portray it, that painter of the abyss. The noise and tumult kept increasing; the air resounded with shouts, blasphemes and roars of triumph. Men and women argued over the abominable honor of dragging the headless, mutilated corpse with a rope, in the gutter."[7] The crowd then headed for the Palais-Royal, to present the princess's remains to the Duc d'Orléans, her brother-in-law. Then, at around seven o'clock in the evening, after the butchery and dancing, a macabre farandole that lasted an entire day, the crowd disposed of the body in a construction site near the Châtelet, where it was left naked all night. In the early morning, they would look for the body to bury it at the Cimetière des Enfants-Trouvés [Foundlings Cemetery].[8]

The princess's body, judged guilty by the people, must thus bear her pain in the eyes of everyone. This law of torture recalls that of the Ancien Régime. "The revealed, paraded, exhibited, tortured body is like the public support of the judiciary procedure. In it, on it, the act of justice must become readable for everyone," wrote Michel Foucault in *Discipline and Punish: The Birth of the Prison*.[9] The truth of pain is connected to the body. This guilty body must proclaim what it was condemned for: it is paraded through the streets, it is discussed, it makes amends, it is exhibited in public spaces so that it can better confess its crime yet again. On this body, moreoever, suffering must appear: the length, the slowness, of the episodes of suffering, of dying, relate a truth, bring a purgation and offer a possible pardon. Its pain, its mutilation, must moreover speak clearly by virtue of a decipherable symbolism: the body returns to the scene of its crime, the form of torture recalls the nature of the fault. Heretics are burned for their impurity, those who have killed have their fists cut off, the tongues of blasphemers are pierced. The penal reform introduced in the early stages of the French Revolution indeed abolished this recourse to bodily torture. It kept capital punishment, carried out publicly, but found an instrument that was supposed to shorten and "despectacularize" the torture: the guillotine, invention of the Age of Enlightenment. The famous machine of Dr. Guillotin allows the duration of the execution to be limited (death is given at lightning speed, when the blade falls and decapitates the body), and also allows the torture to be rationalized and made uniform: all the condemned die in an identical way, and the symbolic localization of the penalty on the body is reduced. Thus, torture on the wheel, quartering, display of the corpse, amputation of the murderer's fist, the burning of heretics—all these are henceforth relegated to the shadows of archaic "barbarism." Starting from March 1791, when the guillotine began its reign, the executioner contented himself with showing the people the most significant decapitated heads, without any other form of corporeal ritual.

At the beginning of the Revolution, however, the ritual of massacre came to perpetuate the old way of punishment, with its scale of tortures and its particular bodily symbolism. Parallel to the reform of justice set in place by the new regime, which tried to drive the previous suffering of the tortured body away from the public gaze, the sudden fits of rage by the people caused the rites of humiliation and mutilation of bodies to be reborn.[10] The violence of these massacres, which horrified the revolutionary elite, caused the reappearance of disembowelments, severed hands, tongues torn out, organs mutilated, as if it were a matter of a punishment corresponding to the expectation of a relatively shared symbolism. One also encounters, in the history of massacres in Paris, numerous cases illustrating this sudden and ephemeral "revival," as if an abrupt return of repression in collective mentality, a return authorized by the exceptional context of a revolution.

But in the particular case of the murder of the Princesse de Lamballe, the ritual of the execution works in conjunction with a phantasmagoric vision. The execution and then, above all, the mutilation, dismembering, tearing apart, and exhibition of the body are like a projection onto the screen of history of a collective mentality that then animated the different protagonists of the Revolution. This corpse, in fact, is essentially a *cosa mentale*. And thus it is revealing: what little objective reality it has is diluted in contradictory narratives, yet on the other hand it possesses the power to captivate and restore intensely the spirits of those who approached it or the thoughts of those who described it. There isn't much objective reality here, for the versions of the massacre attributed above to Jules Michelet or to the various witnesses cited are only minor variations on a narrative that grew out of all proportion in the first days of September 1792. Even more, the probable "truth" of the death of Mme de Lamballe, as many official reports of the period reveal it, decidedly refutes most of the humiliations and assaults that this corpse is supposed to have undergone. The judgment and execution certainly remain unarguable, no doubt rapid, even summary. And likewise, the princess's corpse is quickly decapitated, a relatively customary practice during revolutionary massacres, inaugurated in July 1789 at the time of the murders of Joseph-François Foulon and his son-in-law, Berthier. The head, stuck on the end of a lance, is presented to the people and to its enemies in order to galvanize energies, raise the enthusiasm of Patriots, and spread terror among the counterrevolutionaries. Then the narratives begin, and make use of Lamballe's corpse as an imaginary and fantastic object. For, relying on the reconstruction that the official reports of the *section* of the Quinze-vingts permit, the body was neither stripped naked nor mutilated; even less so was it dismembered, and undoubtedly it was not paraded at the end of a rope through the streets of Paris. "In the Year 1792, the 4th of liberty, on September 3," states the text of one of the first official reports, "the *sieur* Hervelin presented himself at the *section* of the Quinze-vingts, drummer gunner for the *section* of Les Halles; Tirceux, cabinetmaker of the Rue Faubourg-Saint-Antoine; Pouget, gunner for the *section* of Montreuil; Fère, handicraftsman of Rue Popincourt; and Roussel, wage-earner of Rue d'Aval, all of whom were bearers of the headless body of the *ci-devant* Princesse de Lamballe, who had just been killed at the Hôtel de la Force, and whose head was carried by others in the Grand' Rue at the end of a lance, declared to us that in the clothing they had just found, were the following... [a list of objects follows]."[11]

One can thus objectively suppose that, while Lamballe's head was carried to the Temple, the body, covered, preserved even, including the many fetish objects that filled the pockets of the clothes (a portrait-locket of the princess, a little reliquary containing Marie-Antoinette's hair), followed a reversed and relatively rapid path (the victim "had just been killed") along the Rue Saint-Antoine (the "Grand' Rue") to the civil committee of the *section* of the Quinze-vingts. No doubt, to arrive intact at the destination, the body was not dragged at the end of a rope but carried by men or in a wagon. In any case, there is no question in the document of any outrage whatsoever, or of a preliminary procession, even less of an abandoning of the corpse for several hours, let alone an entire night. As for the princess's head, it was carried to the committee of the *section* of the Quinze-vingts the same evening, at seven o'clock, by "Citizen Pointal"—no other than a servant of the Penthièvre house, the family of the victim—to be "buried next to the body" in a tomb in the Foundlings' Cemetery.[12] Judging from the absence of description in this second report, the princess's head seemed to be in a "normal" state. No allusion is made to a mutilation or an outrage, thus invalidating a good number of narratives. Lamballe's corpse was respected, and her head, which was presented to the people and carried to the Temple, is the only bodily symbol of the atrocity worthy of the public gaze. This atrocity thus turns out to be rather ordinary, a killing carried out in haste by modest and conventional political personnel—artisans, soldiers, "wage earners," a picture of the typical Parisian *sans-culotterie.*

PURIFYING SACRIFICE AND NARRATIVE FURY

How, then, should we interpret the numerous narratives that transformed this absent body into a terrifying corpse, and this symbolic head into an object of outrage? The impression left in people's minds by the September massacres was terrible, offering a scene that was at once fascinating and unwatchable. In a letter written to a woman just after the massacres, the deputy Claude Basire expresses this double feeling of excitement and terror in the face of the unleashing of popular violence: "My dear friend, if anything can console me for not seeing you, it is to think that your beautiful eyes have not been sullied by the hideous scenes that have these days formed the heartrending and unbearable spectacle for us all. Mirabeau said: 'Nothing more appalling or more revolting in these details than a revolution, yet nothing finer in its consequences for the regeneration of empires.' The sensitive man must wrap his cloak around his head, and hasten through the corpses to shut himself up in the temple of law, and envisage only the mass."[13]

The "unbearable spectacle" of massacred corpses seems to be thinkable only through the abstraction of "the mass," that is to say the rhetorical justification of the acts of the crowd. The collective is thought of as an active being, an agent of History, embodiment of a national destiny whose most unbearable details can be forgotten. It is into this conceptual framework that, beginning with the September massacres, the language of purgation is immediately deployed, a language of purification by the outpouring of blood, in which the multiplication of enemy corpses is part of a ceremony of sacrifice offered to the revolutionary cause, as if affixed to its historical destiny. At the time, massacres were rarely described by the Republican camp as acts of barbarism, but more as sacrificial rites, acts of justice rendered by the collective and omnipotent being that the people constitute. The September massacres, according to this logic, were not a regression but a step ahead in revolutionary history. And the commentaries of Patriot newspapers and pamphlets abound to feed this process of *rhetorical exuberance* that, in the name of the outpouring of purifying blood, justifies the "vengeance" of the people confronted with the "conspiracy" of its enemies. This exuberance is illustrated by the multiplication in the revolutionary language of neologisms meant to designate the role, even the prestige, of massacre: an ample family of words—"Septembreak (*septembriser*)," "Septembreaking (*septembrisation*)," "Septembreaker (*septembriseur*)," "Septemberist (*septembriste*)," "Septemberade (*septembrisade*)"—which allots a special place to "thugs (*tape-dru*)" and "murderers (*massacreurs*)" in Patriot imagination.[14]

The periodicals and pamphlets of September 1792 are thus haunted by these "restorative corpses," which, left on the pavement, allow the twelve thousand armed men leaving Paris in the night of September 3–4 to fight the Prussians at the frontiers to "leave with a tranquil mind." *La Juste Vengeance du peuple, La Justice du peuple, Le Courroux justifié* [Wrath justified]—these are the titles of the "descriptions," "exact details," "great details" of the September massacres that appeared at the time. At a moment of urgency, of fear, of denunciation of internal conspiracy "fomented in the prisons," the concept of *a priori vengeance* is allowed to be put forward, justifying the massacres in revolutionary language: "France has become a volcano more terrible than Vesuvius, and it is only through the sacrifice of our enemies that we will be able to be conquerors. It is time to show ourselves in the face of our persecutors; they must learn at their expense what an outraged people can do. Let us hope that the earth may be purged of these execrable tyrants. Many heads have been paraded, among others that of the *ci-devant* Princesse de Lamballe, whose body was also dragged almost in pieces. What frights must these perfidious violators of the rights of man experience!"[15] For the author of this pamphlet, the violators of the rights of man are not the murderers but those who plot against the motherland of the Declaration of the Rights of Man and of the Citizen, and their spilled blood is nothing but a just purgation.

"The people did nothing but express its desire to see on the scaffold the *vampires* who devastated it. They began with those who had outraged national majesty, and who had served the tyrants who seek to rob us of our holy freedom. They went to seek them in the depths of the prisons where they were wallowing in the cruel idea of the destruction of the nation. But no, vile slaves, your perfidious conspiracies will be helpless against the sovereignty of the people! They brought them to the court, and, after having examined the causes for their arrest, they handed over to the people these traitors to the motherland, the thieves, taking care to set free those debtors and those detained for delinquency in paying child support. All good, honest and virtuous citizens were beside themselves. They ran to and fro transported by fury, they argued with each other for what they deemed the honor of hitting the traitors with the first blows. Everywhere the same feeling animated citizens and carried them toward the prisons, the same hatred for crime transported them. A great blow was necessary, and the people executed it. Paris is now purged of the horde of regimented brigands that the prisons had been harboring. In the streets, one saw only wagonloads of expired corpses, covered with blood, mud and dust.... But this image of death in action is the spectacle of liberty at present. For, oh my fellow citizens, free men, men of July 14, men of August 10, let us take advantage of the lights that heaven procures for us to thwart once and for all the plans and conspiracies of the crowned tyrants. Once all these villains have become corpses of blood and dust, may union reign among us, may it be the model of our actions, the basis of our holy liberty. May all the French, then, united in thought, equal in sentiments, in virtues, in qualities, form henceforth only one single family."[16] The conspirators, according to this praise of massacre, are only excrescences living as parasites on the great national body: the presence of their corpses in the streets of Paris is the consequence of a necessary sacrifice, of an operation of regeneration.

But the elimination of enemies is not enough to satisfy the rhetoric of massacre: the physical sufferings of execution and the outrages undergone by the corpses fulfill symbolic and political functions that are even more radical. The annihilation of enemies and their values, the terror that must seize them, call for rites of humiliation and dismemberment that exceed death. The blood that is shed washes the nation clean of counterrevolutionary acts, and the fragmentation of massacred corpses is a direct image of the annihilation of conspiracies. These conspiracies are uncovered and then dislocated just as the body of the Princesse de Lamballe was, in Patriot discourse, put to death, laid bare, and then dismembered. Born to justify the fear and vengeance of the people as a collective being, the rhetoric of massacre exaggerates and then finishes off corpses by presenting them in their bloody details, by fragmenting them into so many eloquent bodily pieces. The corpse of the Princesse de Lamballe, a symbol of those September days, stopped being a simple dead body in order to become an essential metaphor for conspiracy, a conspiracy that only the horrifying rhetoric of massacre can avert and tear to pieces. The bloody, macabre, and phantasmagoric exaggeration of this language thus tries to signify the exhaustion of aristocratic conspiracy.

The other characteristic of the tales about the murder of the Princesse de Lamballe lies in the political consensus that supports them. They are Patriot or Royalist, revolutionary or counterrevolutionary. It seems that, at the time, all commentaries, left and right, unite in the enumeration of details of execution. Lamballe's corpse is shared out, and its limbs, scattered by the imagination of the narratives, belong to everyone. For the revolutionaries, this ritual of fragmentation and mutilation embodies the dream of an annihilation of enemy conspiracy. For the Royalists, the same corporeal details, used again and again, signify the regression of the revolutionary man to the state of barbarism. The Royalist rhetoric of massacre teems with these primitive figures, which embody the taboos that the murderers transgress in order to free themselves from the human race: cannibalism, rape of corpses, obscene laughter, denial of burial. The monstrosity of the Revolution is henceforth set in contradiction, like a scene of horror, to the delicacy and refinement of the princess's body: "I saw," asserts a witness about her murder, "a cannibal tear out her smoking heart, squeeze out the blood with one blow, and delightedly quench his thirst with this execrable drink. The executioners, mixing the delirium of debauchery with the horror of this butchery, sullied her body with their unspeakable turpitudes, until, drunk with a cannibal rage, they divided her palpitating limbs amongst themselves! These are men who, with the flesh of men, appease their cannibal appetite! The blood that they have been spilling for days arouses the thirst they have for blood; their arms, tired of slitting throats, relax while still slitting, and they swim in the huge waves of an ocean of crimes."[17] This shaping of the Republican monster is a classic procedure of counterrevolutionary discourse; it haunts, sometimes with a certain magnificence, the pages of Edmund Burke and later of Hippolyte Taine, of James Gillray's drawings, the story of the "crimes of the Revolution" outlined by Royalist writers, lesser or greater.

But it is troubling to note that the imagination of Royalist narrative multiplied the details describing the atrocity of the murder of the Princesse de Lamballe to the point of compulsive obsession, to the extent that one can speak of a form of *narrative fury* (*acharnement narratif*). No part of her body is not soiled, humiliated, taken apart, deformed, ridiculed. This body, through the spectacle of its martyrdom, ends up becoming an autonomous figure, detached from the mere denunciation of its torturers: head cut off, heart torn out, breasts mutilated, sex cut out.... Count Axel von de Fersen illustrates this fury when he writes, on September 19, 1792, "Madame la Princesse de Lamballe was martyred for eight hours in the most horrible way. The pen resists such details; they tore her breasts off with their teeth, and they administered every possible aid to her, for two hours, to make her revive from a faint in order to make her feel her death more keenly." If the Royalist pen claimed to "resist the details," it nonetheless invents two striking "scenes"—her breasts torn off with teeth, and the frightful prolonging of the martyrdom, in the manner of the torture of the Ancien Régime. It is Royalist narrative that certainly shapes this manner of "making her feel her death more keenly" by murdering Lamballe's corpse with words, weirdly exaggerating an already appalling scene. These narratives, while denouncing massacre as barbaric, revel in the murder of the Princesse de Lamballe, annotating, embroidering it ad infinitum with the corpse as starting point, offering a scene made up of multiple details in which excess and pleasure in description are mixed together, conferring on this martyr the status of a collective fantasy. Such a corpse, fruit of the Royalist imagination, in fact embodies an idea that the monarchists take note of but most often refrain from stating explicitly: the internal decomposition of French royalty. The corpse of Lamballe, a princess close to the queen, exercising high functions at the court, appears in this rhetoric of massacre like a substitute for royal denaturation. And if it is the murderers who carry Lamballe's head to the royal family, it is the Royalist narratives that present the monarchy with a dismembered, denatured corpse, a corpse in which the monarchy will recognize itself. The impotence and inconsequence of the king, the tactlessness and unpopularity of the queen, primary causes for the progressive dislocation of royal power in the eyes of the monarchists themselves, find in the poor corpse of a lady of the court the metaphor that these narratives shaped even down to its most minute details.

This murder, and then the narratives that described it and inflated it, are thus much more complex than the simple effects of the unleashing of popular violence. A rite organized itself around Lamballe's corpse; a ceremony was described. And around it an idea of the body (*pensée du corps*) develops (notably in the symbolic localization of faults and tortures); and with it develop too both an esthetic of violence, poised between purifying sacrifice and narrative fury, and an idea of politics (*pensée de la politique*).

A POLITICIZED CORPSE

If tales of murder constructed the corpse of the Princesse de Lamballe, it is undoubtedly because she bore the attributes of her rank and her nature with an obvious ostentation. Even more than the murderers, these narratives, through the misadventures of her corpse, make the Princesse de Lamballe pay for her friendship with the queen, her court favorite aptitudes, and her flaunted femininity. One can thus discern two "states" of the fantasized corpse of Lamballe, which recall two aspects that rumor attributed to the princess: she was a conspirator and a woman of the court. It is starting from these two figures that the tales of murder take shape, and it is these two figures that they keep reinforcing. The former finds its references in the anti-aristocratic literature of the first years of the Revolution, incessant denunciations of conspiracies hatched in the court. This obsessional imagination seems to impose on Lamballe's corpse a certain number of specific ordeals: head cut off, heart torn out, public spreading of an impure blood. The latter figure rests on several linked reputations: the princess was regarded with suspicion as a courtesan, and through her they took aim not only at the friend of Marie-Antoinette but also at the woman and her alleged homosexuality. There again, Lamballe's corpse and its different outrages allowed the tales of butchery to form the reflection of a life. The refinements and frivolity of the court found flesh in which to imprint themselves. Sexuality led astray exposed the sex of the princess to the worst humiliations, and her endlessly asserted femininity was projected onto the immaculate screen of a milk-white skin.

In its September 8, 1792, edition, the *Révolutions de Paris,* the main Patriot newspaper of the time, offers a 'picture from life' of the murder of the Princesse de Lamballe. It is entirely political, and titled "The Justice of the People." Popular violence is first justified as a defense reflex faced with the aristocratic plot fomented in the prisons of the capital: "Around the middle of the following night," the journalist informs us, "at an agreed-upon signal, all the prisons of Paris were supposed to open at the same time; the detained were armed as they left with rifles and other murderous weapons that the aristocrats had hidden. The dungeons of France were fitted out with with munitions for this purpose." This bold and premeditated raid is the signal for the invasion of France by the foreign troops. But the people, "who, like God, see everything," in retaliation make the "extreme decision, but the only suitable one, of averting the horrors that were being prepared for it," and shows itself to be "without pity for those who would have had no pity for it." The specific murder of Lamballe is only an episode in the prevention of this more general political conspiracy. It is an episode, but one that best illustrates the political reflexes of the murderers. Thus, when the prison guards of La Force search the princess before the interrogation, they find among her many effects "irrefutable" signs of her counterrevolutionary action. A small paper image representing two hearts pierced with arrows in a crown of thorns, surmounted by a cross, bears the inscription: "Sacred hearts, protect us." The *Révolutions de Paris* sees in it "a rallying sign, a kind of slogan that the Lamballe and other women of the court carried on their persons." In the same way, the princess's seal seems suspicious, a tree surmounted by the motto, "Rather die than change." Finally, some letters signed by the queen confirm Lamballe's guilt in the eyes of the People's Tribunal and the murderers. These letters embody at once the revolutionaries' obsessive fear, material traces of the enemy networks that threaten them, and irrefutable proofs of guilt that they will exhibit during trials and interrogations. "All the means to keep up a correspondence were attempted," writes a journalist for the *Chronique de Paris,* about the epistolary links that joined the princess and the queen in August 1792. "They have already smuggled letters in the folds of a bodice, in a child's ball, in almond paste, in a pot of ointment."[18] These signs of conspiracy, made public by rumor, very quickly trigger a form of political excitation around the princess: "They found, in the bonnet of the ci-devant princess, a word from Marie-Antoinette. They spread the rumor of her betrayal; in the prison court, around eleven o'clock, they heard many voices in the multitude crying out: la Lamballe! la Lamballe!"[19]

These signs vividly recall to the Parisians the rumors that troubled the fall of 1791, when the princess, having fled Paris on the preceding June 21, following the departure of the king and queen, and having stayed in England, Ostend, Brussels, Aix-la-Chapelle, and then at Spa during the summer, had (courageously) returned to take her place beside Marie-Antoinette, in the heart of revolutionary Paris, on November 4, 1791. If the Royalist press at the time emphasized the beauty of this gesture and the greatness of soul of the "faithful friend," vying with each other to use this phrase attributed to the princess: "The queen wants me; I must live and die beside her," the Patriot papers, on the contrary, welcomed a plotter, a declared enemy of the Revolution, the main activist of conspiracy. Starting in mid-October 1791, fifteen days before her arrival, hostile newspapers and pamphlets "imagined" the princess's return, already imposing on Lamballe an imaginary life parallel to her actual existence. *The Grand détail exact de la réception de Madame de Lamballe à la Cour, et l'agréable accueil qu'elle reçut du roi et de la reine* [Great exact details of the reception of Madame de Lamballe at the Court, and the cordial welcome she received from the king and queen] thus forms the portrayal of the "head traitress," the "worst of conspirators."[20] Similarly, *Les Imitateurs de Charles IX ou les Conspirateurs foudroyés* [The imitators of Charles IX; or, The conspirators struck down], a dramatic parody in five acts written by Gabriel Brizard that met with a certain public success, undertakes to portray "the horrors of the conspiracy of the court." The play goes back to the days that preceded and followed July 14, 1789, and portrays the intrigues of courtiers intent on "destroying the Revolution." Lamballe, at Marie-Antoinette's side, takes the role of a "woman of blood" busily at work in the queen's shadow in order to "have the Parisians massacred": "Fire, iron, swords, poison, bleeding corpses torn into shreds and dragged in the dust, the most horrible carnage, the secret of the most atrocious conspiracies, the most execrable wickedness, the total loss of an entire nation: that is what I undertake to outline in unveiling the intentions of this relentless conspiratress," writes Brizard in presenting the character of the princess.[21] Conforming to this register, the figure of Lamballe appears in other pamphlets from the autumn of 1791 and spring of 1792, for instance in the *Testament de Marie-Antoinette d'Autriche, ci-devant reine de la France* [Testament of Marie-Antoinette of Austria, formerly queen of France], in which the princess actually is the damned soul of her royal friend; or again in the *Désespoir de Marie-Antoinette sur la mort de son frère Léopold II* [Despair of Marie-Antoinette at the death of her brother Leopold II], in which the two women dream together: "Our only desire is to see this capital bathe in its own blood, to make all France into a battlefield. With what pleasure would we direct our greedy gazes over those heaps of corpses. Each French head offered to our eyes will be paid for with its weight in gold. Is there anything sweeter than seeing a detested blood flow? Frenchmen! our hatred for you will be extinguished only in the tomb. We swear here to nurse an implacable hatred for you."[22]

Finally, in a re-publication of the *Essais historiques sur la vie de Marie-Antoinette* [Historical essays on the life of Marie-Antoinette], this common dream finds its terrifying culmination, to drench itself with French blood: "Enervated by our pleasures, exhausted with fatigue, we rested from them only to insult public misery and to drink long draughts from the cup of crime. The beverage that filled it was a sign for us that soon, following the example of Caligula, we would drink French blood from it, and *from their own skulls*."[23] These accusations and this sinister portrayal are repeated and given definitive form in the *Annales patriotiques et littéraires* [Patriotic and literary annals], in May 1792. First in a speech to the Jacobins on May 7 and then in his paper, Carra invents the idea of an "Austrian committee," a veritable malefic counterpower in regular contact with the foreign armies that are advancing toward France. The "dinners at la Lamballe's," in the Pavillon de Flore in the Tuileries, would serve as a meeting spot, where the "Médicis-Antoinettes" would spread their "aristocratic poison."

Again and again, the princess is directly confronted with this reputation. The paper war, which contrives to place in Lamballe's mouth the same words of conspiracy, blood, and cannibalism, thus leaves room for the violence of actions. On June 20, 1792, when the Tuileries palace was first besieged, the Princesse de Lamballe stayed at the queen's side to face the crowd. Insulted, the two women saw themselves presented with "a piece of meat in the form of a bleeding heart, on a board,"[24] symbol of the French blood that they were supposed to have wanted to spill, and of the Patriot flesh that they supposedly wanted to devour. Two months later, on August 20, 1792, when the princess was separated from the queen, at the Temple, to be taken in a carriage to the Prison de la Force, the crowd gathered on the road again insulted her, "brandishing fists reddened with blood," calling her the "villainess of the queen."[25] Finally, the princess's murder, on September 3, 1792, also left political traces of unmasked and dismembered conspiracy on her corpse.

The blood that all the tales of murder emphasize, contrasting with Lamballe's white skin, this spilled blood is in fact a direct response to the bloody dreams that were attributed to her. Her decapitated head, soon paraded at the end of a lance, is also an eminently political punishment, an ignominious and spectacular fate for conspirators caught in the act during the Revolution. The very journey of this head, from La Force to the Temple, reconstructs the political itinerary that leads to the queen; then, when the head is presented to Marie-

Antoinette, it forms with her a derisory parody of the "Austrian committee." Moreover, in certain narratives Lamballe's head becomes a receptacle from which the murderers drink to the health of the nation. That is the case, for instance, in the interrogation of Jacques-Charles Hervelin, which took place almost three years after the fact, on April 30, 1795, by a Thermidor commission of investigation.[26] No credit should be given to this narrative, but we can see in it the use of same bloody mythology that took hold of Lamballe's corpse. This document has the princess's head placed on a bar in a cabaret, serving as carafe, surrounded by a circle of little glasses. The Caligula-like vision of the *Essais historiques sur la vie de Marie-Antoinette* is here taken up and inverted, as if turned back on the princess.

In the same cabaret, the victim's heart was supposedly "roasted on a stove" and eaten. Many other narratives make allusion to Lamballe's heart, notably that of the Abbé Barruel: "The executioners swoop down on her and the redoubled blows of their sabers open her breast and intestines. Her head, remarkable for her long hair, soon appeared on top of a lance, her heart, bitten into by a brigand, was put into a basin. This head, this heart, carried in triumph through the streets of Paris, arrived at the Temple, under the eyes of the king, who was forced to see them."[27] Another Royalist tale takes up and amplifies this legendary image: "One of the brigands carried at the end of a lance the head from which hung blond hair dirtied with blood. He was followed by another, holding in his hand the bleeding heart of the princess, and her entrails twisted around his arm. This is how they appeared when they went under the windows of the Duc de Penthièvre, at the mansion of Toulouse, whom they forced to contemplate the mutilated members of his daughter-in-law, and from there to the Temple, where the royal family was. The queen fainted at this horrible sight. They stopped all the carriages that passed in the street, and they forced everyone who was inside to kiss the princess's head. A monster bragged of having made Madame de Lamballe's heart his dinner."[28] The decapitated head, the heart torn from the chest, sometimes eviscerated entrails—such mutilations compete with each other in "politicizing" Lamballe's corpse. In fact, the tales of butchery recycle the bloody visions that pamphlets had attributed to the princess, and apply them to the fate of her own body.

Moreover, the bodily symbolism of this ceremony is precisely political. Separating the head from the body comes down, in revolutionary rhetoric, to cutting off one of the conspiratorial hydra's heads; to tear out the heart is to deprive the counterrevolution of its will to act. Above all, these acts demand spectacle and publicity. They are enacted in the center of public space. And the most surprising thing is not that these humiliations of the body were a complete fabrication, but rather that they were publicly avowed, fashioned by witnesses, then repeated in the form of eyewitness accounts from narrative to narrative, integrated as such into the martyrology of the princess. The political narrative seems to be able to feed on a kind of collective hallucination while at the same time engendering it. Kissing the princess's mutilated face, saluting her heart, biting it as a sign of allegiance to the Revolution, in the midst of the crowd—all that has become an obvious fable, read in the papers and pamphlets even before Lamballe's actual death, reread at the time of that death, thus seen in the street. In a framework in which each humiliation that marks the corpse finds its political equivalence a priori, as already written, all these tales of murder gain in "realistic effect" what they lose in verisimilitude. The political symbolism attached to the corpse outweighs what the murderers actually did and what the crowd actually saw. In a way, for the tales of murder, the princess had to be publicly dismembered.

THE WOMAN PUNISHED

In June 1768 Marie-Thérèse-Louise de Savoie-Carignan, Princesse de Lamballe, a young widow nineteen years of age, is presented to the court. After a time she becomes the favorite of the old King Louis XV, before Mme du Barry takes on this role. Thus begins, under the best auspices, the womanly career of the Princesse de Lamballe. This career is first that of a courtier, heightened even more by the interest and friendship of the young dauphine, Marie-Antoinette of Austria. The latter, at the age of sixteen, arrives in France in the spring of 1770. On May 14, Lamballe is present at the going-to-bed ceremony of Marie-Antoinette, during her first evening at the Château de Compiègne, and tells her of "her joy to find herself there."[29] The princess then participates for several years in all the daily games of the court at the side of the dauphine—at spectacles, dances, all the "pranks and mockeries." She knows that she will never be able to remarry, because of the wish of her father-in-law, the Duc de Penthièvre; thus she devotes herself wholly to her friendship with Marie-Antoinette. Memoirs and newspapers, as well as secret diplomatic correspondence, often recount the "dinners," "balls," "evenings at the Opera," "sleigh rides," in which the two young women, nearly alone, openly show their complicity. The Comte de Mercy-Argenteau, the ambassador from Austria, scrupulously spies on this relationship, describing to the Empress Marie-Thérèse this "very particular affection," the "favors from which this dear Lamballe benefits," and the visits that the protégée makes to the dauphine "too often alone."[30]

In 1774, when Marie-Antoinette becomes queen of France, this complicity is a little changed by a rigid etiquette that rules all actions and all hierarchies at the Château de Versailles. "My dear Lamballe, I am imprisoned in my Versailles, constrained to all the annoyances of etiquette, of representation," writes the young queen to her friend.[31] But a solution is quickly found when, in February 1775, Marie-Antoinette obtains from the king "a country house where she could do whatever she liked."[32] Far from court etiquette and from the château, the queen takes possession of the Petit Trianon and introduces the Princesse de Lamballe there in a good position, charged with helping the queen plan the English garden and the ornamental sheepfold. This pastoral friendship takes a more official and courtly turn when it is consecrated by the attribution of a high function to the princess: superintendent of the queen's house, an appointment "that had not existed at all at the court of Versailles since the death of Mademoiselle de Clermont in 1741."[33]

The reestablishment and attribution of this honor, on June 16, 1775, provoke numerous intrigues, negotiations, rivalries, and jealousies. The appointment offers the Princesse de Lamballe substantial power and income, but also means a detestable reputation for her. Lamballe is henceforth a figure of satire, almost an object of hatred. Her enemies, notably Mme de Genlis, the Abbé de Vermond, the Comtesse de Dillon, and the Comtesse de Polignac, relay to the chroniclers and gazetteers these "titillating scenes," these "amusing anecdotes," which are inflated into rumors, in which the princess seems "stupid and ignorant," "extravagant," "a plotter," "scornful and haughty."[34] These characterizations are not entirely unjustified, and the princess, once she is superintendent, seems to grasp tightly her duty and power. She is henceforth extremely attached to etiquette, to the point of mania, with a love of ceremony and science of precedence that earn her the accusation of "courtier despotism" and end up exasperating the queen herself. She also seems greedy for property and income: *La Matière préférable à l'esprit* [Matter over mind] is the title of one of the pamphlets about her that attacks her position close to the queen. Finally she is a great arranger, for a time, of the "amusements of the court," which obliges her to run up expenses and follow the fashions, and reinforces her reputation as a "ridiculous and frivolous woman."

In 1777, however, the princess falls out of favor, the queen now preferring to surround herself with the Comtesses de Polignac and de Dillon. "Their relationship, seemingly friendly, is now nothing more than illusory, a form of decorum,"[35] confides Mercy-Argenteau to Marie-Thérèse about this phantom of friendship. Lamballe returns to the shadows, and satires of the court wind up forgetting her. But by October 1789, when the court is installed at the Tuileries and the princess comes to rejoin the queen in adversity, taking charge again of the organization of court ceremony while her rival Polignac flees abroad, the Lamballe figure reappears in the foreground of pamphlets, identical in every respect to that of the middle of the 1770s. The *Description de la ménagerie royale d'animaux vivants, établie aux Tuileries* [Description of the royal zoo of living animals, established at the Tuileries] or the *Galerie des dames françaises* [Gallery of French ladies], for instance, do not spare her but say nothing new about her: rapacious, stupid, and scornful in the former, and greedy, speculating, and plotting in the latter, Lamballe can no longer escape her disastrous courtesan image. Her charitable and philanthropic involvements, her role in French freemasonry at the end of the Ancien Régime, so many elements that could have changed her portrayal, do nothing for her here:[36] the princess is the "slave" of the queen, and it is first with this title that she is chastised by the September 1792 murderers and that her corpse is put on show.[37]

In fact the tales of her killing suggest the execution of a slave, while the imagined parading of her corpse is part of a parody of courtly ritual. The slave, thus, must imitate the gesture of submission at the time of her torture: many narratives mention that the princess "was put on her knees, kneeling before the nation"[38] at the instant of the fatal blow. "A man orders the former princess to bend her knee, to beg forgiveness of the nation. A thousand voices cried out to her: 'To your knees, and beg forgiveness.' Two executioners seized her by the hands, stretching them out sideways, ready to dislocate them, in order to make her kneel. Then she felt redoubled blows of the saber."[39]

As for the procession that leads Lamballe's head from La Force to the Temple, it resembles a form of etiquette gone astray: the final presentation of the princess at court. The king and queen are called to greet this face that, according to a persistent and revelatory legend, a barber had "washed, curled and rouged" on the way.[40] The courtesan's final toilette returns many times in the September stories, an anecdote completely fabricated by three self-proclaimed witnesses—Blanzy, Rétif de la Bretonne, and a historian who has remained anonymous. The first asserts that the daughter of a wig maker in the Rue des Ballets had the head carried to her father's shop so that "it could be curled, made up with vermilion, a tricolor ribbon placed in her hair," a head that the people "want to be beautiful for her friend, who cries behind the somber walls of the Temple, to contemplate."[41] Rétif, in *Vingt nuits à Paris* [Twenty nights in Paris], depicts himself as an alarmed witness of the killing: "I saw a woman appear who was as pale as her linen, held up by a counter clerk. They made her climb up onto a heap of corpses. They told her over and over to cry, Long live the Nation! She refused. Then a killer seized her, tore off her dress, and opened her stomach. She fell and was finished off by the others. Never was a similar horror offered to my imagination. I wanted to flee. My legs weakened. I fainted. . . . When I came to myself, I saw the bleeding head. I was told that they had had it washed at a wig maker's, curled, made up, put on the end of a lance to present it to the Temple. This ill-fated woman was Madame de Lamballe."[42]

The third story is even more explicit on the courtly function of this at once morbid and grotesque ritual: "They requisitioned a wig maker so that the princess might not show herself thus neglected before the queen. He had to wash, untangle, plait and powder the stained blond hair. Then make up the face, give it back some color, like the rouge she wore at the court. 'At least, now, Antoinette will be able to recognize her,' exclaimed the people present."[43] In the course of this final toilette, the courtesan dies: her "mask" is reconstituted, her presentation effected, then it is dislocated by the grotesque and macabre parade that accounts of the murder invented.

Lamballe's murder also keeps intending to show, in contrast with the gushing blood and the displayed organs, the refinement in which the princess wanted to live. This delicate, finely worked, frivolous appearance designates the past and the caste to which the victim belongs: the Ancien Régime, the court. It also designates her condition as a woman. Contrasted with the confident virility of the murderers, this fragility is a sign of guilt. All the descriptions of the Tribunal of the people that worked at La Force, imprecise as they were, insist on this virile presence of the people through its words of command, its bearing, its corporeal manifestations. The femininity of the princess, on the contrary, clashes with this universe of men. It is expressed by her paleness, a sign of innocence for the Royalists attached to the symbolism of the color white, supplementary indication of betrayal and of belonging to the caste of privileged women for the *septembriseurs* ["Septembreakers—a nickname for the sans-culottes and other militants who supported the September Massacres in 1792—TRANS.]. Lamballe is a white spot in the midst of a people of color. Her immaculate dress does not hide for long a body of an "extraordinary pallor."[44] And the blood that soils them plays the role of unveiler: it adds itself to the whiteness to emphasize even more the guilty femininity that is being executed, as if this execution were, to begin with, only a monstrous menstruation.

Lamballe's pallor well before her murder in September, had become a legend. The painted portraits mark her visibly by this trait: pale blue eyes, almost white blond hair, and an immaculate complexion. The absence of color, at a time when this quality is considered a gift of nature, makes the princess's reputation, conferring on her an aura even greater than beauty. And many are the scenes in which the historians describe her with a background as white as her skin, a way of emphasizing Lamballe's singularity: in a sleigh, with Marie-Antoinette, on the snow; in a white dress, powdered wig, adorned with pearls and ivory jewelry; at the Trianon, especially, surrounded by sheep, barely distinguishable from the background of white marble in the royal dairy. Through this insisted-upon whiteness, at once candor, ingenuity, and gentleness, the princess is associated with the queen. And one could say that this pallor will be their downfall, when it is confronted with the colors of the people, with the tricolor and aggressive symbolism of the Revolution. This contrast functions even up to the princess's corpse, as a narrative of her murder describes in detail: "A black man (Delorme) and a cutthroat (Petit-Mamin) regularly sponged the bloody remains to make sure the people noticed the exquisite whiteness of la Lamballe."[45] This whiteness, emphasized here by the spectrum of colors portrayed in the description, is the sign of an extreme, and thus scandalous, femininity. Lamballe is neither a mother nor a virgin; even less is she a revolutionary; she is only a woman irremediably attached to the old France, that is to say a woman who has become useless, harmful.

The other famous sign of Lamballe's femininity stems from her vapors, her faintings, from that "malady of languor" that the doctors of the time saw as the woman's illness par excellence. The *Mémoires secrets pour servir à l'histoire de la République des Lettres en France de 1762 jusqu'à nos jours. 36 vols. Paris, 1777–89* by L. P. de Bachaumont evokes this pathology in the fall of 1767, when the princess's husband, the young Duc de Penthièvre, dies of syphilis: "She contracted a profound melancholy and convulsive vapors."[46] Her frequent swoons, from then on, are famous: a noise that is too loud, the sight of blood, of something dirty, of certain animals, a sudden emotion—each time Lamballe collapses. It is said that she fell into a swoon in front of the painting of a lobster; that was a cause for laughter and even the object of games of parody in certain court coteries. They played "at la Lamballe": a man disguises himself as an animal, acts out the part, and as he passes by, all the women faint into the arms of their cavalier.[47]

The princess's numerous cures at Bourbonne-les-Bains did nothing. In the early 1780s she even became a textbook example through all of Europe, entrusting her illness to Franz Mesmer, famous for his experiments on the "magnetic fluid" that was supposed to be able to pacify Lamballe's fragile nerves. One or two seances around the "mesmeric *baquet* [a bucket or basin that served as an 'accumulator' of mesmeric force; the patient would take hold of an iron rod protruding from the *baquet* and thus receive the healing force—TRANS.]," though, seemed ineffective.[48] She then took on a German doctor, Seiffert, "her Saxon of medicine" according to the pamphlets of the time, which also make him her lover.[49] Seiffert saw in his patient a case of "convulsive weakening" and wrote a treatise on this exemplary specimen of excessive emotionality that has been translated into many languages.[50]

Thus Lamballe carried her femininity to the point of pathology, offered it to charlatanism, and, for many of her contemporaries, embodied the female predicament to ridiculous excess. And this too is what the September 1792 murderers make her pay for. In the stories of her torture, she is in a way taken apart like the crustaceans that she could not bear to see, even in painting. In like manner the ceremonial of her execution parodies her "feminine pathology." The interrogation, the corpses on which she must walk, exaggerate the emotions and visions that make the princess swoon, but, as the Count Fersen invents it, the cruelty of the executioners goes so far as to "administer every possible aid to her, for two hours, to make her revive from a faint in order to make her feel her death more keenly."[51] "How many times, before her last sigh, did this princess die!" continues a historian, stressing this interminable agony.[52] The murderers provoke these celebrated swoons only to cut them short: Lamballe's consciousness is indispensable, and she must not escape the spectacle of her own torture. And what she sees then, in the fantasy of the killers, is a *woman punished.*

The princess also had the well-established reputation of carrying her femininity to its extreme: she could take her pleasure without men. "The queen has the liveliest friendship for the young princess. We know that Her Majesty often has parties with her at the Petit-Trianon or Petit-Vienne, and that she admits only a few ladies of her retinue to them, without any man. There, she gives herself over in freedom to all the adorable extravagances of her age."[53] Thus, in the beginning of 1775, the *Mémoires secrets* by Bachaumont evoke for the first time this pastoral friendship linking Marie-Antoinette to her "beautiful angel" in the fashion of suggestive allusion. This friendship then changes, in the chronicles, into a "rural gaiety," "rustic escapades," "enchanted walks in the sweltering heat of the shrubbery."[54] And the rumors increase. An "epidemic of satirical songs,"[55] evoked by Lamballe in a letter to her mother on November 30, 1775, begins to portray intimate relationships between the two women. These texts revel in the deeds and misdeeds of the "manless (*anandrine*) sect," which "had as its aim to lead France to sterility."[56] This lesbian conspiracy is led by Lamballe, "The Sappho of Trianon."[57] Everything comes together, in these satires, to draw up the portrayal of two women who despise and disparage the masculine ideal. The queen is married to an impotent man who neglects her, and other men are only prey for her, playthings between her thighs. The princess was cheated on and ignored by an ephemeral husband dead of venereal disease, and is kept bridled by a father-in-law who denies her the company of other men.

Little by little, the descriptions become more precise, bolder, explicitly designating this antimasculine sexual plot. "The court was not slow in joining the fashion/ Each woman was at once tribade and trollop/ They no longer made children, that seemed too easy/ The prick was replaced by a lascivious finger," writes the author of the *Fureurs utérines de Marie-Antoinette* [Uterine furies of Marie-Antoinette],[58] to which the author of the *Vie de Marie-Antoinette d'Autriche* [Life of Marie-Antoinette of Austria] responds, describing a pleasure party between the queen and her favorite: "The Princess Lamballe, with her right hand, burrowed into the bush of Venus, which was often moistened with a sweet serous fluid. Her left hand adroitly and rhythmically slapped one of the royal buttocks. She draws from her pockets a kind of dildo, which she applies to that part which gives our pleasures. A large ribbon was attached to it; it passed with grace over the contour of her breasts. Madame Tourzel made a distinct rosette in the small of her back. The bright crimson of this ribbon contrasted wonderfully with the whiteness of her skin."[59] The queen, in the lewd imagination of these pamphlets, exhausts men without loving them, and her only true passion is "lesbian vice": "If one day men abandoned us," she confides to Lamballe in *Les Bordels de Lesbos ou le Génie de Sapho* [The brothels of Lesbos; or, The genius of Sappho], "we would not have to complain since we know how to replace them."[60]

Behind this fantasy of a lesbian conspiracy, there is the fear that the reins of politics might escape men; that, challenged and conquered by courtesans, they would no longer have the upper hand in directing the world. Through her doubly delinquent sexuality, the queen best embodies this fear: she exhausts her lovers, castrates them, emasculates them, with a terrifying distance in relation to pleasure, whose sole enjoyment she reserves for her relationships with women, her accomplices. The ideas and caprices she imposes on men with whom she plays are thus born in the society of "women amongst themselves," and are forged in the course of these relationships against nature. Once more, the September murderers make the Princesse de Lamballe's body pay for this fear. For her execution is described as a rape, as the assertion of a barbaric and primitive virility that would take its revenge on the conspiracy of women: "The monsters tore her from prison, stripped her completely naked, mistreated her, insulted her, exercised on her unspeakable liberties, forced her to kiss bleeding corpses, cut off her breasts and the parts that shame prevents us from naming. At the execution of the princess, there was a well-reared gentleman in the crowd. Seeing the unspeakable fondlings that the assassins permitted themselves with the naked princess, and the extraordinary efforts she made, in defiance of the death with which she was threatened, to conceal from the gazes of these enraged men what nature and shame order us to keep hidden, he cried out in his indignation: 'For shame, wretches! Remember that you have wives and mothers!' He was immediately pierced with a thousand blows, and his destroyed body was torn to pieces."[61]

Similarly, the taking apart of the corpse is often presented like a sexual ceremony in which men's revenge is exercised. These men fall upon parts of the princess's body—the breasts, the sex—which she would have kept from masculine pleasure while she was alive. The mutilation of Lamballe's breasts is a constant in the tales of the murder, generally described through the horror of a wound made by teeth, like a kiss transformed into hateful rage. As for her sex, it is sometimes presented as lacerated by saber blows, but more often as carefully cut off and paraded in the guise of a trophy. E. Roch Mercandier, in his *Histoire des hommes de proie* [History of men of prey], went so far as to form the legend of a *septembriseur* who "cuts off the intimate fleece of the princess and makes himself a mustache from it" before "parading at the head of the bloody procession."[62]

Finally, the finger of scandal remains, that of the pleasure of female masturbation, Lamballe's lewd finger, which the licentious satires of the Ancien Régime and those of the beginning of the Revolution presented as a kind of symbol of the courtesans' lesbian conspiracy. It is this finger that we find at the heart of one tale of the murder, no doubt the most complete and most extravagant in its phantasmagorical rereading of revolutionary history: "The assassins of La Force quarreled with each other, in the middle of blood-filled streets, over the pieces of the princess, which could awaken in them at once feelings of cannibalism and of lewdness. In her, all that is most respectable in sex was the least respected, and some days afterwards, the murderers still publicly showed, in the taverns, the bloody remains that shame does not even allow us to name. It is not enough to have dissected the princess while still alive, to have divided her corpse amongst themselves, and to have dragged it in pieces through rivers of blood; her assassins needed a proof of barbarity for those who had paid for the massacres. The triumvirs are meeting with a few other heads of the *septembrisations.* They are at dinner; four of their agents come and put on the table the princess's right hand. They examine it, they pass it from one comrade to another; they make witticisms about her fingers as atrocious as they are lewd. Robespierre stares at it more attentively and says with his cold contempt, 'She was pretty.' "[63]

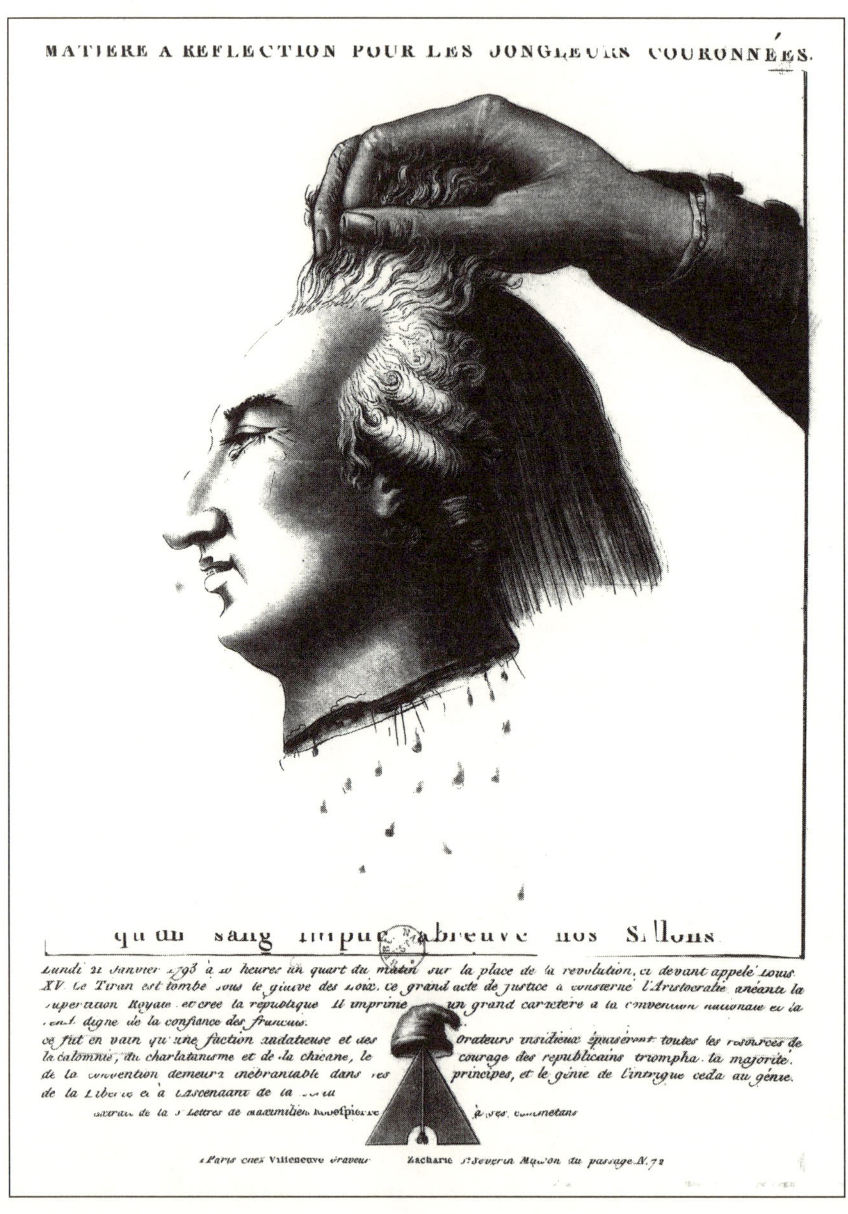

Villanueve, *Matierè à Réflexion Pour les Jongleurs Couronnés*, 1793. Cliché Bibliothèque Nationale de France, Paris.

Louis XVI

OR, THE SACRED REMAINS

When France entered into a republic, in the course of the summer of 1792, it did not solemnly proclaim the foundation of a new regime. The historian can look: nowhere will he unearth an official decree in the archives installing the first French Republic. He will only find, dated September 21, 1792, a suggestion from Camus, responsible for the national archives, henceforth to date the administrative documents from the "Year I of the French Republic."[1] On the other hand, between August 10 and September 21, 1792, the deputies of the National Assembly kept proclaiming, to the whole world, the "suspension," then the "abolition," of the royalty in France. They knew what they wanted to destroy, but not yet necessarily what they needed to construct.

This desire to end the monarchic regime, "withered state of thirteen hundred years," finds its culmination in the execution of Louis XVI, "Louis the last," on Monday, January 21, 1793, at the Place de la Révolution.[2] The abolition of royalty, in these few months, from the assault on the Tuileries palace to the torture of Louis XVI, constructs a public ceremony offered to the eyes of the citizens, through its spectacle, then through stories, speeches, and images.[3] This ceremony is extremely important, for it serves as a founding rite for the young Republic, and in a way replaces the official proclamation of the failing regime. It is a rite of blood that must strike people's minds, and at that instant banishes France from the European nations, both monarchic and traditional. In a precise and detailed way, thanks to studied decrees and composed actions, a scene of sacrifice is instituted. The pride of the French Republican, as well as his isolation, stem wholly from this ritualized spectacle, this ceremony that humiliates, abolishes, and then causes the disappearance of the body of the king.

THE MONARCH HAS LEFT

On the morning of August 10, 1792, on the advice of Roederer, Louis XVI flees his Tuileries palace, which has been besieged by the crowd, to take refuge within the National Assembly.[4] At the announcement of the king's arrival, surrounded by his family, in the fever of this insurrectional day, the Legislative Assembly remains circumspect.[5] The constitution in fact authorizes the king to turn to the representatives whenever he likes, but the deputies, most of whom had become hostile to royal authority, do not in the least wish to seem to take the sovereign's side. Therefore, quickly, under the authority of Pierre Victurnien Vergniaud, president of the Assembly, it is decided to hold strictly to the ritual established by the Legislative Assembly in such a case: a minimal deputation of twenty-four members goes to meet the king in the antechamber of the legislating room, an armchair is hastily placed beside the president's, and the monarch sees himself welcomed without fuss or emotion. In a way, by the nondramatization of this welcoming ceremony, the Assembly wishes to remain neutral: it is a matter of an affair between the king and the people, and the deputies are content to observe. Louis XVI understands the risk of this neutrality and tries to dramatize the scene when he exclaims, as on the stage of tragic theater: "Gentlemen, I came here to avoid a great crisis, and I think that I could not be in greater safety than in your midst." But the Assembly prefers to renounce this role of "savior of the nation," of deus ex machina, that the monarch in his desperate plight suggests. The deputies wash their hands of the matter, politely respecting the sovereign but offering him in sacrifice to the people who, a few feet away, in front of the Château des Tuileries, are demanding his head.

This sort of Pontius Pilate attitude even finds an extremely clear illustration in a clause of ceremonial regulation inside the Assembly: the king, surrounded by his family, before whom the deputies cannot legally deliberate, is in fact placed in a loge behind the president, outside the "sacred enclosure" of political power, among the public. That is how the monarchy is actually circumvented by an Assembly that puts itself in the hands of popular decision. The king, powerless, having become a simple spectator, is in a way guarded in a safe and neutral spot, hostage of a political story in which he no longer participates. He will be, against his will, handed over to the winner of the fight whose echoes the deputies can clearly hear. Moreover, no one has thought of interrupting this bloody street fight, which will claim almost four-thousand victims, but which has become pointless since the king is no longer occupying his palace. For each person awaits the outcome of this struggle, like a kind of political ordeal. It is a matter of extracting the king from the nation, of attributing to him a space in a ridiculous utopia placed outside the Assembly to keep him in reserve. This reserve is no longer an earnest of promises but resembles a brief suspension of time, the time necessary for the definitive victory of the people over the armed elements that have remained faithful to the king. Thus, while still belonging to monarchical chronology, this parliamentary meeting of August 10, 1792, is already a ritual of the Republic: Louis XVI's loge, placed outside of politics, represents this blind point that makes France swing over from one regime to the other.

A few hours later, once the Royalists are eliminated from the street, the deputies decide to "suspend" the monarchy and to convoke a new National Assembly to place the foundations for a new regime "suitable to the temperament of the regenerated French people."[6] The loge attributed to Louis XVI in the course of this decisive meeting symbolized this "suspension." On the other hand, the prison that the Insurrectional Commune of Paris, the power that asserts itself when the National Assembly dissolves, assigns to the fallen monarch is inscribed into a ritual of humiliation. Louis has not only become a simple citizen, named "Capet," but he is no longer a free man, in his body or in his movements. He resides henceforth under strict surveillance at the Temple, not in the town house that used to welcome the family of his young brother, the Comte d'Artois, but in the turret, that cold, dark dungeon, isolated in the heart of popular Paris, in which the slightest actions of the royal family are recorded by the municipal guards.[7]

This humiliation reaches its culmination on December 3, 1792, when the deputies of the new Assembly, having met in Paris for two months, decide that "Louis Capet and his defenders are to be heard at the bar of the National Convention." The trial of the king[8] is the final episode of this political and symbolic struggle that for a long time set the National Assembly, representing the French people, against Louis XVI, symbol of the monarchical tradition. It is a cruel episode: Republican severity triumphs over royal majesty. No one questions the place and ritual actions of humility henceforth imposed on the body of the former king of France. "The monarch has left *(s'est absenté),*"[9] a chronicler can even state after a simple glance at the ritual of the king's first appearance at the bar of the Convention, on Tuesday, December 11, 1792, at three o'clock in the afternoon. Another chronicler offers a revealing description: "Supported by his conscience alone, dressed in a yellowish frock coat and directing his gaze to all parts of the room, led by General Santerre who hastens his gait with a premeditated speed, Louis Capet appears without pomp but with dignity. No doubt he was quite surprised to see no other seat for him than a humble chair in a place where he had more than once deployed all the pride and ceremony of royalty. Remember, readers, the scarlet armchair with fleurs-de-lys which insulted the representatives of the nation. With what surprise would the thirty-one kings of vile Capetian race have been seized by seeing their offspring stripped of all his ceremonies."[10] The king stands at the bar when the president of the Convention, Bertrand Barère, addresses him: "Louis, the French nation accuses you. You are going to hear the reading of the act enumerating the facts. Louis, sit down." That is when, the instant the king sits down on a "humble chair" beneath the eyes of the deputies, who are already seated with their hats on, the ritual of his disappearance is set in motion.

After having "vanished" him by placing him in a box outside political life, after having humiliated him by enclosing him in a medieval tower and then putting him on trial, the new Republican authority concurrently constructs the disappearance of the king. The trial of the king creates a theoretical basis for this disappearance, an imposing theory that, by a slim majority, will be the winning decision of the National Assembly. This disappearance is the exact response to the monarchical theory of the sacred inviolability of the body of the king. Although the century of the Age of Enlightenment had already modified the monarchical concept of divine right, as well as the sacred powers with which the body of the king could be invested,[11] the prestige of the sovereign still remains extremely imposing, even in the constitution of 1791, which, from its second paragraph forward, advances the principle of the inviolability of the royal person.[12] The principal defender of the king before the Convention, the lawyer Raymond de Sèze, clearly makes allusion to it in the text of his speech for the defense: "In our present ideas of equality, we want to see in a king nothing but an ordinary individual, but a king is not at all an individual; he is a privileged being, a moral being and a sacred body, a whole by whom a nation itself forms, for its own felicity, an existence that is entirely different from its own."[13]

The Montagnard [left-wing group headed by Danton and Robespierre—Trans.] theory advocating the immediate execution of Louis XVI rests upon this exception of the person of the king, body and soul of the monarchy, in order better to transform it into a monstrosity. Since Louis is an exceptional being, a "body outside the nation," the Republic can only be installed by annihilating him: an almost organic incompatibility exists between these two sovereigns, the king and the people, the principle of exception and the principle of equality. On December 3, 1792, Robespierre puts forth the argument before the Convention with an unanswerable logic: "Louis was king, and the Republic is founded. . . . Victory and the people have decided that he alone was rebellious: Louis thus cannot be judged; he is already condemned, or the Republic is not absolved. Louis must die because the nation must live." The Montagnards call on the Convention to organize a foundational sacrifice: Louis must die so that equality between citizens can be established, prime principle of the new Republic, the regenerated people. This logic, after a month and a half of stormy, close-fought debates, carries the decision of the Assembly. The decisive vote, public and by roll call, begins on the afternoon of January 15, 1793; thirty-six hours later the deputy from the Gard Voulland contributes to the verdict of immediate death the 361st, and decisive, vote, that of the absolute majority.

By thus sacrificing Louis XVI, the Republic immolates the sacredness with which the body of the king was still invested. This sacrifice cannot be better symbolized, in the eyes of all the citizens, than by the meeting between the king, traditional body of exception, and the guillotine, the new machine of Republican equality.[14] The execution of Louis XVI is in fact a kind of consecration of Guillotin's invention. It is not the first of the tortures brought about with the aid of this machine, since, on the Place du Carrousel, the guillotine has already punished the first ones condemned to death by the Revolutionary Tribunal installed after the August 10, 1792, insurrection. But the king is *the* great victim of it. Above all, the very fact that Louis XVI is decapitated *mechanically* constitutes one of the most graphic rituals, and an irrefutable negation of royal exception. In fact, if the setting of the event must be cloaked in a special solemnity, the death itself and its instrument are ordinary: the head of a king will fall as would the head of anyone else, with the "swiftness of lightning," under the effect of a mechanism common to that trenchant geometry. The guillotine that decapitates Louis XVI, moreover, is exactly the same as that which has already been used since August 1792, and will be used even more thereafter. The scaffold was simply transferred to the Place de la Révolution, between the pedestal on which the statue of Louis XV had stood and the beginning of the Champs-Elysées, to give the ceremony all the room and solemnity it requires. This ceremony of blood in which the exceptional body of the king founders creates the republic of equality. This major encounter is prepared and arranged in minute detail, as if the ritual taking shape had, at once, to speak loud and clear the language of the Republic, and to warn of the unknown, feared effects of this unprecedented execution.

On Sunday, January 20, at two o'clock in the afternoon, a delegation of the executive council of the Commune of Paris, led by Garat, Lebrun, Grouvelle, and Hébert, comes to read the sentence before the monarch at the Temple, a sentence of which Louis XVI has already been informed by his defenders, and makes the "ceremonial arrangements" of the execution known. The king, who will from now on never deviate from an imposing calm, receives these arrangements with a seeming tranquillity of spirit, but makes three requests. A "delay of three days to be able to prepare myself to appear in the presence of God," freedom for his family—two wishes that are immediately refused him by the Convention—and the possibility of confessing in all secrecy and freedom to the priest of his choice, one on one, without the omnipresent surveillance of his guards. Louis XVI chose the Abbé Edgeworth de Firmont, of Irish ancestry, a nonjuring priest, and thus openly counterrevolutionary.[15] The Republic makes this concession, perhaps mistakenly, for it allows the king to compose, with the aid of traditional religion, a counter-ritual that presides over his final moments and provides a competing ceremony. The Abbé de Firmont, having arrived at the Prison du Temple at seven o'clock in the evening on January 20, will remain with the king until the moment of his execution.

At eight o'clock, Louis XVI bids his adieus to his family: his wife, Queen Marie-Antoinette; his sister, Madame Elisabeth; the dauphin; and his daughter, Madame Royale. The scene is watched by the guards through a glass partition, without their being able to hear a word. The most faithful narrative seems written by Cléry, the king's valet, a Republican, appointed to the Prison du Temple by the municipality of Paris but won over, "turned round" by the composure and confidence of Louis XVI: "It was impossible to hear anything; one only saw that after each phrase of the king, the sobs of the princesses redoubled, and that then the king began again to speak. It was easy to judge from their movements that he himself had told them of his condemnation."[16] This meeting lasts for two hours, and Louis puts an end to it by promising a final farewell for the next morning. This promise is a ruse meant to cut short the familial sorrows. The interview on the evening of January 20 is indeed the final scene of a reign that had placed familial virtue at the center of its values, a scene many times reproduced and provided with dialogue by the royal hagiographers, a privileged moment when the tale of martyrdom begins in monarchical tradition. For if the Republic constructs a ritual of foundation through this execution of the royal body and its sacrifice to the equality of all, royalty tries to offer another ceremony. The same gestures, the same deeds, can be interpreted differently. Some see in them a Republican sacrifice; others read them as a new Christ-like passion. Louis XVI, calling to him a nonjuring confessor, calmly wearing a handsome and simple white habit, accepting his sacrifice with grandeur, suggests this reading to his hagiographers: it is a saint that the Republic is putting to death. On January 20, 1793, two rituals are thus set in place through one single ceremony. The king prepares himself as a true Christian and as a monarch, while the men of the municipality, good Republicans, transfer the guillotine to the Place de la Révolution and hand Paris over to the authority of armed citizens. The only link between these two rituals, between the old and the new, is Henri Sanson, the executioner, man of the Ancien Régime—whom some moreover represent as a fervent Royalist—who had previously worked the wheel or the gallows, henceforth officiating by the guillotine, aided by his son, Henri François, and by an assistant, Legros. All these executioners equally prepare themselves for the execution, respecting the old ritual forms (Sanson, on January 20, had requested and received absolution from a priest, the Abbé de Keravenant) and also the new ones (the hinges, the sliding supports, and the uprights of the guillotine were all checked, and the blade itself was sharpened).

But on this day before the execution, it is the Parisian municipality that most actively prepares itself. Cutting off a king's head worries some. How will the people react to this deed, which has absolutely no precedent in French history? Can they allow Louis XVI to utter a final harangue? Even if no one believes in divine intervention—the blade stopping short in its thundering descent or a miraculous reattachment of the head of "Saint Louis"—many fear a final blow from Royalist forces trying to rescue the king along the way. (In fact the reaction was not long in coming: the regicide Lepeletier de Saint-Fargeau would be assassinated by a former Royal Guard on January 20 at six o'clock in the evening, at Février's, the restorer of the Palais Royal.) Thus the

Commune of Paris, and some of the *sections* situated on the route leading from the Prison du Temple to the scaffold, react with dispatch and prepare a plan of action down to the smallest details. On one hand, those individuals suspected of being overfavorable to the king, or even of being sensitive to and compassionate about his fate as a victim, are warned and kept at a distance. Royalists of course, but women too, with humors supposedly more accessible to compassion: "Any man who cries forgiveness or who acts without consideration, will be arrested and led to prison. Women will not leave their homes. The *sections* will be armed at their different posts," states the *section* of Gravilliers in a decree that is immediately adopted by the neighboring *sections.*[17] On the other hand, the management of the ritual is exclusively confided to the armed force. During his final moments, Louis XVI's gaze will meet only armed men. Along the route, 12,000 men of the *sections* of Paris take their places very early in the night of January 20–21, while on the Place de la Révolution almost 80,000 men, national guards, and policemen are deployed, protected by 84 pieces of artillery. Finally, the general attitude of the Parisians—those in arms who approach the scaffold, as well as those who will learn of the details of the execution from the press—must adhere to a particular attitude, a "mournful dignity," according to the words of the notice posted on January 20 on the walls of Paris by the mayor, Chambon: "The sword of the law will strike the greatest and the guiltiest of conspirators. You have, citizens of Paris, during the course of this long trial, maintained the calm that is suitable for free men; you will know how to preserve it at the instant of the execution of the tyrant. You will prove, by the decorum of your behavior, that an act of justice in no way resembles vengeance. That day will be, for kings and for peoples, at once a memorable example of the just punishment of despots and of the mournful dignity that a sovereign people must keep in the exercise of its power."

"From five o'clock onward, the low rumble of cannons and caissons was heard, the galloping of cavalry, the regular tread of the troops; an event is being prepared,"[18] writes a Parisian bourgeois in the early morning of January 21, 1793. Five o'clock is in fact the first decisive moment of that day. Louis XVI had asked Cléry, his valet, to wake him up at that time; just as, for his part, the executioner Sanson had asked his assistant. Cléry does the king's hair, slowly, at great length. The king eats nothing. Fasting accompanies the Catholic last rites, that of the execution of the martyr, as well as the king's last confession, from six to seven o'clock, in the cell of the turret, all alone with the Abbé de Firmont.

Then Louis XVI gets dressed with the help of his valet: a fresh shirt, the off-white waistcoat worn the day before, grey trousers, a light jacket. Early on, though, the guards offer a firm refusal when the king tries to extend monarchical ritual to the Republican acts of humiliation that will punish his body: Cléry is not authorized to cut his hair, or even to accompany him so as to undress him at the bottom of the scaffold. The executioners will take charge of that. Finally, at 7:45, the municipal delegation arrives, led by Santerre, commander of the National Guard of Paris, accompanied by ten soldiers standing at attention in two rows in the antechamber of the Prison du Temple. Louis XVI takes one final moment to kneel down, in his private cell, at the feet of the Abbé de Firmont, who gives him his blessing.

One favor is granted the king: he will go to the execution in a coach—in the carriage of the mayor of Paris—not in the shameful cart of those condemned to death. The solemnity and dignity of the Republican act of justice called for this final compromise. Two policemen accompany the king in it, as well as the Abbé Edgeworth de Firmont, in the front seat. Louis XVI prays, murmuring the prayer of the dying, and nothing on the way will break his silence. The crowd, restrained behind the soldiers, is silent, as planned. The journey, in streets still half obstructed by heaps of snow, takes more than two hours, at the slow pace of the horses, of the 100 mounted police that precede the carriage as well as the 100 horsemen of the National Guard that follow it. The carriage arrives a little after ten o'clock at the Place de la Révolution. It stops there for five minutes in silence, without any movement visible inside the coach. Legros, Sanson's assistant, and a municipal officer finally open the door. The king descends, and with an impatient gesture recalls one last time the lesson in royal ritual that the Republic does not want to observe: he does not permit anyone to touch him. The inviolability of his body is incompatible with the public undressing and the ropes they want to tie on him. The ceremonial conflict culminates in an exchange of glances between the king and his confessor. The latter makes the monarch understand that it is vain to struggle, that dignity is the only possible compromise between the two competing rituals. Louis XVI complies, takes off his coat, opens the neck of his shirt, and, to free his neck, pulls it down to his shoulders. He lets himself be "bound," then, his hands behind his back, lets his hair, which he wears short under his wig, be cut. Leaning on his confessor, he climbs the steep steps leading to the scaffold. When the three executioners seize him and tie him to the board, he cries out, in a strong voice: "People, I die innocent of the crimes that they ascribe to me. I forgive the authors of my death, and I pray to God that the blood that you are about to spill will never fall back on France." Drumrolls then drown out his voice, while "he lifted his eyes for a moment before he was laid beneath the sword that cut off his days." It is 10:22.

THE BLOOD OF THE KING: A REPUBLICAN POETICS

In the *Journal de la République française,* dated January 23, 1793, Marat writes, "The head of the tyrant has just fallen; the same blow has overthrown the foundations of monarchy among us. His life is no more, his body is now nothing but a corpse; at last I believe in the Republic." The execution of Louis XVI, and it alone, ushers in the Republican era. That is how the "friend of the people" presents and justifies the deed of regicide on January 21, 1793. Since this execution is a foundational act, it is quickly situated at the center of the work of representation that establishes it as an essential figure—*exempla*—of French Republican culture. More precisely, the body of Louis XVI—monarchical body from another political tradition, radically foreign to Republican culture—becomes the token of a specific appropriation. How does an inviolable, sacred body, embodiment of the old ideological system, become a symbol proper to Republican culture through his execution? Here is a question that we must try to elucidate by measuring the effects of a representation of the royal corpse that made this unprecedented event in French political culture visible and thinkable.

Once the execution of the king has been carried out, Republican discourse seeks to invert its values. Louis XVI's body, exceptional before, is now made commonplace. The execution, previously described as common, assumes an exceptional quality in Republican imagination through its instrument—the guillotine; its function—a sacrificial rite; and its baptismal quality. The body of the king is made commonplace. It is first a matter of an organic remark: the specialness does not resist its encounter with the guillotine, and the very fact that Louis XVI is decapitated mechanically constitutes an irrefutable negation of monarchical corporeal exception. The setting is solemn, but its procedure and its instrument are absolutely ordinary. The machine remains common: posts, beams, blade, all have already been used, and it cuts off the king's life with all the more symbolic efficacy since the body put to death is exceptional until the precise moment of the execution, which in an instant demotes it to the rank of a very ordinary corpse. The machine seizes royal prestige at the very instant of its action, leading this unique body to common organic rationality.[19]

The fate of Louis XVI's corpse, in Republican ceremony, is furthermore quite explicit in this negation of the traditional body of the monarchy. In fact this corpse becomes the subject of one of the first debates at the Convention even before the king's death. When the condemnation is pronounced, a Royalist asks, in a letter addressed to the president of the Convention, that "Louis Capet not be deprived of the honors of burial" and that "his remains be transported to Sens in order to be buried next to his father."[20] That would involve taking an exceptional measure, one that the members of the Convention refuse categorically, fearing a misappropriation of the king's corpse: pilgrimages and Royalist agitations, sanctification and a sudden cult of the relics of the monarch. On the contrary, the deputy Chabot suggests that "Louis [be] buried in the ordinary place of burial for citizens in the *section* in which he will be executed."[21] This proposition, passed immediately, must avoid the possibility of any cult directed at the body of Louis XVI.

The king's corpse is accordingly transported to the former Church of the Madeleine immediately after the execution. The Republic had granted an exceptional favor to the king in letting him die in the religion of his ancestors, surrounded by religious ritual, supported by a rebel priest. Once the guillotine met the king's body and cut the thread of a sacred life, the corpse belongs to the Republic: two juring priests, loyal to the new regime, officiate at the short funeral service held at the Madeleine. The vicar Damoureau testifies: "Having arrived at the cemetery, I imposed the greatest silence. A detachment of the police presented the body to us. It was clothed in a white piqué waistcoat, trousers of grey silk and stockings of the same. We chanted vespers and recited the prayers of the service for the dead. The body, laid bare on the bier, following the orders of the executive authority, was thrown into the bottom of the ditch, twelve feet deep and about ten feet away from the wall, on a bed of quicklime. The head was placed at its feet. The whole was then covered by another layer of quicklime, then a layer of earth, the whole firmly tamped down, repeatedly."[22] This corpse must be putrefied as quickly as possible. It is mixed up with other corpses, anonymous in a communal burial, without ceremony or distinguishing mark, a corpse returned to its natural fate, that of disappearing little by little, corrupted by time.

"Hatred of kings," the founding emotion of the Republic, manifests in this negation of all sacred values of the monarchical body, a negation that is extended to the king's corpse: it *must* disappear. That is the proud attitude of Republicans in relation to the executed corpse: neither injury nor vandalism nor ostentation, but a terseness recommending self-restraint and neutrality. This body is like others; it is put to death in an instant, and then it must be forgotten as quickly as possible, naturally. There is here no attack on the body, no violent act of desanctification, just a position of principle, secular, clinical: the corpse of Louis Capet is not a "monument," even if, for a few days, a small troop mounts guard around the Madeleine burying ground to prevent any profanation.

This lesson in humility imposed on the king's body, brought down to the rank of commonness by its "guilty" and "decomposable" nature, is placed at the center of Republican narratives of the execution, as the *Journal des hommes libres de tous les pays* [Newspaper of the free men of all countries] reports: "Today the great truth that the prejudiced ones of so many centuries had stifled has been clearly shown; today we have been convinced that a king is nothing but a man, and that no man is above death. Capet is no more. People of the earth! Contemplate thrones, and see that they are nothing but dust."[23]

These narratives construct a radical "non-event," revealed by the imagery of the execution, very sparse and poorly presented in the Republican press. The papers thus insist on the seeming indifference of the people to this body-corpse having lost its traditional exceptionality. "No insult was offered to Louis' corpse: it was put in the basket, placed in a cart that awaited it at the foot of the scaffold, and transported to the Madeleine, to a ditch that was filled with quicklime," reports the *Journal de Perlet* the day after the execution, explaining that the king's body had scarcely become a corpse when it seemed to have lost all political significance for the Republicans: "Blood that had run onto the square was wiped up with paper, with white handkerchiefs, by people who seemed not to attach any political superstition to it."[24] No sacralization of the remains, no insult made to the corpse: neither veneration nor desecration—such is the Republican discourse in which death is muted. "Let them take him where they like! What does it matter to us?" reports *Le Républicain* on the subject, an offhand attitude to the fate of the royal corpse.[25] As for the *Gazette nationale,* it emphasizes this tranquillity that so struck observers: "Louis's head fell at 10:20 in the morning. It was shown to the people. Immediately a thousand cries: Long live the nation! Long live the Republic! were heard. The corpse was at once transported and deposited in the Eglise de la Madeleine, where it was buried between the people who perished on the day of his wedding and the Swiss who were massacred on August 10. His ditch was twelve feet deep and six feet wide; it was filled with lime. Two hours afterward, nothing revealed that the one who a short while ago was the head of the nation had just undergone a criminal's execution. Public tranquillity was not troubled for an instant."[26]

The *Révolutions de Paris* takes the same approach, saying "that they talked about firing the Pont-Neuf cannon at the time of execution," but "that did not take place: the head of a king, in falling, must not make more noise than that of any other scoundrel."[27] This silence with regard to the execution is also justified by Hébert, who as substitute for the prosecutor of the Commune of Paris, must come to a decision on a proposal of the General Council of the *département* of Paris, on "recording all the deeds and gestures of Louis Capet at the time of his execution in order to instruct the people." For Hébert, it is on the contrary the very ordinary fate of the king's body that remains the best lesson for the people. He exclaims, "This proposal would be impolitic and dangerous, for it would place before the people's eyes the kind of firmness that Louis carried to the scaffold. Do you want to make the people pity the tyrant's fate? His head has fallen; we should no longer concern ourselves with him except to recall his infamies. They talk to you of monuments for history, but history has until now told lies to posterity. History must finally be made for the people, and this history must portray Louis's features indelibly as he cut the throat of the citizens on August 10th. But the private life of this despot must be buried in the deepest oblivion as his mutilated corpse will be beneath the lime of the Madeleine cemetery."[28] The corruption of the royal corpse, decomposed by the lime, the ordinary fate of human bodies, is the eloquent representation created by Republican narrative to tell of its victory over the sacred body of tradition.

However, if the ceremony of January 21, 1793 transformed the king's body into an ordinary corpse, it also elicited from the royal presence that it damaged an undeniable share of its sacredness. Marat wrote, "The people seemed animated with a serene joy: one might have said that they had just attended a religious festival."[29] The death of the king is more than the abolition of royalty; it serves as a founding sacrifice. The Royalists interpreted it in this sense: the advent of a new martyr, a tragic revelation of the Christ-like fate of Louis XVI. But the Republicans also understood this event in a mystical logic. The guillotine, as Daniel Arasse has shown, receives its true consecration then, and "the sacrality of the king will henceforth stain the instrument of his execution."[30]

On the other hand, the decapitation of the king, poised at the brink of the French Republic, acquires a baptismal value. And this rite is consecrated by the recurrent and obsessional symbol of the king's blood flowing to engender and regenerate the new Republic, reborn under the protection of the Supreme Being by the rite of immersion in a sacred and purifying liquid. The metaphors for this bloody baptism are innumerable, incorporating in the representation of the king's execution the share of sacredness that Louis XVI's corpse had abandoned at the instant of his death. "By soaking the fields of the nation, his impure blood will save the country,"[31] the editor of the *Républicain* proclaims, explicitly appropriating the phrasing of the "Marseillaise," while the *Révolutions de Paris* deepens the interpretation by defining its meaning: "The blood of Capet, shed by the sword of the law, washes away from us a stain of thirteen hundred years of monarchy. Only since it began to flow are we Republicans: thanks to this blood, we have earned the right to serve as a model to neighboring countries."[32]

An archetypal representation, a Republican icon embodying in itself the event of the king's death, comes to express this founding and baptismal role accorded to the royal blood that flowed on January 21, 1793: the public display of Louis XVI's head, "all dripping with blood." If one systematically consults the reports of the event in the press of the time as well as its images (of the Republican persuasion), one sees this archetype establish itself clearly. "The executor of justice has taken the head and shown it to the people"—that is the phrase, along with a few variants, used again and again in the accounts, as surely as "The head of the tyrant has fallen," much more than any other anecdote (the preparations for death, the climbing of the stairs, the king's last words . . .). Even more, it is the display of the bloody head that, according to all the testimonies, sets off the founding cry of "Long live the nation! Long live the Republic!" The *Journal de Perlet* is explicit: "The head falls, it is 10:15. The executioner picks it up, and raising it in the air to show the people, circles the scaffold twice. A cry rises up from the midst of the silence: Long live the nation! Long live the Republic!"[33]

The Republican illustrations of the event emphasize it endlessly, concentrating almost exclusively on this act of defiance.[34] Less numerous than the Royalist engravings, Republican prints are completely without variety, and the motive of the display of the king's severed head imposes itself without competition, taking the place of images showing the moment immediately after the fall of the blade. As much as what precedes the death can provide material for the dramatic and pathetic peripeteia capable of nourishing Royalist dreams and rereadings, so also are these images of the severed head implacable: the act is brutal, decisive, definitive, fatal, ratified by history. The Republic is born.

One hand holds the king's head by its hair, while its blood flows lavishly. Published after the event, excluding any anecdote, any peripeteia, any overall view of the scene of the execution, the image here is pure moral and political exaltation. The famous engraving by Villeneuve, *Matière à réflexion pour les jongleurs couronnés* [Subject matter for meditation for crowned minstrels], illustrates it directly, isolating the action of the executioner, who has been reduced to an anonymous forearm, the whole meaning of the execution placed in the display of the king's head.[35] This gesture recaptures the force of iconographic tradition, that of Perseus turning Polydectes to stone by showing him the severed head of Medusa. In this ritual of blood, the display terrifies; it "medusas" the enemies of the nation and of the people. As for the blood that, in large drops, flows from the gaping wound of the royal neck, it seems to fortify the Patriot texts inscribed at the bottom of the image. The slogan, "May an impure blood water our fields," immediately gives explicit meaning to this Republican icon. Then a text of a dozen or so lines taken from the third of the *Lettres de Maximilien Robespierre à ses commettants* [Letters from Maximilien Robespierre to his supporters], a legend for the image as well as an interpretation of the event: "The tyrant has fallen beneath the sword of laws. This great act of justice has dismayed the aristocracy, annihilated royal superstition, and created the Republic. It imprints a great characteristic on the National Convention and makes it worthy of the confidence of the French people." At the very bottom of the image, a red bonnet surmounting a carpenter's level completes the composition, a reminder of the red color of royal blood, here associated with the freeing of citizens who are hereafter all equal, since monarchical exception has been overthrown and annihilated. This Medusa-like and bloody function of the image can be found in all the Republican engravings, notably the *Réception de Louis Capet aux enfers* [Reception of Louis Capet in hell] in which the king is welcomed into the other world by a collection of despots, assassins, and counterrevolutionary victims of the massacres of 1789 and 1792.[36] In the center of the legend, a medallion contains the figure of the head of Louis XVI severed and dripping with blood, shown by the hand of the executioner. It is explicitly a variation on the image engraved by Villeneuve, which thus takes the power of signification from a Republican symbol, a bloody form by means of which the "readers" of the image give meaning to the event. The space of Republican representation is entirely filled by this symbol.

However, the properties of royal blood are rich, we know, and, by a very strange spatiotemporal phenomenon, seem to stretch out in time and dilate in space the Republican representation of the death of the king, in the literal sense: the blood flows from the royal corpse, spreads out, and Republican narratives soon begin to swell, in some way making the ordinariness and silence at first associated with the description of the execution implode. And this representation of a proliferation of royal blood also belongs to the Royalists: "The blood of the martyrs is the seed of Christianity." This maxim of Tertullian points a meaning to the numerous funeral orations for Louis XVI spoken in 1814 and 1815. But the metaphor of blood insinuates itself into all the registers of Republican narratives of the execution. If the blood flows "so well" from the king's corpse, it is above all because it symbolically founds a community of sacrifice. The king's blood, on January 21, comes to recall and exalt the Republican blood shed during the struggles of August 10, 1792. This link is tirelessly recalled by the narratives. It is surely a matter of constructing, by this bloody proliferation, the reputation of the "monster-king"—no longer, this time, that of a weak and impotent body faced with the guillotine, a victim's body, but a faithless monster and a traitor sacrificed and put to death by another victim, the real victim, virtuous, wounded, suffering: the French people. Thus the nature of the fraternal link established among Republicans by the founding act of the king's execution is profoundly bloody: it is as a community that the citizens have put the king to death. That is why, if the king's body is almost absent from the narratives and images of the execution, the blood of the monarch is overrepresented. Louis XVI does not have a body, but the blood flows from his corpse since, metaphorically, it joins with that of revolutionary victims, to found a community of martyrs: the wounds of the "martyrs of freedom" (Lepeletier had just died), the victims of August 10 or of the foreign war, are the *bloody evidence* of Republican fraternity ensuing from the "invisible" execution of the king.

Already, at the time of Louis XVI's trial, numerous deputies alluded to the blood of "martyrs," crying for vengeance at the expense of royal blood. Thus the king becomes, very legitimately in the mind of every Republican, an assassin, even a "drinker of blood." Louis XVI, till then ridiculed by the grotesque association with the bestiary of comedy or by the rumors concerning the impotence of his "imbecile body,"[37] metamorphoses into a monster under the effects of this eloquence of blood: "I have seen this thirsty brigand drink in ruby-red cups the sweat and blood of a Frenchman, while that same Frenchman, a soldier crippled for the nation, begged for alms," cries out Citizen Dorfeuille a few days after the execution of the king.[38] François Gamain, locksmith at the Tuileries, who accuses Louis XVI of having poisoned him, also sees his suggestions relayed significantly by Peyssard at the Convention, in the name of the Committee of Public Aid (*Comité des secours publics*): "It is at the tribune of liberty that the crimes of oppressors of the human race must ring out.... Scarcely had he [the king] emerged from infancy when the germ of that ferocious perversity that characterizes a despot was seen to develop in him. His first games were games of blood, and his brutality increasing with age, he took delight in satisfying it on all the animals that he encountered."[39]

Under the pressure of events, the image of the king was turned upside down in revolutionary propaganda: his story is rewritten as the terrible role of a despot. It is to this same genre of bloody accusation that the assassins of all revolutionary heroes and martyrs will conform: "Go on, cowardly assassins who feed on human flesh and who are dripping with Marat's blood; his body calls you, appear, monsters, a thousand times more hideous than those imprisoned in Hell. Your hands and lips are still covered with blood.... May your body dry up, may it never die, and may it find nourishment only in the blood of those whom you have immolated and in the corpse flesh that thousands of worms will fight over with you."[40] One of course encounters these visions of horror in the pamphlets and newspapers of the beginning of the Revolution, but henceforth they will come to feature in official discourse and animate public rituals, worthy pendants of Republican ceremony surrounding the bodies of martyrs. In this emotional logic introduced in the heart of summer 1792, Bourdon de l'Oise suggests to the National Assembly that those wounded on August 10 ought to have a distinguished place on the tribune during Louis XVI's trial: "It is customary, in matters of criminal justice, that one present the accused along with the exhibits for the prosecution."[41] "We must show Louis the bleeding wounds of the citizens whose massacre he ordered," adds Philippeaux afterward, a proposal that is finally effectively refuted by Masuyer:

"Judges do not have brought before their eyes the bleeding bodies that the murderers whose fate they are about to decide have deprived of life."

This link of blood to blood, the corpses of martyrs calling for the sacrifice of the king, is at the heart of the spatial and ceremonial symbolism of the execution of January 21, 1793. On the Place de la Révolution, opposite the Tuileries palace, Louis XVI publicly expiates the "crime" of August 10. It is the soldiers of August 10, notably the Federates from Marseilles, principal victims of the day of insurrection, who are placed by the authorities in the first row in front of the king's scaffold, which their commander recalls in a letter addressed that very evening to his fellow citizens from the south: "Santerre said yesterday that, knowing how much we detested tyrants, and above all those who had shed our brothers' blood, he would place us next to the scaffold, as much to procure for us the satisfaction of seeing that infamous head fall, as to fight his partisans if the need arose. Thus, at one o'clock in the morning, we took up arms to go to the Place de la Révolution, where we had the pleasure of being the first to arrive."[42]

When the royal blood flows, Republican regeneration is underway. That is what, as the weeks go by, comes to inflate the narratives of Louis XVI's corpse to the point of a fantastic vision, one that literally reconstitutes the event, loading it with meaning and description. This Republican regeneration by royal blood starts out with the description of the degeneracy of the body of the monarch faced with the guillotine. While the official silence of the Republic on the day of the execution tended to negate the king's corpse, certain subsequent narratives seem to question this version of a "non-event." On the contrary, killing a king *must* be an event, and the narratives try to give back a presence to Louis XVI's body, even if it means to exaggerate its pathetic and bloody aspects. That which was unrepresentable, unsayable, now becomes visible, even if through a certain overstatement worthy of the morbid novels of the end of Enlightenment, tales of the living dead. *Le Journal français,* on January 29, evokes a king "who did not stay in place," "agitated," "overcome by furious movements," "letting out a terrible cry," and for the first time transforms the fatal instant. Something happened at that moment, when the blade cut off the royal head, something happened, for *it did not go well.* The knife fell on the king's neck when the latter, badly held, badly tied, still resisted. His death is transformed: from serene to shameful, from beautiful to terrible, a bloody tale that gives itself the power to "create an event" by the precision of its macabre details. "At the instant that speech was so brutally taken from him by a deafening beating of drums, Louis entered into a violent anger, stamped his foot, struggled with vigor with the executioner's assistants, let out terrible cries, and fought to the end to such an extent that he had, not his neck, but the back of his head and his jaw horribly mutilated by the fatal knife," states the *Relation des derniers instants de Louis Capet* [Account of Louis Capet's final instants].

The *Thermomètre du jour* also wants to confirm this in its February 13, 1793, edition, three weeks after the event, when recalling the words attributed to the executioner himself, Sanson: "At the instant the condemned climbed up to the scaffold, I was surprised by his confidence and his firmness. But at the drumrolls that interrupted his harangue, and at the simultaneous movement that my boys made to seize the condemned, immediately his face changed dramatically. He cried out three times in a row hurriedly: 'I am lost!' This circumstance, joined to another that Samson also recounted, namely that the condemned had eaten an ample dinner the night before and had had a large breakfast in the morning, teaches us that Louis Capet had been in an illusion until the actual moment of his death, and that he had counted on being reprieved. Those who had kept him in that illusion no doubt had the object of giving him a confident bearing that could impress the spectators and posterity. But the drumrolls dissipated the charm of this false security, and those present, as well as posterity, will know what to make of the condemned tyrant's final moments." One week later, in the same paper, Sanson categorically denies these rumors,[43] but they are already circulating, let loose in the Republican imagination. It is the "eater," the pig-king of Varennes, who thus sees himself inflicted with an infamous death: the blade of the guillotine no longer cuts off the thread of life, it trivially cuts off a head of pork, in the midst of cries, blood, fear, and laughter. These tales culminate in *Le Nouveau Paris* [The new Paris] by Louis-Sébastien Mercier, who transforms Louis XVI's death into a bloody tale oscillating between the burlesque degradation of the pig-king and the most macabre fantasy, a form of Grand Guignol before the term existed: "Is it truly the same individual, crowned and sacred at Reims, mounted on a dais, surrounded by all the great ones, all kneeling, greeted with a thousand acclamations, almost adored like a god, is it truly the same man whom I see knocked over by four executioners' valets, forcefully undressed, his voice drowned out by the drums, only with difficulty tied to the plank, so gross was he from yesterday's meals, still struggling, and receiving the guillotine's blow so badly, that not his neck but the back of his head and jaw were horribly cut. His blood flows. The cries of joy of 80,000 armed men struck the air and my ear. They are repeated all along the quais.... I watched all the people march past arm-in-arm, laughing, chatting familiarly, as when one returns from a festival."[44]

The blood of the king is a representation that little by little becomes fictional in narratives that try to overload the execution with morbid or burlesque visions and to engrave on Louis XVI's corpse a mark of infamy, that of "a bad death," one that is shameful, angry, even grotesque. In these stories, the corpse ends up imposing meaning on the monarch's entire life, a life of luxury, betrayals, and crimes, a "king's life," which can culminate only in this final form, a mutilated and bleeding corpse, terrible and fitting image to revenge the victims of the monarchy and frighten its defenders. Therefore, royal blood takes on an expiatory quality in these narratives. Through its flowing, the king pays for the "crimes" committed, and moreover, this blood seems like the forfeit that guarantees Republican victory and revenge: it becomes the "good-luck charm" of the new man.

This theme of blood as a good-luck charm—for which a cult, parallel to that of the royal "relics," forms in January 1793—is distinctly present in narratives of the execution. "Louis's head has fallen; it has been shown to the people," comments *La Révolution de 92* in its January 22 edition. "Right away volunteers stained their lances, others their handkerchiefs, and then their hands, in the blood of Louis XVI." The *Annales de la République française* returns three times to this flowing blood and its supposed power, each time giving new details, more and more precise and explicit. First on January 22: "The execution over, the executioner presented the head to the people. A number of people hurried to get hold of his hair, others drenched paper and even their handkerchiefs in his blood." Then, on January 25: "It is not only his hair that people have gotten hold of and sold, for they had the same eagerness to get pieces of his clothing. We noticed a young foreigner, well-dressed, who gave fifteen pounds to soak a white handkerchief in the traces of blood. Another seemed to attach a great importance to obtaining some hair, for which he paid a louis. Many drenched their swords or their lances in the blood." Finally, on January 28: "The executioner, surprised at the eagerness of so many to drench their sword or their lance in Louis's blood, cried out: 'Wait a minute, I'll give you a tub in which you can soak them more easily.'"

But the narrative that best exemplifies this bloody rite is Louis Marie Prudhomme's in the *Révolutions de Paris:* "The priests and their devotees, who are already looking on their calendar for a place for Louis XVI among the martyrs, have likened his execution to the Passion of their Christ. Following the example of the Jewish people of Jerusalem, the people of Paris tore Louis's frock coat into two, *scinderunt vestimenta sua* [they divided his garments—TRANS.], and each one wanted to carry a rag of it home; but that was through the pure spirit of Republicanism. 'Do you see this piece of cloth,' grandparents will say to their grandchildren, 'the last of our tyrants was dressed in it on the day he mounted the scaffold to perish by the execution of traitors.' They say that the citizens drenched their handkerchiefs in the blood. That is true. And many volunteers hurried to drench the iron of their lances, the bayonet of their rifles or the blade of their swords in the despot's blood. The police were not the last. Many officers of the battalion from Marseille and others saturated the envelopes of letters they carried on the top of their swords with this impure blood, saying: 'Here is the blood of a tyrant.' One citizen climbed up to the guillotine itself, and plunged his whole bare arm into Capet's blood, which had collected there in abundance; he filled his hand with clots of it, and three times showered the crowd of attendants who pressed up to the foot of the scaffold to receive, each one, a drop on his forehead. 'Brothers,' said the citizen as he sprinkled, 'brothers, they warned us that the blood of Louis Capet might fall back on our heads: well! let it fall there. Louis Capet has washed his hands in our blood so many times! Republicans, the blood of a king brings happiness.'"[45] The blood of a king is the sacred liquid of the founding sacrifice, a liquid able to regenerate the French and to make them enter straightaway into Republican legend, the most fertile symbol of political culture but not the least ambiguous or the least embarrassing.

This richness and this embarrassment linked to the flowing of the royal blood can be found again, a few years later, at the heart of a debate agitating the Republicans of the Directory. By decrees of the Convention, on the 2 Pluviôse and 18 Floréal, Year II, confirmed on the 21 and 26 Nivôse, Year III, there was in fact instituted in the program of national celebrations a day devoted to recalling to everyone the "execution of the tyrant," an official recognition of a founding event of the French Republic. This day is fixed for 1 Pluviôse, but every year, without fail, during the month that precedes it, debates are reborn in the assemblies concerning the necessity and usefulness of such a celebration. On one hand, as certain deputies recall, the baptismal value of the execution of Louis XVI remains whole, even three or four years after the fact. François Riou, president of the Council of the Five Hundred (*Conseil des*

Cinq-Cents), asserts on the 1 Pluviôse, Year V, that the republic "founded on September 21" was "consolidated on January 21, as if cemented by the king's blood."[46] And he continues, emphasizing the impact of the monarch's execution, "transforming into a corpse a body whose communal idolatry was part of the beliefs of the old times," "presenting a great lesson to all the kings who believed themselves to be gods."

The following year, Bailleul, when he "renews the oath to live free or die," recalls the "misdeeds of the kings of France," and offers to plant trees of liberty in the courtyard of the palace of the Council of the Five Hundred, since, he says, "they grow better when they are planted on January 21," the roots symbolically watered with royal blood.[47] Finally, in Year VII, on the pediment of Notre-Dame transformed into a Temple of Victory, the citizens can read these slogans inscribed in large letters: "To the 1st Pluviôse, day of terror for traitors and betrayers," "May an impure blood water our fields," or "The corpse of the king makes the pride of Republicans."[48] In a long speech at the Five Hundred on 17 Nivôse, Year V, fifteen days before the celebration commemorating January 21, Pierre Guyomar also strongly supports the necessity of swearing hatred to royalty every year. For the Republican, it is a matter of "reassuring worried citizens of our faithfulness in keeping intact the precious deposit that is confided to us by the social pact by recalling each year the opprobrium attached to the corpse of Louis Capet."[49] The idea that the fraternal link of Republicans was born from a form of original sin, from the royal blood, this shared sacrifice, this ritual murder, is thus not dead four years after the execution of Louis XVI.

But this idea remains problematic. For to associate the Republic with the king's blood, and thus with the guillotine and the corpse of a great victim, directly poses the question of the political legitimacy of the Terror. Isn't the king the first victim of the Terror, since he is a corpse sacrificed to the origins of the Republic? The use of the guillotine, and its ever-burgeoning imagery, thus repel some Republicans of the Directory who question the validity of the celebration of 1 Pluviôse. Maximin Isnard, former Girondin, publishes, for instance, the *Réflexions sur la fête du 21 janvier* [Thoughts on the festival of January 21] denouncing this "strange anniversary": "Has anyone ever seen, among any people, the execution of a man being celebrated? Will we dance around a corpse that falls from the scaffold? This frightful pleasure is worthy only of Robespierre, and is like those cannibal rites that engulf vanquished foes that tribes are about to slit open and devour. To command the multitude to witness the shedding of blood, even the most impure, with transports of elation, is to trample all natural sentiments underfoot. If, in a living body, all the limbs were gifted with emotion, could they rejoice at the amputation of one of them, even if the amputation were judged indispensable? Would the day when this cruel operation had been performed be a day of celebration and triumph for the whole body? That is a monstrosity that, in the human body, would cause one to tremble. Can we then transform it into a duty and a merit in the body politic? To link the establishment of the Republic with this catastrophe comes down to abandoning humanity, and exposing ourselves to the hatred of other men. Far be from us an execrable celebration at which the altar is the scaffold, the sacrificer an executioner, the victim a mutilated corpse, and in which the initiates, full of a delirious fury, are sprinkled with human blood! From this dire spectacle even a druid would have recoiled with terror."

Dissociating the celebration of the origins of the Republic from an execution and from a corpse, Isnard suggests rather to associate it with the date of September 21, the first day of the new regime in the Republican calendar. Similarly, a few days later, Dusaulchoy, at the end of Nivôse, Year V, becomes indignant at the sacrificial and "blood-stained" speech given by Guyomar before the Council of the Five Hundred. He says he rises up "not against the Republic" but against the assimilation of the Republic with the Terror: "By taking Republicans who knew best how to ally humanity and civic virtues with energy, and proclaiming them henchmen of the Terror, like cannibals thirsty for blood, we are going to ruin them completely in the opinion of the people." Dusaulchoy recommends "letting the remains of corpses already forgotten rest in peace" and rejects any oath of hatred to royalty as a token of anarchy: "You will prove that a dead king, indeed even a simple guillotined corpse, will always be infinitely more valuable than all the live churls in the world. One must never stop kneeling before a corpse, however noxious it may be."[50]

The authorities of the Directory are aware of the danger involved in too explicitly linking regicide to the mythology of blood, the corpse of Louis XVI with those of the Terror. But they are also fully aware of the foundational and symbolic importance of the execution of the king for the Republican regime. How then can they commemorate the death of the king without speaking of his corpse; how can they celebrate a principle and a slogan, "Death to tyrants," without evoking the king's blood? That is the ceremonial dilemma of the

Directory. The regime tries to resolve it by attaching the founding act of the Republic more to antidespotic sentiment than to the executed body of the king. Soon only the oath of hatred to royalty, and of loyalty to the constitution, is imposed, and it alone. The celebrations of 1 Pluviôse are in fact organized around the words of an oath, not a reconstruction of the execution. Republican enthusiasm is now born from words cried out, from a speech, from an oath, and no longer from the vision of a mutilated and bleeding corpse. Louis XVI's head has stopped being shown to the people. In Year VII, encyclical letters addressed to the administrators of the Republic by François de Neufchâteau, minister of the interior, concerning the organization of the celebration of 1 Pluviôse, all insist on this "religion of the oath": "You must truly seize the spirit of solemnity that presides over the anniversary of the just punishment of the last of the French kings. Solemn in its subject, imposing in its details, it reminds you of the religion of the oaths."[51] The ceremonial of these celebrations is entirely centered on the oath and the Republican enthusiasm that must be born from it, as the report of the Parisian ceremony of 1 Pluviôse, Year V, shows. The ceremony lasts two hours, organized around the five directors, who proceed from the Palais National to the Ecole Militaire, and then to the Champ-de-Mars. Bands, artillery salvos, the "Marseillaise," processions of soldiers and public functionaries, and a speech by Jean-François Reubell, president of the Executive Directory, precede the taking of the oath, at noon, pronounced by more than 100,000 people: "I swear to be sincerely attached to the Republic, and I vow an eternal hatred for royalty."[52] The king's corpse is the unspoken part of an oath commemorating his execution in a public square.

However, through narrative and representation, often satirical and disrespectful, royal blood, the unspoken of the Directory celebrations—that bloody corpse which is allied at once both with symbol and embarrassment in the Republican imagination—can rise up again in an impromptu and inopportune way. A symbol, since royal blood flowed for the Republic to be born; an embarrassment, since this blood called for that of the victims of the Terror. How to get rid of this cumbersome but obsessive corpse? It is this macabre piece of comic theater that certain Directory narratives offer. While official ceremony conceals the king's corpse, this bloody figure returns in ridicule and satire. A pamphlet from Year IV, *La Tête ou l'oreille de cochon* [The head or ear of the pig], unhesitatingly steps right into the political thick of it, making the "proposal that all citizens celebrate the epochs of the Revolution in the bosom of their family, and, in commemoration of the events of January 21, eat a head or an ear of pork." "We must have symbols, characteristic signs that trace on our tables such famous landmarks," continues the author, who remained anonymous. "Let us hurry to substitute, for festivals as unsuitable as the carnival or the abominable Roiboit ["King Drink"], institutions that agree better with the events of our fortunate revolution." On the occasion of July 14, the Republican gourmet suggests a "bastille of biscuits"; for August 10, a "fat chicken from India which will remind everyone of the turkey [fool, *dindon*] of political farce"; and for January 21, "in imitation of the English Patriots who eat a head of veal on the day of the beheading of Charles 1st," the pamphlet-writer suggests that "everyone hurry to kill his pig so as to decorate with the head of that animal the banquet that every pater familias should offer on that day to his relatives and friends." Before this symbolic morsel, one should hear recited the oath of hatred to royalty and loyalty to the constitution. This pamphlet ironically recalls the couple that had been broken up by the Directory celebration: words rediscover here the corpse of a king symbolized by the pig's head, an animal that had been grotesquely associated with him since the king's flight to Varennes. Thus the story redirects the founding archetype of the exhibition of the royal decapitated head.

The following year, "Citizen Emmanuel" suggests to his readers a "project for a festival to celebrate fittingly the death of Louis XVI." The work has all the signs of Republicanism, but it multiplies them so much that it ends up being suspect: isn't it really a satire working with exaggeration as an act of political provocation? Using a fantastic and macabre vision, the narrative presents the ceremony of January 21, organized at the Champ-de-Mars, around a basin where an "immense crowd" has gathered. "The shape of the basin is semicircular," states the author. "The entire base of its curve represents a sea of boiling blood. In the midst of its turbulent waves, one sees Despotism expiring, vainly struggling; he succumbs, he drowns forever under the vengeful waves, while Liberty swims over holding in her hand a branch of the sacred tree that marks her, and happily reaches the shore. This sea of blood is formed from the blood of all perfidious aristocrats, emigrated traitors, cowardly slaves who had to be immolated to obtain the inestimable goods that we enjoy. Rivers of blood hurl themselves into this sea, and names set at their mouths identify the traitors who supplied them. Thus we read these words: bandits from the Vendée, emigrated traitors.... All the rest of the decoration is filled with the heads of the principal immolated aristocrats. The head of the tyrant, larger than life, occupies the center of the basin. At the sides, to make it pleasing to the eye, they have placed great borders that depict the massacres perpetrated by kings over fourteen centuries."[53]

Through its bloody delirium and morbid exaggeration, this narrative of celebration tracks down and brutally shines the light of day upon the taboo but inevitable symbol of the Republican political culture in France, the royal corpse, and its mutilated and bleeding head. This phantom resurges from the past as soon as the Republic turns its attention to its origins. Republicans tried to hide it, since it spoke too openly of the inaugural violence of the regime. But history often took charge of laying it bare, the living dead slowly advancing, terrible, to the front of the stage. For a long time it terrifies "honest people"; for almost a century it repels Republican hopes of establishing their regime in stability. A corpse disturbed these dreams of serenity, royal blood besmirched any legitimacy, execution demanded expiation.

THE "SACRED REMAINS," A MONARCHICAL PATRIMONY

The presence in history of the corpse of Louis XVI, his memory and his power, kept tormenting the minds and monopolizing the preoccupations of the Royalists. Louis XVI's remains formed a patrimony that monarchists wanted to establish in the name of the entire nation as a sign of expiation for revolutionary "crimes."[54] The object to be preserved stems from the royal tradition and carries a strong symbolic and emotional charge. Monarchists in fact turned their attention to the body of the king, the incarnate, charismatic center of traditional majesty.[55] The narration that takes charge of this body is intensely mystical: even before his death, we have seen that the king tries to entrust his fate to the narrative of religious sacrifice—a Christ-like model endlessly affirmed by his acts and words. Later the Royalists take the preservation, exhumation, and transferal of the sacred remains—which establish Louis XVI's corpse precisely as an expiatory heritage—and raise them to the dimension of a providential miracle.[56] It is the "finger of God," to use an expression of Chateaubriand,[57] that touches the body of King Louis XVI and raises him into a monument. And we must understand this "monument" in both its meanings. On one hand, the king's remains become "readable": narratives take it up, the bones speak, they are the founding corpus of the monarchical revival of 1814, a monument in the sense of a canonical text on which a regime and a politics can be founded. On the other hand, the king's remains are at the source of a monumental work: images have fixed his glory at the instant of execution; soon stones rise up on the very place of his burial and his execution to build an expiatory chapel and a statue that should testify, in the eyes of the faithful, the pilgrims, the curious, the French, to the final transformation of Louis XVI's corpse, preserved and saved, into a national treasure.

The raising of the king's death into a Royalist literary monument, a corpus forever taken up and quoted by narratives, edifying anecdotes, significant deeds and gestures, begins even before the sovereign's head falls. In fact, on Sunday, January 20, once the verdict is announced, the king asks for the possibility of making confession in complete freedom before the Abbé Edgeworth de Firmont. The Republic grants him this privilege, opening up the religious narrative of the royal execution. It is the moment when the narrative of the martyr in monarchical tradition begins: a Most Christian Majesty, innocent, mounts the scaffold; he is a good father and a king of France. It is a saint that the Revolution is putting to death. Beginning on the morning of January 21, several ritual stages pursue this religious scenario, as befits the monumental legend of the death of Louis XVI. Fasting accompanies this ritual of *appearing in the presence of God,* as well as the final confession, from six to seven o'clock in the morning, one on one, in the cell of the turret of the Temple, with the Abbé de Firmont. During this time Cléry, the king's valet, places in Louis XVI's room, arranged as on an altar, the sacred objects requisitioned the day before by the municipality from the Capuchin church of the Marais for the final Eucharist before the execution, this execution that the Royalists will soon compare to the sacrifice of Christ offering his blood to save humanity. Secretly, Louis then confides a few objects to Cléry, the first relics whose distribution a particularly active cult will assure in the next century: a royal cachet for the dauphin, the coronation ring for Marie-Antoinette, a little box holding locks of hair of all the members of the Bourbon family for his daughter. The final stations of this Passion illustrate the climbing of the scaffold, associated with the Way of the Cross leading to Golgotha: the humiliation of the king, undressed and tied by the executioners, the steep staircase that he must climb to go to the guillotine, the final oration of Louis XVI, illustrating the sovereign's magnanimity and his forgiveness, interrupted by the drumrolls ordered by Santerre, and finally the words of the confessor at the instant when the royal head will fall, the Abbé de Firmont and his "Son of Saint Louis, climb to the sky," which appears in multiple versions in the monarchist narratives of the event.[58]

Once the king of France is decapitated, the primary process is to take up the mystical tale of the sovereign's final acts, giving profundity to this death, reality to the distinctive substance of the royal body, and an exceptional quality to this corpse—all the many elements that the official Republican ceremony tried to deny by silence or scanty reporting. In fact Louis XVI's body finds multiple reflections in the immediate fragmentation and diffusion of his souvenirs. First come the organic: tufts of hair, cloth, and handkerchiefs soaked in his sweat and blood, pieces of fabric torn from his stained waistcoat. An initial patrimony is formed, or rather reformed: the martyr's relics are used to reconstitute royal identity through networks of clandestine celebrations, secret masses, forbidden exchanges.[59] In France, as Honoré de Balzac will magnificently show in a short story entitled "Un Épisode sous la Terreur" [An episode under the Terror], but also abroad, with the émigrés, the cult of the king's relics is the bedrock of counterrevolutionary identity. Balzac's description of the mass organized on the very evening of the execution around a handkerchief stained with the king's blood and sweat is a perfect example. Ardent chapels are formed; simple as they are, they are the first, fragile monumentalization of the cult devoted to the body of Louis XVI. "Everything had been prepared for the ceremony," writes Balzac. "Between two chimney pipes, the two nuns had brought the old chest of drawers, whose antique contours were shrouded under a magnificent altarcloth in green moiré silk. A large crucifix of ebony and ivory attached to the yellow wall made the bareness stand out and compelled people's gaze. Four slender little candles, which the sisters had succeeded in setting up on this improvised altar by embedding them in sealing wax, threw a pale gleam badly reflected by the wall. This weak light scarcely illumined the rest of the room; but, in giving its brilliance only to holy things, it was like a ray of light fallen from heaven on this unadorned altar. Nothing was less pompous, and yet perhaps nothing was more solemn than this lugubrious ceremony. A profound silence spread a sort of somber majesty over this nocturnal scene. Finally the grandeur of the action contrasted so strongly with the poverty of the objects and with the pious relic that there resulted a feeling of religious awe.... Everything was immense, but small; poor, but noble; profane and holy at the same time."[60]

The second heritage forming at the time, and feeding on innumerable elements thanks to Royalist memory, is a burgeoning corpus of texts and pictures of the event, describing and illustrating the stages of the martyrdom, from his pious patience as he waited for death to the sacred corpse of the "Son of Saint Louis." As poor and repetitive as Republican representation is, centered on the exhibition of the royal head, so is Royalist imagery abundant,[61] international, diverse, lingering on each moment of the martyrdom of the king. Narratives are equally numerous and abound with quotations progressively clarified, moments, obligatory stages: these are the Stations of the Cross that are illustrated and recounted. Through text and image, a monument is constituted in the literal and historic sense of the term,[62] piously collected in Royalist compilations, a monument on which the cult of the martyred king is founded.

The next stage concerns the corpse itself of the monarch, the preservation of his remains. Some loyal Royalists have not lost all trace of the king's body, and have undertaken to preserve his corpse: they have placed it in reserve for the monarchy, as one says of a painting that is kept in the reserves of a museum to be restored. Two Royalists, Descloseaux and Danjou, who lived close to the cemetery of the Madeleine, were in fact present at the burial of Louis XVI's remains, keeping in memory the exact location of the corpse. Two years later, the cemetery was closed for fear of a "morbific contamination," due to the complaints of the neighbors: there were too many bodies there, far too many. Included among them were the hundred or so victims who were crushed and trampled in this very place, irony of fate, during the festivals celebrating the marriage of Louis and Marie-Antoinette in 1770; some four hundred Swiss soldiers massacred on August 10, 1792, in front of the Tuileries; and 1,343 victims of the guillotine, including Louis XVI, his wife, and his sister. Then, in 1800, the cemetery was put up for sale as acreage for development. Descloseaux bought this abandoned parcel and attentively marked the supposed location of the king's body. In order to discourage curious onlookers and protect his property, he raised walls and surrounded the square of burial mounds with an enclosed arbor. Thus the preservation of a heritage, a heritage of land, but also an organic, symbolic, and political heritage, has been carried out.[63]

Descloseaux intends to "exploit" this property that he has acquired through his pecuniary investment and his Royalist devotion. This property is the body of the king himself, and Descloseaux, without ever exhuming it, nonetheless "organizes the place" and makes it "visitable"—exactly the way certain museums of the time, Lenoir's for instance, collected fragments snatched from the royal tombs of the Basilica of Saint-Denis to put them on exhibit. Descloseaux thought carefully about the location of his "museum" and himself edited a guide[64] of this "sacred place," drawing up the list and exact placement of the 1,343 corpses guillotined during the Terror, and precisely delimiting the ground containing the remains of the king and queen. He sells to visitors—guided by his daughter—the fruit of this labor to preserve the patrimony. The visit to the Madeleine cemetery, thus organized, becomes a regular pilgrimage for Royalists, who take advantage of the relative tolerance of the Empire in this matter. Beginning in 1801, and later even more between 1810 and 1814, a number of works on the Madeleine cemetery are published.[65] And from the registers kept by Descloseaux's daughter, no less than 1,200 visitors are counted between 1811 and 1814, even before the restoration of the monarchy. We can imagine that these visitors bought the pamphlet published by Descloseaux, of which many editions succeed each other in this period. This group of Royalist militants traces a symbolic, political, and curatorial itinerary through the corpses of the executed, and especially that of Louis XVI.

This conservation of the royal heritage culminates in an official recognition during the Restoration. In May 1814 the chancellor of Louis XVIII, brother of Louis XVI, conducts an official investigation into the location of the king's remains and listens to the testimony of Descloseaux and Danjou, as well as one of the vicars who presided over the burial of the corpse. The following August, the monarchical state puts in a bid for the land and Descloseaux agrees to sell, albeit for a good price. Thereafter, the heritage of the royal remains leaves the private sphere, the militant underground that witnessed its formation, and gains the status of a national monument.[66] The excavations, conducted in the presence of the principal ministers and princes of the court, begin on January 18, 1815. That day, the queen's remains are found; the next day, the king's.

The stories of these exhumations, recorded in detail and full of providential miracles, soon make their way into many funeral orations, elegies, historical accounts, guides to the new "holy places" of the capital. It reaches the point where we must speak of a *poetics of the remains* of Louis XVI, magnificently illustrated by Chateaubriand. The writer ponders on how to expiate the crime of the Republic and, a few days before the fateful date, publishes a long political dissertation, *Le vingt et un janvier mil huit cent quinze* [The twenty-first of January, eighteen hundred and fifteen]: "January 21 is approaching. We have long been wondering: what will we do? What will France do? Will we again let this day of grief pass by without any sign of regret? Where are the ashes of Louis XVI? What hand has gathered them?... If we would aspire to virtue, we must have the courage to be men: our character must, following the example of the peoples of Antiquity, be virile enough to endure the sight of our own faults. Whoever is afraid of repentance draws no fruit from his mistakes. Let us forget criminals then, but let us always remember the crime.... We are about to see accomplished what we have always desired, what all Europe awaited: our grief, so long repressed, will finally emerge from the depths of our souls just as this corpse will be extracted from the earth. The king comes, so to speak, ahead of our hearts' need: he will satisfy the piety of his people, will bring back moral and religious ideas to us. We did not want to move the earth before the moment of exhumation. Nothing must be hidden from this holy act. All France watched its king die, all France must watch his mortal remains reappear at the same instant. Ah! What won't the spectators feel when the raised earth exposes the bleached bones of Louis XVI, his mutilated trunk, his head displaced and deposited at the other end of his body, a sign by which we must recognize the descendent of so many kings! Let us envision carefully the three princes falling to their knees with the clergy at that overwhelming moment, religion striking up its hymn of peace and glory, the martyr's relics leaving the earth's embrace triumphantly to protect our nation from now on, and to bring, by their intercession, the blessing of heaven down on all the French!"[67]

Others, like the author of the *Notice sur l'exhumation de Leurs Majestés Louis XVI et Marie-Antoinette* [Notice on the exhumation of Their Majesties Louis XVI and Marie-Antoinette], attempt to narrate the return of the royal corpse to broad daylight: "After long and arduous research to which these gentlemen brought extreme care, the mortal remains of the Holy King were found. But here the lime had been moved: impious hands had perhaps sought to mix his remains with other bones which lay there. Nonetheless these precious remains were recognized in a definitive way; the bed of lime identified them. Thus, O profundity of secret aims of Providence, in this narrow enclosure where so many victims were mixed together, the mortal remains of Louis XVI and Marie-Antoinette were preserved, and their burial places marked precisely by the very means that the guilty parties had thought to use to annihilate them. Their fury intended only to destroy these corpses. But He who reads the minds of the perverse as well as the heart of the just, sees them and their own hands are condemned to preserve these precious remains against which they directed their impotent rage out of their damnation. And, in fact, under this miraculous lime, the bones were found perfectly preserved. The king's head was recognized, placed, as all the early testimony had insisted, between the two legs. . . ."[68]

This exhumation, in the obvious religious sense—even if it was at the time stated that the king, by the fact of his actual death, was distinct from the risen Christ—takes on, as Chateaubriand had hoped, a political sense of national import: the new regime, restored, founds itself on this miraculously preserved and reconstituted monument. Descriptions in official documents as well as the funeral oration of Louis XVI given at Saint-Denis lean on this interpretation: Louis XVI's remains become a national heritage, for they serve as a legitimate foundation of the Restoration, equal to a constitutional text. Thus the *Journal royal* can say, "In one single instant, so to speak, the usurper has fallen, tyranny has been annihilated, and the remains of the royal victim, profaned by factions, forgotten perhaps by tyranny, but watered with the tears of solitary felicity, have come forth from their humble tomb, and in their august and triumphal march, surrounded by the love of the people, have brought the solemn day of expiation, the era of clemency, the return to order, the respect for customs and religion, and the restoration of public and private virtue."[69]

This "return of the legitimate bones" is at the heart of the funeral oration of January 21, 1815, preached twenty-two years after the execution of the king by the bishop of Troyes in the Saint-Denis basilica: "How did these sacred remains escape those doubly sacrilegious hands that violated at once altars and tombs? How did the parricides, intent on snatching them away from our veneration, not succeed in making them vanish, down to the last vestiges of these formidable ashes? Let us have no doubt, it is the miracle of Providence that has saved these mortal remains; and it is the same miracle that saved the monarchy. What an inheritance for his august family, what a treasure for the nation! And what object more fitting to awaken in us these feelings of repentance, of sadness and of expiation that are so suitable to this solemn and deplorable anniversary."[70]

In fact, after having been exhibited to the fervor of several thousand Royalists in an improvised chapel of repose at the Descloseaux house, the king's remains are solemnly transferred on January 21, 1815 to the royal Basilica of Saint-Denis[71]—quite recently restored, even though the tombs of the kings of France no longer exist there. This convergence of heritage is significant: the restoration of the holy place is reinforced by the restoration and restitution of the king's bones, a corpse that symbolically represents the totality of the bodies of all the kings of France, and reconstitutes in a charismatic way the body of the nation itself. The coffins containing the royal remains, carried by imposing funeral chariots, followed by eight carriages of princes of the blood, cross Paris in a slow and solemn procession, and then are placed in the restored crypt of the basilica, where the traditional inscription is engraved on a vermilion plaque: "Here is the body of the most high, most puissant and most excellent prince Louis XVI called by the grace of God, King of France and of Navarre."

This expiation takes on its ultimate monumental form when at the very moment Louis XVI's funeral cortege sets off, his younger brother, Monsieur, the future Charles X, surrounded by his two sons, places the first stone of the expiatory chapel on the very site of the ditch that had held the king's corpse for twenty-two years. The chapel, along with the project to erect a statue to Louis XVI on the exact spot of his execution, is the monumental trace that must confer on the king's body the value of a communal heritage. Monarchical ceremony, restored, now tries to expiate the ritual and bloody sacrifice that founded the French Republic. From this rivalry, however, no conqueror yet emerges. For the whole history of the nineteenth century, in France, can be read as the prolongation of this ritual battle over the corpse of a king.

Jacques Louis Perée, *Allegorie Homme Régéneré*, 1795. Cliché Bibliothèque Nationale de France, Paris.

Geffroy

OR, THE FEAR OF OTHERS

At one o'clock in the morning on 4 Prairial, Year II, while patrolling the outskirts of the Théâtre Favart square, some citizens from the Lepeletier *section,* armed with their lances, hear a shout: "Help me, I'm being murdered by a gunman!"[1] Patriotic and bold, four of them rush to the door of 4, Rue Favart, whence the call for help has come. There, the citizens discover, bareheaded and shaken, Jean-Marie Collot d'Herbois, deputy, member of the Committee of Public Safety. A man in the stairway of the house has just hurled himself on him, armed with two pistols. One misfired, flaming only in the pan. The other missed its mark when Collot d'Herbois ducked. The bullet embedded itself in the wall. The assassin took refuge in a room on the fourth floor; he is still armed with a rifle. One of the citizens of the guard, Jean-Baptiste Pelletier, restrains Collot d'Herbois, who wants to avenge himself by getting hold of the murderer: "We will not let you risk your life, it is too precious to the Republic. Have no fear that the villain will escape, the armed force is here and we will do our duty."[2] His three companions have already gone to the fourth floor, where they are getting ready to force open up the door. A frenzied cry resounds: "Come on, villains, I'll kill you!"[3] A pistol shot initiates the general confusion. The assassin is arrested and led to the police station on the Rue Favart,[4] but a wounded man is discovered among the ranks of the citizens. The former is named L'Amiral, fifty years of age, an employee in the office of the National Lottery. He confesses to having waited all day for Robespierre, first on the Rue Saint-Honoré and then outside the Feuillants, to kill him, before attacking Collot d'Herbois, "since he lives in the same house as I do"; the latter is named Geffroy, father of a family, locksmith on the Rue Favart, and has been gravely wounded in the shoulder, the bullet having gone right through him.

Le Crime et la Vertu, ou L'Amiral et Geffroy [Crime and Virtue, or L'Amiral and Geffroy]: that is what a playwright will title a play performed in the following days on the stage of the great theater of Rouen, and then repeated, appropriately enough, at the Théâtre Favart.[5] In fact, from the morning of 4 Prairial on, when the news spreads, the Convention tries to transform this trivial news item into an exemplary case, an edifying narrative: a new martyr has shed his blood, but his sacrifice was not useless, for it saved the life of a representative of the people. An actual cult of Geffroy is formed: the wounded man is honored, viewed as an example by hundreds of delegations that present themselves before the Convention, and canonized by hymns, poems, paintings, engravings, festivals. Finally, political discourse takes possession of this wounded body: Geffroy's wound is quickly adduced as an illustration of the necessity of the new impetus to the Terror called for by the Committee of Public Safety. The healing of the martyr is placed directly under the auspices of the Supreme Being protecting the Convention's Republic, while his wound accuses the implacable enemy, the Englishman who purchased the services of the assassin. The cure calls for a vengeance that will terrify the adversaries of the Republic: it is the Great Terror, decreed a few days later. Geffroy denounces the enemy, commands his terrible punishment, and announces the birth of a new man, virtuous, devoted to the Supreme Being, citizen to the point of sacrificing his life. The "course of the wound," designating the bullet's journey through the wounded flesh, the path forming this so honored and commented-on wound, leads from corruption to regeneration. For around the "brave Geffroy" this discourse of regeneration that has haunted the Revolution since 1789 and that the Convention thinks it can finally, in Prairial, Year II, impose on the Republic is put back in place. Geffroy is the embodiment of this dream, and his wound leads the spirit toward this absolute purgation: not only is it the sign that the corruption of the conspirators has been discovered and seen through; not only does it call for an organized vengeance, the blood of sacrifice demanding the blood of restitution; but the wound is actually cured, the flesh closes up and is regenerated. "Pitt has made assassination the order of the day. The sources of corruption are opened up, and the faction of atheists and foreigners wants to drink the blood of intrepid defenders of the people in long draughts. Steel threatens the nation's representatives, but the Supreme Being watched over their destinies: Pitt's fury is impotent, the brave Geffroy appears, his blood flows, the lives of Collot d'Herbois and Robespierre are saved. Blessed be your name, O virtuous citizen! For your sacrifice is recompensed: you will recover and see the corrupt end their days beneath the terrible vengeance of national steel, and Republicans begin to enjoy the benefits of regeneration,"[6] declares the delegation of the revolutionary committee of Saint-Ouen at the Convention on 15 Prairial, thus making all the possible ways leading to regeneration converge in one single example, one single body, one single wound. Geffroy offers this "textbook example": his sacrifice is the desired regeneration, regeneration incarnate.

The "Geffroy case," intervening at the moment of truth of the Terror—the victories of the French armies are announced by Bertrand Barère de Vieuzac on 5 Prairial, but the Terror continues and intensifies despite this relaxing of foreign threats—best illustrates the snowballing of Terrorist discourse: the political certainty of the Convention stems from this multitude of examples of the perversity of enemies, from these numerous anonymous martyrs that file before the deputies bearing the stigmata of conspiracies threatening the Republicans, a scar of the Republic of which Geffroy offers the emotional peak. This political discourse that demands the Great Terror never remains abstract; on the contrary, it is endlessly illustrated by heroic deeds, edifying examples, moral anecdotes, large and small sacrifices. It ends up promoting the narrative of a *Martyrology as History* to which the Convention, the revolutionary committees, the clubs and militants, all fully adhere, a narrative determining the political decision making without much relationship to actual men (who are, as a general rule, neither martyrs nor assassins, neither reborn nor corrupt), a narrative that we could compare to a "stereotype incarnate."[7] The Terror is the opposite of the rule of the arbitrary: rather, it is a system in which reason itself has gotten carried away. It is always trying to count and multiply the evidence of the guilt of its enemies (who then, for that very reason, multiply), just as it insists on counting and caring for the wounds of its own children (which also multiply, to the point of taking the place of discourse). The proof of guilt and the scars of sacrifice are the two obsessions of the Terror, held on each side of a diptych structuring Terrorist legitimacy: the corruption that must be punished, the regeneration that must be promoted. The status of the proof of guilt and that of the glorious wound strangely resemble each other: proofs and wounds found the very legitimacy of the regime, and call for the legal violence of the Terror. As such, they are the "documents" that endlessly feed the political discourse of Year II, they make up the framework through which Terrorists read the world; they are as well the basic "documentary archives" for any study of the Terrorist moment. The martyr's wound, that essential embodiment of political narrative, the only thing that can relate the decisions of the Terror to "good and just" emotions and justify the horror of the guillotine by the glory of the sacrificed heroes who demand reparation, was clearly never offered with so much fanfare as in the case of the "brave locksmith" Geffroy. Here is his story, and here is his wound.

THE CONVENTION AND THE TALE OF A MARTYR

On 4 Prairial, midmorning, a member of the Convention, Charlier, announces to his colleagues the assassination attempt of which Collot was the victim.[8] Two reactions are immediately distinguished among those present: an interpretation of the event, and a way of learning about it. The assassin is not the only one responsible; on the contrary, he allows a network of much more considerable enemies to be discussed, the "ultimate obstacles" to happiness, whom Charlier designates under the name of "corrupt and corrupting men": "The party from abroad and the aristocrats from within, feeling that they will never be able to conquer us, have fomented a new plot, their last before our victory: they want to assassinate the national representatives." The reception of the message characterizes a way of learning about the narrative of the event with an ever marked and endlessly renewed emotion. The Convention learns the news from the world outside through the omnipresent reporters and delegations, an assembly that has become at once stage and audience, as if "representation" literally took its most spectacular and most moving sense. The first account of the event, although terse and sparing in anecdotes, is thus already the occasion for accesses of rage and emotional traffic that go beyond mere group responses and actually influence dramatically the political decision making itself. "The spent bullet which was supposed to pierce Collot struck a wall instead," announces Charlier in a report punctuated by "reactions of horror" and "final applause" noted by the journalists present.[9] This interpretation—assassination as the last weapon of the corrupt—will, like this emotionality, punctuate the entire affair, and, through obsession with conspiracy and the emotional presence of the martyrs, provide a psychological history of the management of political decisions under the Terror.

Early in the afternoon, on that 4 Prairial, the affair begins to come clear in the eyes of the deputies. Barère comes to report the facts in the name of the Committee of Public Safety.[10] The orator takes up the first interpretation of the event: the assassination attempt "reveals the corrupting schemes of our enemies," that "fatal genius of the Englishman, buyer of assassins and corrupter of domestic factions," which from now on is a classic thesis of foreign conspiracy stretching its tentacles into the very body of the Republic. But Barère goes further. On one hand, he calls for an intensification of the Terror, a renewing of punishment: "Our enemies are like those venomous plants that proliferate as soon as the cultivator forgets to root them up completely. We must resume this task with the most extreme fervor." On the other hand, he sees in the fortunate outcome of the attempt a justification, or rather a consequence, of the decree of 18 Floréal recognizing, fifteen days before the affair, the omnipotence of the Supreme Being: "Providence has watched over the life of the Republic as over the life of Collot d'Herbois. The dangers that he has run are incalculable, and the fortunate outcome of this horrible plot is thanks to a miracle."

Couthon, taking the rostrum after Barère, confirms this idea of a "providential miracle" that has saved Collot d'Herbois and Robespierre: "The monsters, they act in vain, the Supreme Being, guiding the eyes of a people regenerated by virtue, unmasks them wherever they hide. We would have seen nothing if the system of immorality, of atheism, of corruption of the Héberts, the Dantons, the Fabre d'Eglantines, and other villains paid by the tyrants of Europe, had succeeded. But since justice and virtue have been made the order of the day, since we have proclaimed with all nature the existence of the Supreme Being and the immortality of the soul, Providence protects the nation's representatives. . . . Freedom is a present from heaven that heaven does not withdraw from virtuous men: the human race needs this example, for the Supreme Being, whom the corrupt have so outraged, arranged for Collot d'Herbois to be saved." To this proof-by-miracle of the greatness of the Convention's decisions, we soon find added another way toward the promised regeneration, that of Geffroy's sacrifice.

This tale of sacrifice is introduced by an address of the revolutionary committee of the Lepeletier *section,* an address read by Barère himself in the midst of his report. It offers a portrait of Geffroy: "We announce with pleasure that a good Patriot, family man, locksmith of this *section,* was the first to arrest the monster. Then he commanded, in the name of the people, that his representative [Collot] withdraw; after having been wounded, he himself seized the assassin. Reading this news, you shudder with horror, citizens, but (as if the Supreme Being had wanted to compensate humanity at the same time) He showed it, in the same scene, a generous Patriot, a firm Republican who wanted to defend and avenge national representation. . . . The Citizen Geffroy will not die from his wound, but this very wound will be presented to your eyes as the mark of devotion that virtue owes to the Republic, it will be the mark of the Republic itself." The emblem of this sacrifice, the wound, must be constantly visible to the representatives of the people. The *section* then proposes to link the fate of the Republic to the healing of Geffroy's wound: "The National Convention would like to be informed of the state of the wounds of this good citizen. There was a time of degradation and shame in the Constituent Assembly when the insignificant and disgusting bulletins on the health of a faithless king were read in the presence of the deputies. Well, we will make civic expiation by reading, in the midst of the National Convention, in the presence of the people, the bulletin on the state of the wounds of a citizen who sacrificed himself to stop a villain corrupted by a foreign power. Woe to the frigid souls who cannot feel the value of such information proclaimed! They are neither citizens, nor children of the Republic, and never will the regeneration promised to the virtuous be able to brush them with its benevolent wing." Geffroy's wound allows the Republicans to expiate the "ague"[11] of Louis XVI, whose convalescence the Constituent Assembly had followed day after day in March 1791: the "degradation" of former times has changed into the "kindly regeneration" of today.

Collot d'Herbois, who finally addresses the Convention to give his testimony, confirms this vision, consolidating into a few sentences the collection of interpretations and consequences of the event. "I recognized the moment had come when I could not save my life without a miracle," he first declares to the deputies, explicitly taking up the association of his rescue with the blessings of the Supreme Being. "Of all the means that you can use to suppress this long series of crimes and assassinations that the tyrants have made the order of the day, the honor accorded to Geffroy seems to me the most apt to attain the goal that you set for yourselves. It will throw terror among our enemies, who will read in it each day the homage that you make to virtue and civic devotion," continues Collot, identifying Geffroy's sacrifice with the pursuit of the Terror, calling in his name for a just and severe vengeance. But Collot seeks to attach this double consequence of the attack to the very image of the martyred body. Thus he adopts the proposal of the revolutionary committee of the

Lepeletier *section* as the only way to emphasize with enough insistence that "the blood of a Republican has flowed," and to identify the Republic with this glorious wound: "I request that each day, until his recovery, the state of his wounds be appraised, and then announced to all of us. But it is not only the representatives who should take interest in the health of this generous citizen, not only the people of Paris, but the entire Republic. I demand that we insert into the bulletin of the Convention the report about Geffroy." Georges Couthon raises this identification to the love of the moral edification of all the peoples of Europe: "They have demanded the printing and distributing to the *départements* and armies of Barère's decree and the bulletin on the health of the brave Geffroy: that is not enough. The tyrants whom you have sentenced to death by proclaiming the Republic must still be condemned by you to the torture of reading, in their own language, this extract of the long list of their infamies transformed by the sacrifice of a French citizen into a bloody and glorious wound. The peoples whom they keep in chains will perhaps at last blush with shame to see themselves governed by monsters and assassins." These propositions are "unanimously decreed."

REGENERATION FACED WITH CORRUPTION

Geffroy's wound in itself bears the mark of three simultaneous regenerations, and occupies a truly strategic position at the beginning of Prairial, Year II, a necessary passage in the discourse of the Terror. It is first, clinically, the space of a physical regeneration: Geffroy's body is not only, in the primary sense of the word, in the process of regenerating itself, of recovering, of being cured, but it has also become, metaphorically, a "rampart" placed between the blows of enemies and the Republic itself. Next, this wound is the concrete, earthly manifestation of a miracle attributed by Barère, Couthon, Collot, or Robespierre to a providential protection by the Supreme Being. Collot d'Herbois says it himself: in an instant, he passed from the other side of the world of the living, he returned from among the dead, which Geffroy's wound evidentially proves in the eyes of all the Republicans. The sacrifice of the brave locksmith gains a spiritual quality: it is regarded as an oblation, a total devotion to the Republic and to the mystical power that protects it. Finally, Geffroy's wound commands a third regeneration, this one political, allied with the "regeneration" of society that is underway: a purification, a purgation of all those corrupt men who were judged enemies of the Republic after the execution of the followers of Hébert and Danton. The wound supporting this political regeneration is clearly a summons to the pursuit and intensification of the Terror.

Through this triple regenerative movement, the concept itself finds its actual force and its entire definition, in some way absorbing the various traditions attached to this word that has been filling people's mouths and flowing from all pens since the beginning of the Revolution.[12] Regeneration is in fact a concept charged with a singularly rich meaning at the end of the eighteenth century. Explicitly linked on the one hand to theological vocabulary, the word indicates two aspects of renewal: baptism and resurrection, the path for Christians to try to imitate the mystical journey of Jesus Christ. Regeneration has also been attached to scientific vocabulary, since at least the sixteenth century and the experiments of Ambroise Paré on the "regenerative faculty" of the flesh during operations on wounds and ulcerated flesh. The *Encyclopédie* records examples of this double meaning in a rather long article.[13] The outset is strictly theological: "By the sin of Adam, we are all born children of wrath. To erase this original stain that makes us children of the demon, we must have, according to the order of grace, a new birth to make us children of God. For that is what happens to us in baptism by the unction of the Holy Spirit, of which this sacrament is the sign and the proof. The second acceptation consecrated by religion concerns a kind of rebirth for another life, for immortality. The first regeneration makes us children of God and gives us the right to eternal life; the second regeneration lets us enter into possession of this heritage." Next, the article offers a definition stemming from the surgical art: "Commonly used in treatises on wounds and ulcers to express the repair of lost tissue. Wounds with loss of tissue close up by the subsidence of open vessels whose orifices collapse and adhere to each other from the circumference to the center. This occlusion by regeneration of flesh forms the scar."

Some years later, by the time of the Revolution, regeneration has also entered into the political vocabulary. It has not lost its force of religious conviction but is charged with the meaning of reform of a society; the revival still designates the physical body but now also touches on the social body. Dictionaries of the revolutionary period canonize this widening of meaning, this essential triplicity, as for instance in *Le Néologiste français; ou, Vocabulaire portatif des mots les plus nouveaux* [The French neologist; or, Portable vocabulary of the newest words],[14] which, in 1796, offers an illuminating definition:

"Term of theology and chemistry. It has been given, of late, a greater latitude. It now signifies the ameliorated, perfected reproduction of a physical, spiritual, or political object." The author of the dictionary illustrates this extension of meaning by some examples drawn from the political language at the beginning of the Revolution: "A nation that works seriously on a *regeneration* must necessarily purge itself of its vices and its immorality." The author concludes, however, with a disavowal of the word, stating that "the term has been harped on to the point of satiety," which he also illustrates by the declensions of the word offered by the discourse of the Terror: "The Jacobins claimed to be the *regenerators* of the human race, imposing *regenerative* decrees and a *regenerating* Republic of the universe that formed a *regenerated* political society, which we could more discerningly call a bloody dictatorship." It is certain that Geffroy's wound relates to these three meanings, and follows a course similar in every respect to that of the word in the dictionaries of the time: it little by little regenerates itself into a scar; it offers the martyr a sacrificial itinerary close to that of Christ, which leads him to immortality under the providential auspices of the Supreme Being; finally, it is a summons to regenerative purgation, to the state's organized revenge by means of the Terror.

To this portrayal of Geffroy as a regenerated man there corresponds a counterportrayal, that of the corrupt man. The latter is not a creation of Prairial, Year II; he has haunted conspiracies since 1789, personifying French "degeneracy" in a good number of writings from the second half of the eighteenth century. He nevertheless manifests, during the time of the Terror, a singular precision of traits associated with anxiety about the proliferation of his nefarious deeds. One by one, between 18 Floréal and 7 Prairial, Robespierre and Barère endeavor to construct the character of the "corrupt." This figure drinks from two sources: atheist conspiracy and foreign agitation. Robespierre denounces the former in his report of 18 Floréal on *décadaire* festivals.[15] [The "décades" were the ten-day weeks of the Revolutionary calendar.—TRANS.] If the Convention then solemnly recognizes the existence of the Supreme Being and the immortality of the soul, it is to struggle against the conspiracy of the atheists: "It is a question of considering atheism as nothing other than national corruption tied to a system of conspiracy against the Republic." It is a conspiracy whose ambitions Robespierre reveals: "What had the conspirators set in the place of what they destroyed? Nothing, if not chaos, emptiness and violence. They despised the people too much to take the trouble to persuade them; instead of enlightening them, they wanted only to irritate, shock or deprave them," an ambition that gathers together the orator's recent adversaries, communally accused of corruption, Hébert and his "24 pounds of salt pork hidden from the very eyes of the Patriots he deceived," Danton "who smiled pityingly at words like virtue, glory and providence," Danton again "whose system was to degrade that which can raise up the soul." As for Barère, in his report of 7 Prairial on "the perfidies and all the kinds of corruption and crimes employed by the English government,"[16] he defines, almost fantastically, the "foreign party," in this case the supposed ramifications of English conspiracy against France. All the recent assassination attempts, absolutely all, are linked by the orator to the corrupting money coming from Albion. There again, for Barère as for Robespierre, the danger of corruption is real: the ramifications of the foreign party plunge into the very heart of the Republic—not only into its prisons, those places of conspiracy par excellence, but also into the people of federalist *départements,* or, even more, into the very midst of a political class that Robespierre judges, not without some truth, to be corrupt in the extreme and susceptible to arguments of money.[17] Its "mad pride" and "cannibalistic ambition" lead Barère to consider that the "English race" has single-handedly placed itself outside the human species, an atrocious statement leading to the terrible decree: "No English or Hanoverian prisoner will be taken." Expelled from the human race, the Englishman is no longer an adversary: he has become a barbarian whose only ambition is to assassinate Republicans, a barbarian who no longer has the right to any respect and whom Republicans can exterminate.

Faced with the atheists, then, the Revolution is now nothing but a struggle to the death between regeneration and corruption, to which Geffroy's body can testify in the eyes of all Republicans: "The French Revolution, immortal as the virtue that caused its birth, is a fight to the death between corrupt ambition, streaming with blood, and the natural rights rediscovered by a regenerated man, sources of his happiness and foundations of his liberty, that only a long series of crimes could take from him. . . . The Republic will thrust away from its bosom the perfidious and faithless corrupt just as we see the vast ocean push onto the shore its own foam and the heterogeneous bodies that soil its surface."[18] On 7 Prairial, Robespierre completes the portrayal of the corrupt man during the course of another speech, directly placed under the rubric of the threats of attacks against the representatives of the nation (and against him in particular), a "discourse on betrayals, methods of corruption and assassination attempts."[19] This text is literally haunted by the figure of the assassin, the great fear of Republicans embodied by the omnipresent wounds of martyrs—Geffroy, if he offers the most glorious of wounds, is not alone, far from that, in coming and presenting his wounded body to the deputies.[20] Great fear creates in Robespierre's speech a rhetoric exemplarily balanced between an excessive siege mentality and devotion to the Republic: "They have tried to deprave public morality, and to extinguish the generous sentiments with which love of liberty and country is composed, by banishing from the Republic good sense, virtue and Divinity. We have proclaimed Divinity and the immortality of the soul; we have commanded virtue in the name of the Republic; all they have left is the resource of assassinating us. In brief, calumnies, burnings, poisonings, atheism, corruption, famine, assassination attempts—they have been unstinting in all crimes; now they still have assassination left, and assassination, and again assassination.... In saying these things, I may be sharpening daggers against me, and it is for that very reason that I say them: Representatives of the people, persevere in your principles and in your triumphant march! Stifle crimes, and save the country! As for me, I have lived long enough."

Pushing the discourse of the struggle against corruption to the point of seeing himself already dead, a martyred corpse offered to the Convention so that it can pursue the momentum of the Revolution, Robespierre consciously adopts in this speech the same trajectory as Geffroy's very recent wound: regeneration will be able to vanquish corruption only by the excess of evil, by enduring it, by forcing assassins to commit their crimes in order better to reveal them, better to punish them, better to glorify the sacrifice and save virtuous men. Robespierre ended up by convincing himself—and the obsessive recurrence in his speech of the word "assassination" associated with the frightening generalization of "they" demonstrates this to the utmost—that every individual is subject to the temptation of corruption. Terrible statement: the Incorruptible, on one hand, sees himself isolated, a body promised to the multiple blows of his innumerable enemies. On the other hand, the politician, the great organizer of festivals and civic ceremonies, has become aware that only the tragic ritual of martyrdom can now save the Republic, only the sight or story of Geffroy's wound (and the other martyrs' wounds) can effect the salutary rectification, can complete the Revolution. It is on this condition that regeneration can conquer corruption, by blood and in blood, total devotion leading to virtue. This sacrifice bears a name: the Terror.[21]

A MYSTIQUE OF TERROR

It is in this context, in the course of this struggle to the death between the corrupt man and the regenerated man, a struggle illustrated by the wounds of martyrs, that the cult of Geffroy is born. The Convention paid homage to this sacrifice on 4 Prairial. The next day, and for over two months, it is the *sections,* the clubs, the committees, and the popular societies that proceed to the rostrum to congratulate Geffroy. Two hundred and eighteen delegations formally present themselves before the deputies, while 244 speeches are addressed to the Convention, forming, by 9 Thermidor, a corpus of 462 texts and speeches written in homage to the "brave locksmith." Extremely repetitive, these praises are the foundation of the "incarnate political stereotypes" of the Terrorist moment. Between 5 and 10 Prairial, the *sections* and committees file by, offering a discourse that is then repeated without any real innovation by the suburban and then provincial societies. The Jacobins of Paris make up the very first delegation, received on 5 Prairial at morning's end.[22] The deputation reiterates the interpretations elaborated on the day before by the Convention members almost word for word, insisting particularly on Geffroy's link with the cult of the Supreme Being, linking his presence and the "rampart made of his body" to a "blessing from Providence." The martyr's act, his very presence on the scene of the attack, henceforth transcends a completely trivial event and attains spiritual necessity: the atheists' "chance" here finds a categorical refutation. Similarly, the Jacobins imitate the most honorable considerations the Convention tenders to Geffroy: the locksmith is immediately admitted to the list of club members, while a delegation visits his bedside to "inform itself on the state of his wound."

The 217 delegations that obey this impulse unsurprisingly repeat this praise of Geffroy's sacrifice, illustrating with lyricism the three successive regenerations that the martyr has embodied. It is surely enough to quote one orator to hear all the others: "Robespierre, Collot d'Herbois, a celestial genius, the Supreme Being, has averted from above your heads the dangers that threatened them and of which the Republic was to be the victim. The brave Geffroy has sacrificed his body; he has been rewarded. His wound is the sign of an atrocious conspiracy; this wound both foils and accuses it, while his cure is the work of divine Providence, and gives thanks for this protection granted the most virtuous of citizens. Geffroy, receive our salute, you have saved for France one of its most fervent defenders. Your danger and your wound are the envy of all Republicans. May they honor you! Your name wins a place in our hearts and we offer, like you, our bodies to make a rampart for legislators who must face daring assassins. Yes, Legislators, we swear to you that in imitation of Geffroy, our bodies will join together like a shield that will serve to ward off the blows directed at you by the corrupt assassins [hired by] the execrable Pitt. Continue, Legislators, make the Republic triumph completely to avenge this sacrifice! May domestic enemies fall under the sword of the law; our surveillance will help you find them out."[23] The consecration of Geffroy to the Supreme Being, the identification of the entire Republic with his wound, and the necessity of healing it, to make it form a scar by the violence of the state, are the three obligatory topics of the speech, all three repeated like a refrain by successive delegations.

Thus the diffusion of the cult of Geffroy precisely conforms with the destiny of festivals, speeches, and hymns saluting the Supreme Being, this cult so linked to the Great Terror. On 20 Prairial, at the Champ-de-Mars, during the festival of the Supreme Being, the locksmith's sacrifice is explicitly evoked: in the procession of Parisian *sections,* when the turn comes of the Lepeletier *section,* a "chariot of blind children" carries a portrait of Geffroy surmounted by a civic crown on which a tricolor strip of cloth is placed with this inscription: "He saved a representative of the people."[24] Moreover, the children sing a hymn to the divinity written by Deschamp, the final stanza of which is devoted to the martyr: "We want only to defend our rights. Supreme Being, support a cause so just! Protect the august Senate! And cure the brave Geffroy!"[25]

On this model, provincial festivals take up the homage to the locksmith's wounds, linking his sacrifice to a regeneration of a Christ-like type. In the discourse read at Armentières (North), on 20 Prairial, Geffroy has become a sort of divine creature sent to earth by the Supreme Being to protect the nation's representatives: "Benevolent genius, tutelary genius of our Republic, continue to watch over the conservation of our incorruptible representatives; create everywhere new Geffroys whose bodies serve as sure shields against parricidal steel and cowardly assassins."[26] At Grenoble, the national agent of the district dedicates his speech to Geffroy, comparing him to the yeast of national renewal: "Receive, brave martyr, the pure homage of a regenerated people who in the midst of corruption, for centuries bent under the harness of degradation and opprobrium, could, in the image of your example, resume its rights, break the chains of slavery and be reborn to happiness under the aegis of the Supreme Being."[27]

Similar homage can be found in the festivals in Blois,[28] Nevers, Pontgibaud, Villefranche-sur-Saône, Nice, Rodez, Port-Solidor in the Côtes-du-Nord, and Lunéville: "And you, Robespierre, if the parricidal steel had cut the thread of your days, if the brave Geffroy delegated by the Supreme Being had not stopped the blow that struck Collot d'Herbois, would you both have gone down completely into the eternal shadows of a sterile tomb? No, generous defenders of the rights of man; from your ashes fertilized by the blood of martyrs new Scaevolas would have been born, and immortality would have raised to you in all French hearts an eternal monument of gratitude."[29]

These speeches and hymns, these ceremonies and homages, form a religious narrative of the Revolution in which the Terror, at once a punishment of the wicked, and immortality offered under the auspices of the Supreme Being to the just and to martyrs, seems to be the essential stage of regeneration, and is explicitly identified with the Last Judgment. The Terror in this narrative of miraculous regeneration separates the virtuous from the corrupt. Geffroy in this context holds a role in the center of the narrative: he is the martyr placed at the decisive moment of the Judgment, the one who is reborn from his wound; he is a Phoenix, or rather an obviously Christ-like figure, in whom one must believe to gain immortality. It is this process that dozens of addresses sent to the Convention in the days that followed the festivals of 20 Prairial describe, an almost mystical rereading of the Terror construed (spontaneously? naively?) on the basis of biblical narrative: "What a day of terror for the wicked when, Legislators, you recalled man to his primal dignity, to a new life, that day when you interested Divinity itself in the cause of freedom! What a day of dread for the corrupt when martyrs rise up by the thousands to make a rampart of their bodies against the blows of assassins. They do not know that the reign of the virtuous has created millions of Geffroys in the Republic! Our regeneration will be sublime, it will consume the old man to form the new man: it will annihilate kings and priests. In their place it will offer a God, virtue, law; it will present a great country of thinking beings, free, happy. Yes! a people who recognize the Supreme Being, a people ready to sacrifice itself wholly for law, is a virtuous people, and a virtuous people never perishes: it has the right to the immortality of the soul."[30] Geffroy's sacrifice offers all those who recognize it the immortality of the soul: this is the way the Terror poses as the Last Judgment, and rewrites politics in the rhetoric of religion.

THE WOUND AND THE TERROR

How should Geffroy's sacrifice be recognized? The delegations and their speeches do not accept only one proof of it; the wound, that which must be offered to every gaze, is linked to the stigmata of regeneration. The wound is the proof that conspiracies exist, the proof that they have failed, the proof that the martyr has a right to immortality, as an orator from the Republican society of Dormans (Marne) describes, on 13 Prairial, before the deputies: "Faced with this holy wound, we are all ready to trace with our blood the route that will lead you to immortality."[31] Each delegation, too, without exception, insists on emphasizing the interest it feels in Geffroy's wounds: "Brave Geffroy, whose blood flowed to prevent the effusion of the nation's representative's, your wounds will be dressed by the people you have so courageously served! Your health sparks the greatest interest in all! Live to enjoy it! Your existence from now on is for all of us a national debt,"[32] writes the popular society of Saint-Flour, while the Alençon society continues: "Fortunate Geffroy, brave Republican, how worthy of envy is your wound! You will live forever in History, and the heart of all the French will be your Panthéon. The bulletin of your wounds will tell us of your cure and then we will repeat this cry of elation: Long live the Republic, long live the Montagne [the radical faction—TRANS.]!"[33]

Thus the very state of the Republic is mapped onto Geffroy's medical bulletin; furthermore, the national body is metaphorically brought closer to the physical body of the martyr, an anthropomorphic parallel often used by the orators of the delegations, who compare Geffroy's wound, exposed to danger and suffering yet surrounded by a living body that protects and cures it, to the relationships established between the Convention and the French people. The Convention is exposed to attacks of all kinds, must work in adversity and anxiety, but the people, "making a rampart of its body" (a slogan associated with the homage to Geffroy), protects it and attentively watches over it: "Citizen representatives, all arms are raised at once for your defense; speak! and the friends of the nation will gird them round you. They will shield you with their bodies. All France will form a human fortress, and you will have nothing more to fear from assassins,"[34] write the administrators of the district of Chalonsur-Saône, duplicated by the inhabitants of the rural commune of Mailly (Somme): "The French of today, gathered into a Republican society, now form but a single body, of which the Convention is the acting heart. The time is approaching when the united tyrants who try to pierce it with blows will feel all the vigor and energy of this human rampart. Then they will repent having attacked it."[35]

This metaphor of the "Republican body," of which Geffroy can be the symbol, is meticulously embodied by the writing, distribution, and even translation of the martyr's medical bulletins. Why is such precision, such a sense of bloody and clinical detail, so insisted upon? No doubt the revolutionary committee of the rural district of Lille explains this obsession: "Legislators, you will find in our proceedings the expression of extreme interest that we take in the honorable wounds of Geffroy. May we find the occasion to avenge them one by one by sacrificing to liberty as many enemies as the pains the brave Geffroy has suffered."[36] It is a question, then, of counting these "pains." That is the main function of the cult of Geffroy's wound: to give a density to the martyred body that roots it firmly in political decision making, but also "quantifies" the pain, to estimate the wrongs that must be accordingly punished. The Terror counts and regulates, constructs a system of equivalence made to terrify its enemies. Suspects, the condemned, the proofs of guilt no less than the wounds of martyrs—all must be itemized, a rational system (which stems from reason and justice), a mechanism for measurement that will effect a harmonized balance between pain and punishment. Suffering, then, has to be terrible for the punishment to be so too; this is the role that devolved upon Geffroy's wounds. Thus Geffroy involves not only a physical regeneration (the progressive cure) but a political purgation: each pain described, in astonishing detail, day after day, in twenty-four successive bulletins, is a debt of blood to be paid by the guilty who, the more they are described, see their numbers and their crimes disproportionately inflated. Geffroy's bulletin is a medical report and, at the same time, a judicial writ. Regeneration simultaneously touches on these two domains: while the bulletins of Geffroy's wounds proliferate—relating the progressive cure of the martyr but overwhelming the deputies with emotions and compassionate feelings—fifty-four guilty people climb the scaffold together. Soon, in order to respond justly to the sufferings and wounds of martyrs, the Great Terror is decreed.

Medicine and justice, the physical and the political, are indissociable. While the first "state of the wounds" is dressed by the two officers of medicine from the Lepeletier *section,* Ruffin and Legras, the trial of conspiracy is elaborated, with its interrogations and search for proofs, under the direction of the president of the revolutionary tribunal. This "state of the wounds" is severe: "Requested to determine the cause and state of the wounds, we declare, after examination, to have found: 1st a contusion with ecchymoses on the cheek and lower jaw on the left side; 2nd a wound circular in shape and as large as a three-pound crown coin, three inches from the left clavicule, penetrating all the muscles, covering a portion of the neck and ending in a second wound, of the same size as the first, about four inches away, damage that we attribute to the action of a firearm shot at point-blank range, said wounds exhaling a nitro-sulfurous smell. We judge that the wounded has the greatest need to be bandaged and drugged according to his state, not now being able to determine when he is likely to be cured, in view of subsequent accidents that might be foreseen."[37]

Justice must be just as severe, punishment equal to the suffering experienced by the martyr. Accordingly, as Geffroy's bulletins are read by the president of the Convention at the beginning of each meeting, between 5 and 9 Messidor, the guilty multiply: L'Amiral, of course, who is seized immediately; then Cécile Regnault, arrested the next day, in front of Robespierre's dwelling with two daggers hidden in her bag; then fifty-two other prisoners who, according to the report of Elie Lacoste, on 26 Prairial fomented a great rebellion of Paris prisons, instigated by the English, inspired by the example of L'Amiral. The search for proofs of this collusion is as detailed as the writing of Geffroy's medical bulletins, the fifty-four people charged being carefully interrogated by Dumas, the president of the Revolutionary Tribunal.[38]

Geffroy's first bulletins are somewhat worrisome, describing the "strong fever of irritation," the "very painful throat affections occasioned by swelling of the wounds," the "lack of sleep inseparable from the sufferings that accompany gunshot wounds."[39] Then, little by little, comes the time of the "falling away of the scabs," which entrains other sufferings of which the deputies are kept daily informed by the public reading and concerned commentaries of the delegations: "Sharp pains through the course of the wounds have continued with force as well as purulent discharge. Last night these accidents increased to the point that he could not win a moment of sleep. This whole great labor of the body, painful as it is, causes us to hope that the scabs will hasten their shedding."[40] Finally, after eight days of suffering, calm and rest progressively establish themselves: "This betterment is due to the purulent discharge, which was considerable; it cleansed the wounded areas, and weakened the scabs. We must hope that this necessary purification continues so that the wounded man can sleep more tranquilly."[41]

Despite some relapses, as on the 14 Prairial, when "a hemorrhage of vessels destroyed by the bullet and whose orifices the scab was occluding caused some anxiety,"[42] recuperation is established around 20 Prairial: "Yesterday [20 Prairial], the wounded man spent the best day he has had since his accident; a good night's sleep, no pangs or shooting pains in the wounds; this morning the pulse is calm."[43] The deputies applaud this news, reassured about the martyr Geffroy's fate. Hereafter, the pain diminishes and the wound closes up, so that by the end of Prairial the bulletins are spaced two, three, and then five days apart. Geffroy is cured; soon he will be able to come on his own and present himself before the representatives of the people and thank them for their concern. This physiological narrative of a body in the process of regeneration, followed with much emotion by the deputies and delegations, is also a "physical" tale of the politics of the Terror. For this body attacked by pain, wounded, surrounded by anxieties and assassins, is an image of the state of the Republic, besieged by outer and inner conspiracy, a *Republic awaiting delivery*. Similarly, the purification of the course of his wounds, the cleansing of bad humors, this way of curing by the very excess of sickness, is a metaphor for the Terror: continual purification of a political body in the process of "regeneration." It is thus not at all surprising that the readings of the bulletin about Geffroy's wounds are punctuated by the great Terrorist measures of Prairial.

This comparison is not forced: it is a matter of a physicopolitical parallel impossible to ignore, and in any case inseparable from the passage from corruption to regeneration that the members of the Committee of Public Safety wish to carry out—a passage the deputies too believe in, and to which the orators of the deputations adhere. Geffroy's wound in fact calls for vengeance, and becomes the occasion for a new outburst of legal violence. Just as the *sections* of Paris demanded the legalization of the Terror by speaking in the name of the martyred corpse of Marat during the summer of 1793, these *sections* now renew their demand for bloody reparation. The political decision to inaugurate the Great Terror is the work of Robespierrists, but the pressure of the *sections* is constant through Prairial, using Geffroy's wound as an exhibit implicating an increasing number of the guilty, and as a lever able to increase the measures necessary for the accomplishment of the Terror.

The Committee of Public Safety seems to profit from this conjuncture. Barère, presenting the martyrdom of Geffroy, demands the final uprooting of "venomous plants" growing in the very interior of the Republic. The *sections* respond to this metaphor: "The Unité *section* presents itself en masse before you. Here are the agriculturists that Barère requested, ready to extirpate these venomous plants down to the last one that seem still to pullulate at the feet of the Montagne. The people is here! It forms a sentinel, its glance surer and quicker than lightning, its wielding of the scythe more terrible than thunder. It will mark the enemies of freedom that the scaffold awaits."[44] This dynamics of Terror founded on the body of the martyr is illustrated, on 6 Prairial, by the orator of the Brutus *section:* "Representatives of the people, listen to our wish. The death of Lepeletier gave an impetus salutary to the cause of liberty. That of Marat caused a great step towards equality. May the new crime plotted against us not be lost to the people, may it serve to strengthen and complete our great revolution. Turn against our enemies their own perfidies, so that national vigilance may become more severe as they become more malicious and cruel. May the Terror henceforth come back to the authors of crimes, never again to abandon them, and let it be for kings and their corrupt accomplices to worry about it. Geffroy's wound demands that the national sword make itself more active."[45]

In this vein, dozens of delegations come, between 5 and 22 Prairial, to demand the "holy purgation that will cause our felicity," "the bolt of lightning striking the new conspirators to exterminate them completely," a movement that is launched again by the announcement, on the afternoon of 5 Prairial, of the assassination attempt of Cécile Regnault against Robespierre. Thus, Couthon, Barère, and Robespierre, when they vehemently defend the law of 22 Prairial that reorganizes the Revolutionary Tribunal in a much more severe and streamlined way, do nothing but profit from this Terrorist fervor deployed by the *sections* around Geffroy's wound. The wound itself is directly avenged on 29 Prairial, when Antoine Fouquier-Tinville demands the condemnation to death of the fifty-four conspirators brought together around L'Amiral, a verdict carried out during the ensuing hours on the former Place de la Barrière du Trône. Geffroy's medical bulletin thus sowed the Terror, the heads falling into the basket being as numerous as scabs that fall from his wounds, which the delegations that are received at the Convention in the beginning of Messidor, after the adoption of the Great Terror and the execution of L'Amiral, designate by a terrible play on the very name of the martyr: "Geffroy-*effroi* [Geffroy-terror]." The locksmith's wound has taken on this power of evocation: his name must elicit, by itself alone, the fear of the corrupt and of the enemies of the Republic. "The very name of Geffroy will always carry fear [*effroy*] into the soul of despots and conspirators"[46]—this is what is spoken, on the evening of 29 Prairial, to a Convention that knows that the assassin L'Amiral, dressed in the red shirt of parricides, is just on his way to the guillotine.

VIRTUE; OR REGENERATION ACCOMPLISHED

It is time for Geffroy, finally back on his feet, to come to thank the Convention and the Jacobins, the two assemblies that had been kept informed daily on the state of his wounds. On 10 and 11 Messidor, the martyr visits both the Convention[47] and the Jacobins Club.[48] The two ceremonies are alike in every detail. On 10 Messidor Geffroy is presented before the Convention by the Lepeletier *section,* "arriving in a body," and "filing in to the sound of drums." He is surrounded by his family, his wife and his three children, accompanied by the two medical officers who had taken care of him. The minutes state, but we doubt it, that "applause precedes, accompanies and follows them everywhere." The orator of the deputation takes it upon himself to present the great man: "Citizen representatives, the Lepeletier *section* hastens to reveal to you the brave Geffroy, who comes to bear witness to the Convention about his gratitude for the lively solicitude that it maintained for his well-being. Here he is!" The martyr comes forward and speaks, regretting not having had himself carried to the assembly to show his bleeding wound on the 4 Prairial, overcome with modesty, "filled with tenderness and gratefulness" for the representatives who have granted him a pension of 1,500 livres. Concluding his short speech, he introduces a theme that, if it had already been evoked in the course of his convalescence, had remained somewhat discreet, hidden by the essentially pathetic and bloody nature of an omnipresent wound supposed to lead the gaze toward the Supreme Being and incite minds to the Great Terror: private virtue, good public morals. After having indicated by his wound the path toward future regeneration, Geffroy now cured offers a result: regeneration is no longer an evolution but has discovered a figure of stability, a fixed point, an ideal of serenity. "All your decrees have made me see it: you have founded the Republic on virtuous customs; and that is why you give such praise to laudable actions, so that all citizens learn that what you cherish most is virtue," exclaims Geffroy in the midst of redoubled applause.

The president of the Convention, Elie Lacoste, thanks the martyr, that robust man, good husband, good father, whom Collot d'Herbois, true actor that he is, seizes by the hand, embraces, and leads to the presidential office to receive the fraternal embrace. The mother and children follow, and Collot discusses them in a long speech intent essentially on honoring the "family values" to which the martyr's good morality and private life testify: "I hesitate to retrace before you what the sight of him in the bosom of his family since I entered here has made me observe, or rather since I took part in the proceedings: but in saying what struck me, I render homage to the virtues common to all true Republicans. It is useful, in fact, to observe that wherever profound hatred of corruption, devotion to the country, and all public virtues are found, there also are found the private virtues, love and the activity of labor, unselfishness, loyal and frank fraternity, happy spouses, parents worthily respected, children who burn to avenge the young heroes who died fighting for liberty, and even younger children, whose tongue has scarcely loosened, and who raise their tender hands to heaven and seem to swear to it that they will henceforth live only for the Republic. That is what I saw in Geffroy. Yes, citizens, there are millions of families in the Republic who think and who act in the same way. There are in the Republic millions of virtuous and revolutionary families. For, Citizen Representatives, you have brought about such a state of things, that revolution is nothing but the simple and daily practice of austere and fruitful virtues. And the heart of the millions of Geffroys who people our Republic is an inexhaustible source of virtues that regenerate the human race and prepare the felicity of future generations."

Collot d'Herbois's vision carries the enthusiasm of the hall: each Republican has become a Geffroy, and regeneration, the reign of an austere and virtuous happiness, is established. Geffroy and the Republic have finally arrived at the other side of the historic break initiated by the 1789 turbulence, at the shores of regeneration, a journey symbolized by the wound itself and its progressive cure, a path symbolized by the sheaves of wheat given, at the beginning of this summer, to the wife and children of the locksmith. Natural, physical, and political rebirths blend together into a definitive tableau, that of the happy end of history. Thus Geffroy loses his status of martyr to become a less tragic model of private life, a model of an ideal life for millions of Frenchmen. He is no longer a glorious exception, though that indeed is an important role, if still limited to revolutionary combat against enemies; now his image must be anchored in the daily life of the people, as if regeneration, leaving the sphere of politics, could extend to all of society. The Terror is animated by this ambition—once enemies have been punished, to pacify the whole of the social body by respect for virtue—an ambition that reached its apogee in Messidor, after the introduction of the law of 22 Prairial, before the turbulence of Thermidor. As if the Republic, at that precise instant, had arrived at a terrifying tranquillity: the eye of the cyclone. Geffroy's visit articulates precisely this desire for appeasement, this wish to stop revolutionary time, which is a way of regenerating men. Virtue no longer demands of the French the sacrifice of their lives but, more accessibly, the respect for family values that produce the happiness and tranquillity of the hearth, good education, and moral probity. Geffroy thus has transformed the virtue of exceptional sacrifice to that of daily private life, the ultimate metamorphosis of a character who closes the history of regeneration under the Terror. The bloody wound has left the brave locksmith: he has resumed the role of good family man. Geffroy is cured, the Republic is regenerated, Republicans are virtuous: it is this equation established by the Terror that the deputies consecrate ritually by coming, one by one, to embrace the brave locksmith whom Collot has guided up to the most elevated seats of the hall, even unto the "sacred Montagne." Triumphant, always holding his martyr by the hand, Collot d'Herbois can then exclaim to all, coming to declare the closure of the revolutionary period: "Crime had combined all its resources, and by a species of excessive and impious scruple, it had given itself security. Well! the eye of Providence has kept watch, and the Supreme Being has interposed in the form of a glorious wound. The villains are on the scaffold, Geffroy is saved. So it will go for everything that our enemies attempt. The most infected wounds will be cured, and the people will be strong, vigorous, virtuous, and invincible. The regeneration of the Republic is accomplished."

EPILOGUE

We must believe that Collot d'Herbois was mistaken: one month later, history, immobilized by the Terror and the stereotypes of political rhetoric, resumed its course; the circle of "virtuous perfection" was broken, and the "corrupt" overthrew the Robespierrists, and soon Collot himself. Once again, regeneration would resemble an uncertain evolution, while Geffroy would fall into oblivion.

Replica of Robespierre's Death Mask. Musée Carnavalet, Paris. Copyright © Photothèque des Musées de la ville de Paris. Photo: Degraces

Robespierre

OR, THE TERRIBLE TABLEAU

When, at two-thirty in the morning of the night between 9 and 10 Thermidor, Year II, in the chamber of the Maison Commune de Paris, a bullet pierces the jaw of Maximilien Robespierre, the agony of the Incorruptible begins. It lasts more than seventeen hours, haunting various places, up to the communal ditch of the Errancis cemetery, near the Parc Monceau. The circumstances of this agony as well as the succeeding peripeteia have been amply commented on, and we will restrict ourselves at the outset to recalling them very briefly.[1] The conspirators, at the head of the General Council of the Commune, are at bay: Robespierre, his younger brother Saint-Just, Lebas, Couthon, Hanriot, in the course of the night all see themselves surrounded in the Maison Commune, where they have taken refuge from the Parisian troops who have remained loyal to the Convention. When the place is attacked, in the heart of the night, they are lost. Some try to flee, such as Hanriot or Couthon; others commit suicide, like Lebas, the younger Robespierre—whose attempt fails when he leaps out the window—and, perhaps, Maximilien Robespierre. Does the bullet that shatters his jaw comes from his own pistol or from that of the policeman Charles-André Merda? Or are there even two bullets?[2] Scholars have been quarreling over this point for centuries. That of course is not our object here. The fact remains that the survivors, for the most part in pitiable condition, are conveyed to the Tuileries in the night. At three-thirty in the morning it is announced at the Convention, which is in permanent session, that the "tyrant" can appear before it. The assembly refuses, and Robespierre, whose physical condition seems to be worsening, is carried under escort into the audience hall of the Committee of Public Safety. There he is laid out on a table where the curious are able to come look at him. At six o'clock in the morning, two surgeons clean his wounds and bandage him. At eleven o'clock, the conspirators are transferred to the Conciergerie. After a short judicial procedure, and on a simple recognition of identity, they are condemned to death. But the path to the guillotine is at once swift and slowed down, since the Robespierrists wait for seven more hours in the Conciergerie, where Robespierre is again stretched out on a table. His strength leaves him little by little. It is not until six o'clock in the evening, on 10 Thermidor, Year II, that three wagons, carrying twenty-two people condemned to death, set off for the Place de la Révolution, where the scaffold has been set up. The journey is slow, for the crowd is extremely numerous all along the way, and there are many halts. At seven-thirty, finally, the execution of the twenty-two Robespierrists is completed, Robespierre himself being the last but one to die.

Immediately a narrative of this agony was formed—contradictory, meticulous or exaggerated, precise and imprecise all at once—in the newspapers, pamphlets, reports of the Convention, and commissions of inquiry, thanks to the minutes and testimonies of various actors in the event. It reached a point where Robespierre's death could quickly become a symbol of political formation, a *forma* in the Latin sense of "configuration allowing one to understand the world."[3] The wounded body of Robespierre, subject matter of these narratives and testimonies, was supposed to permit a conspiracy to be revealed, a discourse on the Terror to be constructed; it was supposed to edify, like a physical and moral spectacle. It is this tableau, composed by the various words of these numerous and contradictory narratives, that is at the heart of this study, the tableau of a corpse, that of Robespierre, who, from the Thermidorians to the Robespierrists of the following century, had the mission of embodying a political philosophy. "The story of his temperament is a great part of his history," wrote Merlin de Thionville about Robespierre,[4] describing the succession of his humors as a chronology of his life and a history of the phases of the Revolution itself. Here we will show that the tale of his agony, the tales of his corpse, are a "great part of the history" of the Terror, at least of its interpretations.[5]

ROBESPIERRE'S DEATH: A TABLEAU OF WORDS

Immediately after Robespierre's death, dozens of accounts of the event appear. Under various forms, official reports are edited into pamphlet form with "political poems" in alexandrine. This editorial efflorescence is animated by a single ambition: to edify through the tale of a death, while at the same time satisfying the rather morbid thirst of curiosity the Parisians felt about this long agony, till then unprecedented in the history of the Revolution. There is in this narrative procedure a strangely repetitive visual construct, a common focus that offers a framework of perception and interpretation of the event. Thus, "Le Cri de la vengeance" [The cry of revenge], one of the short poems composed to draw a lesson from 10 Thermidor, rhetorically presents the death of Robespierre and his friends in two "tableaus." Addressing the "citizen reader," the poem sings: "I must present the tableau of their crimes to you." Then, in the next stanza: "I must present the tableau of their fall to you."[6] The balance and progression of the two statements summon a composition of the "scene of the Republic" in two scenes of equal importance, linked by a logic of causality, the "crimes of Robespierre" and then the "ruin of Robespierre," the Terror and then agony. In the same vein, "Le Tombeau des vivants" [The tomb of the living], another Thermidor pamphlet, takes up the edifying parallel, associating the sight of these two "political spectacles" with an emotional impulse supposed to govern the reader.[7] This path of the senses leads from pity for the collective wounds inflicted on the French body to the satisfaction of seeing the "tyrant" punished by "the most atrocious suffering": "It is in the portrayal of the evils he was made to suffer in prison that the indignation of good citizens must find its nourishment," this edifying narrative states right away before pursuing its logic: "It is in the portrayal of the misfortunes that the tyrant suffered that the satisfaction of good citizens must find its nourishment."

This wish for edification is not in itself surprising, since the subject lends itself to it, reconstructing a classic parable: the fallen tyrant, haunted by his crimes, punished by the same crimes he had committed, that is to say by the suffering he had imposed on the body of the community. More surprising is this constantly asserted desire to visualize the scene, to portray it, to offer a picture of it, when to the best of my knowledge—and up to the middle of the following century—no visual image appears that illustrates Robespierre's agony itself. We do find a few engravings immortalizing the opening scene at the Hôtel de Ville, when Robespierre is wounded by Merda's gunshot. We also come across images—ritual and repetitive—of the execution itself, the head of the "tyrant" shown to the people, the scaffold seen full-frame on the Place de la Révolution. But there seem to exist only two engravings, scarcely explicit, not very skillful, that offer a view of Robespierre's agony in the audience hall of the Committee of Public Safety and later at the Conciergerie. On the other hand, the verbal narratives of these scenes are innumerable, but they all present themselves as explicit "pictures," like visual constructs created by words.

For example, the "cage of Robespierre" was no doubt the finest metaphor thought up in this visual construct; through the bars of it the two final months of the Incorruptible are shown, following the successive and deteriorating changes of his physical state. This cage is placed, as it must be, in hell: "Pluto, wanting to procure for the inhabitants of hell the satisfaction of beholding, whenever they wished, the man (or rather the monster) who would have destroyed the human species if he had remained at the head of the French Republic one more year, had him shut up, just as he was on his scaffold, in a barred box where everyone can easily see him."[8] Danton, accompanied by Camille Desmoulins, comes to contemplate this spectacle of the "last arrival," but the "most hideous of them all." The function of this "barred box" is very precisely visual, as the author of this pamphlet indicates in his preface: "An engraver had promised to make a print representing Robespierre enclosed in a cage. But this engraving lacked language. We are distressed at this. For the rest, it is easy to picture Robespierre enclosed. It is not the image that is most essential to know, but the written work, and words subtly portray what a print could only cursorily describe."

This "written work," which one can define as a "political spectacle," a "visual scene," or a "reconstituted picture," is undertaken by numerous narratives. Even Edme Bonaventure Courtois, deputy of the Aube, reporter for the commission charged with the examination of the papers found at Robespierre's house, cannot keep himself from recomposing this edifying visual construct in the course of the speech that he gives before his colleagues on 16 Nivôse, Year III: "A great spectacle, a great example, has been given to all the tyrants of the universe. Ah! Would that they could all be present here, those hangmen of humanity, those tiger-men! Would that I could show them the dying Robespierre, portray for them the corpse laid on the table of the anteroom of the Committee where he used to dictate his laws; he had a pine box for a pillow, and slowly wiped away with bits of paper the pus that emerged from his bloody mouth, and holding in his hands, by one of those plays of fate that escape neither the painter nor the observer, the pistol case which bore the address of the merchant who had sold it to him, whose sign, 'At the Great Monarch,' reminded Robespierre of the goal his ambition had chosen."[9] The play of gazes, here, is triple, even quadruple. Robespierre has first of all seen himself undone, eaten away by the suffering of a terrible agony. Then, the "painter" historian "sees" the scene, and "shows it" to two types of "observers"—the citizen, instructed and edified; then the tyrants of the world, accused and terrified. Each time, however, these gazes rest on all the details of the scene—physical details, material details, psychological details, the only things able to recompose the whole of the tableau by conferring its true meaning on it, its true interpretation.

In this sense, this *tableau of the Terror* seen played on the corpse of Robespierre is fully inscribed in the dramaturgical ideas of the time, renewed by Denis Diderot and his theory of the "composed scene," a scene that achieves edification by the minutiae of the details, the density conferred on the spectacle by the words and the dramatic mise-en-scène, what Diderot, in the scientific language of the time, calls a "dynamic of affections." Words, thanks to detailed description, seem more able to compose the scene than images, which risk fixing attitudes and bodies in an expression less conducive to the edification of "observers." The dynamic of the composed scene is contrasted with the static quality of the engraved or painted image. It is a tableau of words, then, that takes charge of Robespierre's agony, like the visual sequences rearranged by Louis-Sébastian Mercier in his *Tableau de Paris*. The mechanism of the "tableau" inaugurated by Mercier is explicit: "The curtain is drawn in an instant; it is up to the eye to be just as prompt to grasp what is happening through this open and closed cloud; then to the pen to be lively enough to bring knowledge of it to the reader."[10] The narrative, by this glance and by the vivacity of the pen, offers a vision of the curtain abolished. This cliché of the writing of the time theorized by Diderot and best illustrated by Mercier can be found again, after the morning of 10 Thermidor, in the mouths and from the pens of the Thermidorians. Comte Antoine-Claire Thibaudeau exclaims, "The mask falls, the 'virtuous Robespierre' disappears, and the most hideous tyrant is exposed to the view of all. We must tear away the veil, and then truths too long hidden are proclaimed."[11] Portiez de l'Oise continues, "Night had covered with its crêpe the upwelling of a horrible conspiracy. Sun illumined everything, showed everything, and the sun had not yet finished its course before the head of the guilty ones had fallen beneath the avenging axe."[12] And Jean Lambert Tallien repeats the word hurled at Saint-Just during the meeting of the Convention, on 9 Thermidor: "I demand that the veil be completely torn away." It is this construct of the "composed scene" that was the Robespierrists' undoing, since they themselves did not know how to use it with enough conviction against their enemies; it is also this visual construct that assures the distribution of the tales of Robespierre's agony, "for the instruction of the good and the terror of the bad," insist the *Nouveaux et intéressants détails de l'horrible con-*

spiration de Robespierre [New and interesting details of the horrible conspiracy of Robespierre],[13] starting on the morning of 11 Thermidor, Year II.

TALES OF AN INTERMINABLE AGONY

If the form of a "tableau of words," of the studied scene, takes over the narrative of Robespierre's agony, it must be emphasized that these tableaux and scenes are conjugated in the plural. The narrative of the seventeen hours of the "death of Robespierre" tends to be organized into a montage of successive visual sequences rather than into a linear narrative. Most of the sources that allow us to reconstitute the drama, in the moment itself, offer this story by intermittent lighting, a discontinued story, punctuated by successive scenes. Starting in 1795, the biographies of Robespierre will try to offer logical links to this agony, and will study the "between-tableaus." Previously, each narrative, including the report of the investigative commission of the Convention, chose the form of "revelatory testimony," descriptions that followed the different stations of this agony and their edifying quality. The three main sources of this narrative follow the particular narrative form of "successive tableaus": newspaper accounts, eyewitness accounts published at the time, and the reports presented at the Convention.

Each time, these tableaux offer a physical description of Robespierre faced with death, as if at the exact instant when the "veil is torn away," when the tableaus is made into truth. "In everything else, there can be a mask. But in this final role, this is the master-day, it is the day that is judge of all the others," writes Merlin de Thionville as a prelude to his testimony on the Incorruptible—as if at that decisive moment the body had to say everything and the corpse had to reveal a politics, a "portrait from life." Yet, in an entirely explicit way, this corpse was withdrawn from view as quickly as possible, once Robespierre's head was shown to the people by the executioner who officiated at the scaffold on 10 Thermidor. Contrary to the legends that were spread, not only was no death mask of Robespierre taken in wax, before or after the execution, but we also find in the archives of the two committees, the Committee of Public Safety and the Committee of General Security, an order of 10 Thermidor "relative to disposing of the conspirators." It recommends "the acquisition of a great quantity of lime," of which, it then says, "a substantial layer will be spread over the remains of the tyrants to corrupt them and prevent them from one day being deified."[14] A series of measures is thus taken in the immediacy of events. The final disappearance of the corpses of the Robespierrists must be hastened, the Incorruptible corrupted: decomposition of the bodies is accelerated, the communal ditch of the Errancis closely guarded, as well as the Rue du Rocher, which leads to it, to avoid any theft of "relics," and a death mask is prohibited, setting this apart from other famous victims of the guillotine, executions in the course of which the executioners were less scrupulous.

This rapid disappearance of the corpse is one more unshowable characteristic: it confirms the poverty of images showing Robespierre's agony. In a way, that enriches the precision, minuteness, and number of the verbal descriptions. Although these descriptions deal almost exclusively with the scenes of agony, they do so the better to propose an edifying interpretation. This narrative—which can be qualified as "Thermidorian"—tries to degrade the physical appearance of Robespierre just before he is executed, a degradation that is not an invitation to compassion but rather an esthetic and moral judgment: the tyrant brought to his dying body the outer form of the political monster that he had become. On this subject, the descriptions are innumerable: "Robespierre, extraordinarily pale, lowered his eyes when climbing the scaffold, and lowered his head, horribly misshapen by the dirty and bloody cloth wrapped around it, down to his chest. This deformity with which he presented himself to the eyes of his fellow citizens at the final instant of his life, seemed to even the least religious man a punishment from Heaven. A tyrant, in fact, who after having bathed himself in blood, was completely soiled with it when descending to the tomb, bore witness in a striking way that divine justice was exercising its terrible vengeance on him, and wanted to inspire a great horror of his murders. On the scaffold, Robespierre had a new suffering to endure. Before stretching him out on the plank where he would welcome death, the executioner suddenly ripped off the apparatus binding his wounds. The lower jaw then detached itself from the upper one, and, making streams of blood gush forth, made a monstrous object of his head. And then, when this head had been cut off, and when the executioner, holding it by the hair, showed it to the people, it presented the most hideous image that one can envision."[15]

The few engravings picturing this final scene, either shown from too far away, or kept within decency by the convention of the genre, are incapable of conveying this "hideousness," this radical dehumanization, that words, through pathos of description, through monstrous evocation, and through the physical and moral resources that they harbor, are able to offer in terms of *edification through horror.* The "spectacle of horror" imposed on the dying body of

Robespierre is a final lesson: confronting the people, at the dramatized instant of execution in which the truth of the soul is revealed in the face of a man in the final moments of life, the tyrant is powerless to embody any dignity whatsoever, or even any humanity, before the gazes that judge him. The blood that he had caused to flow covers him, the heads that he had caused to fall now show in him a "horrible deformity," and the refined appearance that he had affected is decomposed by agony, his white shirt stained with blood, his blue vest torn apart, his sleeves torn off, his shoes lost, his socks "fallen past his ankles down to the instep," his trousers "unbuttoned."[16] It is this esthetic judgment faced with the proof of death that the *Journal de Perlet* expresses in its 12 Thermidor edition: "No man could be more hideous or more cowardly: he was dismal and beaten. . . . All those who surrounded him had, like him, lost their audacity. Their baseness added to the indignation against them. One was reminded that at least the conspirators who had preceded them had known how to die. These ones did not even have the strength to talk to each other, or to address the smallest word to the people. They had lost everything, their face as well as their courage."

This confrontation between a monstrous body, a denatured appearance, and the "people-public," did not, according to these tales of agony, wait for the hour of execution. It had *already* taken place during the preceding "tableau," during the long wagon journey separating the Conciergerie from the Place de la Révolution. Many halts slowed down the procession, chiefly in front of the Duplay house on Rue Saint-Honoré, where Robespierre lodged. According to these chronicles, a child, soaking some cloth in a basin of beef blood, smeared the door of the building as the wagon went by. This new tableau is completely occupied by the narrative portrayal of a "striking contrast." On one hand, the people massing into a throng all along the way, unanimously described as joyous: "As soon as the sun rose, the people took their places on the route of the fatal wagon. Joy already shone on all faces, and this immense gathering on all the avenues of the Palais National presented nothing more than the image of a great people gathered together to celebrate the triumph of liberty. The terror that the audacity of the conspirator brigands had tried to inspire was succeeded by the elation that the destruction of the tyrants produced. This day has been one of the finest days of a free people."[17] On the other hand, there is the "somber spectacle" of the Robespierrists led to execution: "Men more dead than alive went to the scaffold. As a whole, they were plunged into the most profound consternation; cowardliness, terror, shame, physical distress were painted on their cadaverous faces."[18] Pushing this contrast further, most of the Thermidor pamphlets emphasize the opposition between the life of the public (be it a "citizen's" life or sometimes an "indecent" one) and the premature death crowding the carts of the condemned that day: "Never was there seen, at the passage of those about to be executed, such an excess of people. The streets were blocked. Spectators of every age, every sex, filled the windows; one could see men who had climbed up to the rooftops of houses. The universal exhilaration manifested with a kind of furor. Above all, the wagon that carried the two Robespierres, Couthon, and Hanriot, drew people's gazes. That is where all eyes rested and to which they were glued. The wretched men, mutilated, disfigured, completely covered with blood, resembled corpses still promised yet another death."[19]

These descriptions offer the readers a double interpretation of Robespierre's death. On one hand, these narratives "collectivize" the scene: the wounded body of Robespierre is here the embodiment of a collective rout, carried along by the three carts in which the bodies discourse with each other in suffering, mutilation, disfiguration. If the "Robespierrist body" is monstrous, and has literally lost a human face, it is also because of this heterogeneous regrouping, this hybridization: tyranny is embodied by this body with many degenerate heads, this new version of the obsessive hydra whose physical wounds and moral defects only Robespierre can gather together. Already, we observe both the emblematic and metonymic quality in these narratives of Robespierre's body: it assembles defects like the monstrosity of the other bodies, and at the same time it is the visible part of a like-natured whole, the main disfigured body continuing the general deformity of its own group. Moreover, the second line of interpretation, the tableaus of words, have the ambition of prolonging Robespierre's death by accentuating his "corpse-like state." The head brandished on the scaffold by the executioner, monstrous, is nothing more than the outcome of a long morbid process of *cadaverization* of the Incorruptible. Already, on the cart, a living dead man is headed for the guillotine—in the name of others, his friends, and the others who still survive. It is not a living being that Thermidor is putting to death, but a being *already* dead, a "phantom" as the chronicles repeat in unison, a corpse on temporary reprieve, a "corpse promised yet another death."[20]

Moving from one tableau to another in such a way, the narratives of the long wait in the audience hall of the Committee of Public Safety, then in the Conciergerie, obsessively insist, even when it is a question of official reports with the most objective intentions, on this stretching out of the corpse-state in Robespierre. Even more, it is at this precise moment that the visual construct assumes its place in the account of Robespierre's death. We are edified by means of a spectacle, as during the tableau of the scaffold; already two gazes are opposed, that of the deformed tyrant facing the people-public, as during the passage of the last wagon. The narratives describe this "public" in detail, its reactions to the spectacle of agony, its comments on the scene so composed, most often a fictive public whose dialogue tries to establish a correct view of this morbid tableau. There is only one single object of the spectacle, one single object of this public's gaze: Robespierre's corpse, a corpse that I keep trying to bring back to the source of life but that the narratives nevertheless always describe as a corpse. A rotting corpse in the common ditch of the Errancis cemetery, corpse when he climbs the scaffold, corpse when he leaves the Conciergerie, corpse when he is laid down on the table of the Committee of Public Safety, Robespierre is thus all the more a corpse as we return to the place where he wielded political power. This paradox is richly illustrated: "Robespierre, his face pale, his head bare, his features hideously deformed, blood gushing out of his eyes, nostrils, and mouth, was stretched out on a table of the audience hall of the Committee of Public Safety. He seemed to be patiently suffering the burning fever that was devouring him, the fierce pains that were torturing his body: no complaint escaped him. He remained for two hours among his colleagues of the Committee in this attitude. So much so that we ended up thinking of him as a living corpse."[21]

This paradox is discussed by all the chroniclers, including two surgeons who, a priori, had to stay away from political and moral considerations to concentrate on describing the clinical symptoms of the wound. Yet, reading their report, or their testimony concerning their visits and their tasks, one finds this same judgment of Robespierre as a living corpse: "Cloth and shredded linen are prepared. When all is ready, the surgeon comes forward and has the wounded man brought to the edge of the table. He is raised to a sitting position. He supports himself on his hands. The surgeon washes his face. He is turned away from the light to bandage him more easily. The surgeon puts a key between his teeth, searches with his fingers the inside of the jaw, finds two teeth uprooted, and pulls them with a pair of tongs; he says that the lower jaw is broken. He stuffs many strips of cloth into the mouth to soak up the blood with which it is filled; he puts a larding-needle repeatedly through the bullet hole and makes it come out of the mouth; once more he washes the face and then puts a strip of linen on the wound, on which he winds a ribbon that passes around the chin; he dresses the upper part of the head with a cloth. During the entire time, Robespierre remained on the table, and watched all those who surrounded him with the fixity of death, especially the employees of the Committee of Public Safety whom he recognized; sometimes he raised his eyes to the ceiling, but aside from a few convulsive movements, there was constantly noted in him a great impassivity, even in the moments of the bandaging of his wound which must have caused him intense pain. His complexion, ordinarily yellow and bilious, had already taken on the lividity of death."[22]

This impassivity that everyone describes is not any kind of dignity but death already there, having taken hold of the body and imprinted on it its funereal traces. This description is quite distinctive among most of the other narratives of the final hours of those condemned to death during the Terror, narratives that are so numerous and so present in people's minds that we must suppose that the specifics of Robespierre's agony struck readers and witnesses alike. If it is no story of an ordinary death, that is surely because the guillotine no longer plays the leading role in it; in a sense the decisive, unspeakable instant when the thread of life is cut clean suddenly no longer matters. Most of the narratives are constructed around this contrast: the great man, the young woman, the old man, die in an instant under the guillotine's blade, stolen from life before they were able to accomplish their destiny, before they were able to live, denied the right to the deeds or repose that is due them. The living corpse of Robespierre, however, makes the execution seem interminable. The notion in fact is quite common in these narratives that the guillotine may have been too gentle a death for Robespierre, as this "historic poem" entitled "La Journée du 9 thermidor" [The day of 9 Thermidor] expresses:

> Death's agonies show too much moderation
> For a man who guillotined the entire nation.[23]

This wish to prolong a corpselike state by narrative finds a precise meaning here: an interminable agony, inflicted by long, cruel sufferings, is the only punishment that can correspond to the Robespierrist crime denounced by the Thermidorians. The phantasmagoric construction of this Robespierre-corpse finally appears, even with the doctors who had promoted the apparatus of the guillotine as a means of lessening all suffering, as the only way to rediscover, through narrative, through the edifying tableau, that ancient scale of punishments that could make the execution of the body of the condemned fit his crime, that Ancien Régime balance between the crime committed and the public punishment. The instant of the guillotine is too quick. Robespierre's body, deformed, erases it by the tale of horror, slows down death to the point of an infinite, painful drawing out, transforming the instant of death into a passage to the corpselike state that would last seventeen hours, the duration of the agony of someone broken on the wheel during the ancien régime. The duration of this passage from life to death, and its handling by the Thermidor narratives, is thus the worst of the tortures inflicted on Robespierre's body, as Audouin writes in his account in the *Journal Universel* on 11 Thermidor, inventing a terrible oxymoron: "Robespierre meurt longtemps [Robespierre dies for a long time]." Numerous historians show this, in the fashion of the time, in Roman dress, constructing a regular parallel between the agony of a living-dead Robespierre and that of Nero, emperor who died of terror in his own funeral cave: "The tyrant, struck with terror, remained impassive in the chamber in front of the meeting place of the Committee of Public Safety, like Nero in his cave,"[24] writes the author of *Robespierre peint par lui-même* [Robespierre portrayed by himself].

There is no question, though, of stretching out this agony to the point of offering Robespierre another role, that of martyr, as one historian fears: "By prolonging the tyrant's life, he might be given the time to suffer even more, to manifest this pain to the world, so that a martyr would be born from his agony."[25] On the contrary, the ceremony established around Robespierre's agony aims to make this corpse speak, but in a Thermidorian language. That is what Jacques Thuriot sets about to do when, at the gates of the Convention, Robespierre's body is presented in the early morning of 10 Thermidor: "They announce that the Maison Commune is fallen and that they are bringing the elder Robespierre on a stretcher," states the official report of the Convention. "Charlier takes the president's chair and says: 'The coward Robespierre is there. You don't want him to enter, do you?' 'No, no,' they shout out from all parts of the room. Thuriot takes the stand: 'To bring the body of a man covered with all his crimes into the heart of the Convention would be to take away from this fair day all the brilliance that belongs to it. The corpse of a tyrant can carry only the plague. The place that is marked for him and his accomplices is the Place de la Révolution. The two committees must take the necessary measures for the sword of the law to strike them without delay.'" Thus withdrawn from the sight of the deputies, his peers, the "infested corpse" of Robespierre crosses other symbolic spaces that are more fitting for the edification imposed on it. The Thermidorian narratives even make this undone body converse with the places that he passes through during his agony: Robespierre's corpse speaks of the Committee of Public Safety, an organization that the "tyrant" is supposed to have "perverted," then of the Conciergerie, symbol of his power of life and death over the French. It is surely Germaine de Staël who best improvised this dialogue by contamination between a body and a place in her *Considérations sur les principaux événements de la Révolution française* [Considerations on the main events of the French Revolution]: "Thus we saw this man who had signed an unprecedented number of death sentences for more than a year, himself lying down, covered with blood, on the same table on which he affixed his name to his death sentences. His jaw was broken by a pistol shot; he could not even speak to defend himself, he who had spoken so much to proscribe! May we not reflect that divine justice does not scorn, when punishing bodies, to strike the imagination of men by all the circumstances that can most act on it."[26]

Still, it is narratives that strike Robespierre as much as divine justice: mute, reduced to nothing but a body prematurely deprived of life: words can construct this "studied scene" without constraint. Silent, Robespierre could undoubtedly never have spoken as much as he did at that time, by his simple and terrible physiognomy, during the seven hours when he was stretched out, bleeding, on a table of the Committee of Public Safety, and later the next seven hours when he was again stretched out, bleeding, on another table, at the Conciergerie. For these Thermidorian narratives function not only as "studied scenes" but also, almost all of them, as portraits. During the fall of Robespierre, the question, How and why did this man become the head of the Republic? is found in all thoughts. And the answer to this question starts by drawing up the psychological and physical, or rather even psychopathological, portrait of the individual. Rarely have descriptions of the body and character of a political figure been as numerous as at that time, as if all narratives attracted readers by saying to them: "Come see the body, come see the character of a tyrant. . . ." The portrait offered immediately by Merlin de Thionville,

Thermidorian deputy among others, illustrates this concern for portraiture: "People who take pleasure in finding relationships between faces and moral qualities, between human faces and those of animals, have noticed that, as Danton had the head of a mastiff, Marat that of an eagle, Mirabeau that of a lion, Robespierre had that of a cat. But this face changed its physiognomy; it was first the anxious but gentle demeanor of the domestic cat; then the savage demeanor of the wild cat; then the ferocious demeanor of the *tiger-cat*. Robespierre's temperament was first melancholic, then ended up being bilious. At the Constituent Assembly he had a pale and lackluster complexion and spoke only in moans; at the Convention he turned first yellow, then livid like a corpse, but a speaking corpse, one that could only speak by frothing at the mouth. The history of his temperament is a great part of his history."[27]

Starting from this scene of agony and this portrayal of Robespierre as a living corpse, the Thermidor narratives complete the image by offering a final tableau in words. In fact, if it is not prudent, in view of the compassionate moods of public opinion, to let Robespierre suffer too long a time by indefinitely delaying his execution, it is on the other hand possible to prolong the time of agony backward, to rewrite his life, his final months, the way his final day was related. We are thus present, in Thermidorian narrative, at the phenomenon of an almost infinite expansion of Robespierre's death: as if this Robespierre-corpse had won an inordinate temporal density. What narratives in fact rewrite as the "death of Robespierre" are his final months: Thermidor indeed goes back to the beginning of Prairial, Year II, the supreme moment of anxiety for Robespierre, when at the bar of the Convention he describes himself as being menaced every day by assassination, and when the laws of the Great Terror come to crown this obsessive fit. Robespierre lent his own words to this morbid rereading of his physiognomy, since his long speech of 7 Prairial, Year II, is literally haunted by descriptions of his assassination, the obsessive figures of his own death, and the images of his fate as a body sacrificed to the common good, of a "Republican corpse." The Thermidor narratives seize hold of this vision and turn it against Robespierre with a virtuosity in their morbid attack on the body that only Hippolyte Taine will later rediscover in the magnificent and unsettling portrait that he draws up of the Incorruptible: "Never does he weary of killing his guillotined adversaries all over again. On these still warm corpses, his hatred oozes in affected slander, in palpable counter-truths. Thus eaten away inside by the cadaverous venom that he distills, his physical machinery breaks down, like that of Marat, but with other symptoms. When he speaks at the rostrum, he wrings his hands in a sort of nervous contraction, sudden spasms run through his shoulders and down his neck, which he shakes convulsively from right to left. His complexion is bilious, livid; his eyes blink under his glasses. He is in the process of becoming a corpse himself, and the shadow of death has already seized hold of his mask."[28]

Similarly, many testimonies of the Thermidorians reinforce this hypothesis that allows the "duration of life" of Robespierre-the-corpse to be lengthened from seventeen hours of agony to more than two months of supreme political power. Paul Vicomte de Barras, to use only one example, left the memory of a strange visit to Robespierre at the end of Prairial, Year II, a visit that supports the Thermidorian hypothesis of a body becoming a corpse well before death itself: "When I was introduced to him, he did not answer one word, made no gesture, and gave no sign of any emotion whatsoever by his physiognomy. I have seen nothing so impassive even in the frozen marble of statues or on the cold face of corpses at wakes."[29] In his report to the Convention, Courtois repeats this interpretation and forms a portrait of the Incorruptible as a man haunted psychologically and physically by death: "Seeing nothing around him except dead or dying people, hearing nothing but the cries of victims, or the subterranean voices from the tombs that called to him, and thinking that he already felt, like the bull at the altar who is about to fall, the blow of the ax that awaits him, Robespierre no longer breathed. He stayed at home, livid, cringing like an animal, no longer acted except to ward off this blow, wandered, like a stricken bacchante with a thyrsus, in the company of the accomplices in his crimes. They want to assassinate me! he exclaims. I will drain Socrates' cup, I will not abandon my days. Robespierre's threat was henceforth nothing more than a coup de grâce, his movements were the shudders of the death throes, he was already pale with his future death."[30]

To this stretching out of time is added a spatial expansion of Robespierre's body-corpse. It is France itself, its territory and its inhabitants, that for some decades has become a dead body. Many cartoons of the time expressed this with black humor, since it is a matter here of a metaphor and not of a direct representation of death at work. We know of three: *Robespierre guillotinant le bourreau après avoir fait guillotiner tous les Français* [Robespierre guillotining the executioner after having had all the French guillotined], *Le Gouvernement de Robespierre* [Robespierre's government], and *Le Peuple français ou le régime de Robespierre* [The French people; or, the regime of Robespierre]. Each time, in these images,[31] France is transformed into an immense cemetery, and the bodies of all citizens of the Republic have joined the condition reserved in the Thermidorian political imagination for the "first" among them, the tyrant: that of corpse. Bodies are amassed, heads pile up, and Robespierre reigns, master corpse in the republic of corpses. That is also what Dussault writes as he establishes a parallel between 1789 and 1794, between two "tyrannies," the regime of Louis XVI and that of Robespierre: "In 1789, as in the second Year, France had the repose of a corpse."[32] Robespierre's body, in the drawings as in this parallel, has become a metonymy for all of France: the tyrant's corpse designates the entirety, the corpse that the Republic has become. Robespierre's body is the macabre symbol for a country deprived of life.

This temporal and spatial expansion of Robespierre's corpse is not just a rhetorical image. It also leads its meaning to the political interpretation of the Terror in Thermidor: having become a phantom, Robespierre rules over a graveyard. That is a way of constructing a correlation between the physical and mental state of the country and the physical and mental state of a man, a correlation that allows the Terror to be explained as a nightmarish identification, a morbid hypnosis. This interpretation has the advantage of refusing the collective responsibilities of the citizens as well as those of the deputies of the Convention for the establishment and government of the Reign of Terror. The guilty one, in the first and only place, is the original corpse, which has expanded in time as well as in space until it completely covers the France of the Terror. It is enough to separate the whole from this morbid original part for the body suddenly to regain life, as after the removal of a "morbific tumor." The agony and death of Robespierre fill precisely this role: phantom, living dead, the "tyrant" can be chased from the mind like a bad dream; metonymic corpse, he can be taken out of the body politic and decomposed under quicklime. First, though, this dying body must tell its truth to everyone—the hideous corpse reflecting the moral monstrosity of the tyrant—and publicly expiate its faults by the sufferings of a long death. This morbid edification constructed on the corpse of Robespierre is the keystone of Thermidorian discourse.

THE TAIL OF THE CORPSE: A SHOCKING TALE

But can this phantom easily be chased away, can this morbid tumor be eradicated, this corpse buried? Quite quickly, in fact, the body of the dead man rises again, not only under the form of "obsessive memories" of the Terror,[33] but also, through the words of narratives, as an unsettling organic matter, through the irony of a shocking obscenity. This physical continuation against nature, this morbid reproduction, is introduced into narratives just a few days after Robespierre's death, more precisely in a pamphlet entitled *Testament de Maximilien Robespierre trouvé à la Maison commune* [The last will of Maximilien Robespierre found at the Maison Commune]. This text, which begins with a rather common fiction at the time—the apocryphal last wishes of the great man—invents a cock-and-bull story and a successful organic metaphor.[34] Before trying to kill himself, Robespierre is supposed to have isolated himself in a remote room to "set his last wishes down on paper." It is this "document" that the pamphlet discloses with an ironic complicity: "I bequeath my soul to the Supreme Being," begins the anonymous author of this pamphlet unsurprisingly, before going on to list all the physical parts that can possibly be bequeathed. "I bequeath to [Jacques-Louis] David my face, with the wish that my features be passed on to posterity," it begins, and the sexual organ closes it: "Finally, to give all my brave lieutenants a rallying point, I bequeath to them, in the guise of a standard, *my tail.*" Meantime, the pamphleteer had reserved a special fate for Robespierre's corpse, reviving, through ironic and polemic words, the fear that had led the Thermidorians to make the actual body of the Incorruptible disappear without delay: "If Jesus of Nazareth, who was only a little boy compared to me, once had the power to send the devil into the bodies of two thousand pigs, I should easily be able to pass into the bodies of thirty or forty Jacobin leaders; I bequeath to them my corpse, which they will feed on to find those words and actions that will perpetuate my will. And the French people will have lost nothing from my death, for my blood will be a fertile seed whence the inheritors of my plans will be born."

This apocryphal will launches not only the saucy play on words in vogue on Robespierre's "tail [*queue*]," but also the idea that, just as narratives had dragged Robespierre's corpse upstream, back through his existence, one could also stretch it indefinitely downstream into the future. This has a direct political consequence: the indictment of the "accomplices of the tyrant"—Collot d'Herbois, Jean-Nicolas Billaud-Varenne, Thuriot, Marc-Guillaume Vadier, Terrorists who had gone round to the Thermidorians' side in the precipitation of the coup d'état that overthrew the Robespierrists. Both the play on words and the political accusation are drawn from the corpse of Robespierre itself. That tells us how much vitality this form could wield in the anxious imaginations of the times. It also prolongs—is this one of the profound reasons for the success of these figures?—the association of Robespierre with royalty, one of the most persistent and common rumors at the time:[35] if Robespierre were a king, then his body, like that of the sovereign of France, would possess the power to perpetuate itself infinitely through his descendants. One single body succeeds itself politically in an identical lineage with Robespierre as with the Bourbons. And if, in monarchical tradition, this bodily transmission is the symbol of life, in Robespierre's case it passes through the corpse. A fantasy of death takes shape here through this morbid perpetuation, associating Robespierre with a deathly royalty, a degenerate religion (in allusion to the resurrection of Christ), and more prosaically through an obscene tableau (the final seed of the dying man: Robespierre's "tail" becomes a group of political followers).

This last theme is explored with delight and virtuosity by a whole vein of Thermidorian literature, a literature that is very much in vogue—there are about thirty pamphlets written one after the other—saucy and subtly political. These lampoons, in the name of a struggle for a return to freedom of the press, attack the "successors of the tyrant," to use the consecrated expression.[36] On 9 Fructidor, Year II, Méhée de la Touche in fact publishes the first pamphlet[37] of a long series, *La Queue de Robespierre* [The tail of Robespierre]. The argument is clever, as is its presentation: the fight for freedom of the press goes through the genres most exposed to censure, genres that are here intimately mixed together, the political and the obscene. Méhée insists on political argument in the main body of the text: he aims at Billaud-Varenne, Collot d'Herbois, Thuriot, Vadier, the Robespierrists who made Robespierre fall by turning against him but who are, according to the author, the "successors" of his politics. As for the titles of these pamphlets, they are a call to libertine imagination: *La Queue de Robespierre, Suite à la queue de Robespierre* [Robespierre's Tail, Continued], *Rendez-moi ma queue* [Give me back my tail]. . . . The association between the two registers is reserved for the domain of wit, of a saucy play on words: it is the successors of Robespierre who form a group mockingly called his "tail."

Corporeally, this play on words makes sense. It directly replaces the prevailing metaphor so useful at the beginning of the Revolution in designating the dangerous resurgences of aristocratic conspiracy, the hydra, whose heads keep growing back as long as the last one has not been cut off. Henceforth, it is the "rings" of the tail that infinitely continue to grow, to use the metaphoric animal register, or the semen of the "dying tail" that has produced multiple offspring, to use the vocabulary of begetting. Corporeally, this play on words makes more sense when it is employed and made explicit in many lampoons. From then on, in fact, the association of Robespierre's agony with a final orgasm is a constant of the pamphleteers' pens. If Robespierre found his "state of happiness" in a France transformed into a graveyard, if he took pleasure in the blood of victims of the Terror till he became a corpse himself before the hour of judgment, then his agony, that state of living death prolonged for seventeen hours, coincided with a final and perverse pleasure. From this final pleasure the "tail" of Robespierre was born: monstrous bliss (*jouissance*) and fertility were in this pain, in this hideous state. Ange Pitou, a satirist who was at the time close to Méhée de la Touche, wonderfully illustrates this association of Robespierre's corpse with the pleasure of the senses in *La Queue, la tête et le front de Robespierre* [The tail, head, and forehead of Robespierre] by comparing the tyrant's sex with the instrument of pleasure of women under the Terror, but a pleasure that is in and through pain:

> Robespierre's tail is most in fashion
> To soothe and still the ladies' passion.
> When his tail and his sharp blade
> Penetrate some charming glade,
> I hear a young virgin's plea:
> O how this knife stabs me!
> This Robespierre of a tail
> With blood will gorge and swell;
> Squeeze it if you dare
> Till pleasure wakes up there.
> The murderer's huge tail
> Makes the whole world quail;
> This tail bears a deep stain
> Of pleasure, love, and pain.[38]

This vaudeville, as Pitou calls it, is clear enough in its telling rhymes: Robespierre's power is associated with that which a degenerate seducer could exercise over women. Another theme in fashion at the time is that of the "great priest" and his "devotees": "It is especially women (called in Paris the devotees of Robespierre) that the tyrant moved to tears. However far away they saw him, their heart, teeth, feet, hands, everything trembled in them. They pointed him out to each other, they stifled him with caresses, they pinched him, bit him, devoured him with the whites of their eyes,"[39] reports a Swiss journalist at the end of the month of Fructidor, Year II. In this sense death is the frame for a final erotic scene: the morbid pleasure found in blood and the pangs of agony. In the course of this final pleasure, Robespierre would thus give birth to his "continuators," the ones that are suspected and accused, starting in Fructidor, Year II.

Faced with this lewd return of Robespierre's corpse, the new heads of the Convention try to reply by appeasement: let's allow the bodies of the conspirators to sleep in peace. At the time the Thermidor narrative took it upon itself to mark these bodies with an infamous mark. Robespierre's corpse had been separated from the Republic. Now it is a matter of forgetting this morbid organism. That is the reply given to the "excessives" by the author, for instance, of *La Réponse à la queue de Robespierre par un franc républicain* [The response to Robespierre's tail by an honest Republican]: "The more one disturbs a quagmire, the stronger the stench becomes. Today, they speak of a tail, tomorrow, it will be claws. For goodness' sake, let Robespierre's corpse sleep in peace. It was hideous enough, and his agony was terrible. He has suffered enough. Under the lime of the Errancis, may his body, his head, and his tail be forgotten. That was his punishment, and the massacre is over."[40] Once again, corporeal metaphor tells of political tensions. But this organic register leans more to the side of the excess and the stirring up of emotions. Obscene pamphlets continue winning in this fight by lexical nuance—one series is in fact launched around the *Parties honteuses de Robespierre* [Robespierre's parts (or parties) of shame] and *Parties honteuses du tyran aux Jacobins* [Parts (or Parties) of shame from the tyrant to the Jacobins]—always demanding the punishment of the "successors" of Robespierre, the fiercest acting representatives, or calling for the closing of the Jacobins Club. Quickly, in this radical narrative, the only expiation possible for the Terror becomes terror itself, the only definitive burial of Robespierre's corpse the massacre of the body. Ending the Terror consists of turning the Terror back against the old Terrorists, judging all the accomplices and all the successors of the Incorruptible, a role that the few great trials of Year III will try to play politically. Burying Robespierre's corpse definitively, to judge by the metaphors chosen, comes down to radicalizing the execution of the tyrant—massacring the body and emasculating the corpse. The ceremony of punishment of the Ancien Régime, inflicted on the dying body of Robespierre by the Thermidor narratives, is transformed a few weeks later into a rite of massacre in the most violent pamphlets of Fructidor, Year II.

That is what the two last titles of the series of "Tails" of Robespierre explain clearly: the *Plan de conduite pour tous les anneaux de la queue* [Plan of conduct for all the rings of the tail] and a blunt and incisive *Coupons-lui la queue* [Let's cut off his tail]. In these narratives,[41] we discover Robespierre's corpse come from the common ditch of the Errancis, a corpse "living from the NECK to the TAIL," that is to say a horrible body without a head that seminal energy has alone succeeded in reanimating, a monster worthy of the morbid fantasies that populate certain Thermidorian engravings, and then animate the magic lantern spectacle perfected by Robertson in 1798. This monster associates the Incorruptible with his political descendants—the "*COL* [NECK]," written in capital letters, indeed answers to the word "*QUEUE* [TAIL]," but it is also a transparent allusion to Collot d'Herbois, main "successor" to Robespierre, along with Billaud-Varenne—while at the same time drawing up a horrible portrait: the living corpse without a head but with an all-powerful reproductive organ, political version of the ecstatic (*jouissant*) death, the "orgasmic (*bandant*) death" that is found at the same period in Sade's novels. Using the "we" of the successors of Robespierre, the pamphleteer writes: "No doubt the NECK was greatly mistaken to mix itself up with the HEAD [an allusion to 9 Thermidor and the return of the alliances that led to the fall of Robespierre]. This imprudence almost cost all of us our lives. We escaped it beautifully! Fortunately the TAIL remained intact at the instant of the execution. And by the vigor of the lower half, we nullified the shaking of the upper half. Now we have pretty well extricated ourselves from that misstep. May this experience make us strong: let us occupy ourselves in seeking this power of the TAIL." This monster can be eradicated only by massacre, the dispersion of the "NECK" and the rings of the "TAIL," emasculation. The agony reconstituted by the narrative of Thermidor branches off to a Saint Bartholomew's Massacre in Fructidor. The horror of the metaphor of the corpse living from the "NECK to the TAIL" calls for massacre. By this logic, all the old Robespierrist members of the Committee of Public Safety must pay the death penalty.

A ROBESPIERRIST POETICS

Another group turned its attention with growing interest to Robespierre's corpse: Robespierrists themselves. They also saw astounding shapes in it. Thermidorian narratives were composed in successive tableaus. It is another language of tableaus that the Robespierrist tradition privileges: the theater.

Since the theater was a very fertile genre under the Revolution, there were some Thermidorian plays composed at the time or some months later. Godineau, for instance, offers a *Mort de Robespierre* [Death of Robespierre] in Fructidor, Year II, a drama in three acts that is particularly virulent against the "furious tyrant."[42] Antoine Sérieys writes a similar play in 1800, using an identical title.[43] In this play, the third act ends with the arrival at the Convention of the "completely disfigured tyrant the way he looked on 10 Thermidor," a half-corpse acknowledging his faults to his peers in a final confession before the guillotine:

> Senators! My presence brings you at this site
> A hideous spectacle to affright.

But, with the chronological gap necessary to the establishment of a literary and political tradition, the Robespierrists make use of the theatrical genre a century later. Between 1882 and 1939 this tradition offers no less than seven great historical dramas on the Incorruptible. These accompany a cult of Robespierre that follows the path of works of militant scholarship—the *Histoire de Robespierre* in three volumes by Ernest Hamel, completed in 1867—which tries to restore, conserve, and open to visitors the Incorruptible's house in Arras; this cult is also at work in great historical paintings. The academic and Robespierrist painter Lucien Mélingue is first to use the agony of Robespierre to "restore his just and male pride" to him. This spectacular historical tableau, very large, *Le Matin du 10 thermidor an II* [The morning of 10 Thermidor, Year II], representing the Incorruptible wounded and stretched out on the table of the Committee of Public Safety, makes a sensation at the Salon of 1877. After 1878, it is widely reproduced and distributed in Robespierrist circles thanks to the procedure of photoengraving.

These circles organize themselves into militant and academic networks of scholarly societies, an organizing tendency that culminates in 1907 in the founding by Albert Mathiez of the Society of Robespierrist Studies (*Société des études robespierristes*), a society that soon publishes its journal, the *Annales révolutionnaires* [Revolutionary annals]. A good number of "men of letters," including Hippolyte Buffenoir, Jean Bernard, Lucien Descaves, and Hector Fleischmann belong to this Robespierrist association, which was quite strong at the time. They are the ones who breathe an epic dimension into the character of Robespierre, particularly into his tragic fate and his death. Their lyricism radically overturns the image of his agony, and manages to *poeticize* the tableau of his death. Robespierre's body—as in any cult devoted to a martyr—is often positioned at the heart of this communion and this renewed narrative. The Robespierrist network thus reactivates, by conferring a militant sense on it, the until then merely morbid and anecdotal interest roused by the death mask of Robespierre, a mask preserved—or rather invented—by certain wax museums, Curtius and Madame Tussaud, at the end of the eighteenth century.[44] Many death masks of Robespierre exist, all false, reconstituted after the fact from portraits, and their conservation, exhibition, and sometimes even their invention from whole cloth occupy an important place in Robespierrist memory and cult. The dead man's face becomes a place of communion, inspiration, and of vows; obviously it is no longer the hideous face, the degenerate and dehumanized head that is described, but on the contrary his serenity, defiance, and glory tragically shattered: "Before this mask imprinted with the painful and profound melancholy of death, and on which a supreme smile seems still to float, born of disdainful irony at the slaves of yesterday become triumphant executioners, our pen hesitates and trembles. That is because never did a more terribly sublime face arrest History," writes Armand Dayot, one of the erudite Robespierrists of the time, faced with one of the masks exhibited in 1911 at the Musée Carnavalet.[45]

"To arrest History"—that, finally, is the role that Robespierre plays in this rewriting, as if, by the two aspects of his corpse, the history of the Revolution were radically divided. Ernest Hamel writes: "The Republic offered on that day [10 Thermidor] the spectacle of his immense suicide. As prelude, they held in the street the vile Thermidorian comedy known by the name of "Ball of the Victims." One thing to be seen around Robespierre's scaffold was the start of the reign of the strumpets and prostitutes from all walks of life, the speculators and knaves. The actual public stood apart, concerned. The Robespierrists all died without boastfulness and without weakness, bravely, as people who defied the future and embraced death with the serenity of a pure conscience and the conviction of having fulfilled their duty to the end. As a fervent Royalist, the executioner must have quivered with pleasure, for he felt deeply that he had just immolated the Revolution and decapitated the Republic in the body of its most illustrious representative, Maximilien Robespierre."[46]

Aside from the play by Victorien Sardou, *Thermidor,* written in 1906 from the Girondin point of view, all the other dramas composed about Robespierre are Robespierrist: the *Monologue de Robespierre allant à l'échafaud* [Monologue of Robespierre going to the scaffold] by Hippolyte Buffenoir in 1882, *Robespierre* by Louis Combet in 1888, *Robespierre* by Robert Griepenkerl, *Danton et Robespierre* by Robert Hamerling—both translated from the German by August Dietrich in 1892 and 1893—*Le Dernier Songe de Robespierre* [Robespierre's last dream] by Hector Fleischmann in 1909, *L'Incorruptible* by Rumsard in 1927, and, finally, *Robespierre* by Romain Rolland, the most famous of them all, written in November and December 1938. What is mainly at stake in these plays, aside from their strictly militant dimension, is solving the challenge posed by Thermidor: how is one to transform this suffering, wounded, deformed body into a hero's body? The Thermidorians, at the time, had made a monstrous corpse of Robespierre; the Robespierrists, almost a century later, propose another fate for him: his sacrifice makes a living, suffering, sometimes shouting, often visionary, body of him, but no longer a corpse. Robespierre's body has become a lyric promise and has left behind its impassive and frozen shell. Life is returned to it thanks to speech and vision, but—since historical objectivity imposes silence on the broken jaw—a speech that sounds internally, and a prophetic vision. It becomes the central issue of these plays: how to make a silenced man "speak," especially on the stage? Most of these dramas find the same answer: Robespierre, dozing during his agony, awaiting death in a serene sleep and no longer like a hideous corpse, is transformed into a *character in a dream*. The first playwright to advance this poetic and theatrical idea is Hippolyte Buffenoir, who in sixty-six lines offers a long interior monologue spoken by Robespierre as in a dream when he is in agony on the table of the Committee of Public Safety. It begins:

> Death comes. I am calm, and nothing frightens me,
> The world will thank us for their living freedom . . .

And it ends, faced with the guillotine, thus:

> Let us go! Mount to the zenith, sun of Thermidor!
> Before this scaffold, I salute thee once more!

The last of the Robespierrist playwrights, Romain Rolland, takes advantage of the cinematographic art to stock Robespierre's agony with sublime visions, projected on a screen placed at the back of the stage. Thus the hero's life, as moving scenes, goes by during his death. Robespierre is no longer in any way a cold, opaque corpse immured in silence, but projects his ideas, his actions, his prophecies, in splendor thanks to the living image. He has become a source of life. It is a matter of returning the power of life to his agony—not following some final perverted procreation, as the obscene pamphlets of Fructidor, Year II, imagined it, but thanks to an unsurpassable epic force. Suddenly, in these plays, agony is transformed naturally into an ascension.

Death throes "full of life" are in fact a paradox that can only be resolved by apotheosis. That is the meaning of the finale of the most militant of these plays, Louis Combet's *Robespierre,* where the two final scenes explicitly associate Robespierre's body with that of Christ. The penultimate scene, entitled "Golgotha," lets us glimpse a reenactment of the execution, through a "cloud tinted with red": "The cloud opens up and we see a part of the Place de la Révolution, with the scaffold and the wagon of the condemned, among whom we make out Robespierre, his head high, and swathed in bloody rags. Thunder sounds, then a black cloud passes in front of this horrible scene, and everything becomes dark." Nothing of the execution itself is seen. The final scene, "The Champs-Élysées," raises Robespierre to Olympian paradise, a syncretic paradise where the goddesses Justice, Truth, and History are grouped together, next to great men, from Plato to Rousseau, from Vercingetorix and Confucius to Jesus, to welcome the Incorruptible, "shining, carried on a cloud," while the following mottoes appear at the back of the stage in letters of fire: "Universal Republic," "United States of Europe," "Alliance of peoples." The hideous corpse of Thermidor has here been visited by a Christ-like apotheosis combined with admission to the civic pantheon.

This, minus the solemn pomp, is the same procedure that Romain Rolland uses. In the finale of his play, first the "Chariot of the Revolution" appears, an image undoubtedly drawn from Abel Gance's "Napoléon," in which all the famous dead of 1793 and 1794 come to offer France its revolutionary heritage. Here Robespierre's final vision before execution is projected on the great screen that backs the stage. Death itself attains that blinding flash refused by the Thermidorian narratives, with Robespierre's execution invisible on the stage but punctuated by an "enormous cry" emitted by the actors. Finally the Robespierrists, as if resuscitated, grouped around their hero, take the center of the stage, joined by the main figures of the "Chariot of the Revolution," such as Collot d'Herbois or François Noël Babeuf. All struggle together against "the hydra of royalism," make a barricade with their bodies faced with the rising tide of perils (remember we are in December 1938). Thus, mingled by the fight, the Robespierrists now form one single body, that of the revolutionary bloc that faces the traditional enemy. This united body is the vital force of Robespierre as exalted by his most ardent defenders, close to the Communist Party in 1938. Ever after, in the cart, then on the scaffold, and finally in his posterity, Robespierre carries this glory through his serenity when faced with suffering, through his visions and his immortality. He has become a pure fantasy of life answering, feature for feature, the morbid fantasy of Thermidor.

It is this vision that Hector Fleischmann portrays, offering his own account in 1909 of the scene of Robespierre's journey to the scaffold, transforming it into a tale of the "heroic age" of France: "It is well that his throat was cut on the eve of decline. With Robespierre dead, the heroic age is finished. It is right that the jolting cart dragged him to the Place de la Révolution, since he is not made for those times! France gave itself to the Directory. What did he still have to ask of posterity, this Robespierre standing upright, his jaw broken, livid, bloody, silent in the storm of vociferations? Certainly, he had sinned; certainly, he had failed; but in his role of expiation, what brilliance, and on his blood-covered body, what majestic horror! He, Catiline, the tiger, the dictator, Robespierre, he dominated them all with the loftiness of his double execution, with that heroic majesty endured by his dying, yet upright, straight, proud body. Men were in the street, women rested in windows. He saw them wavering, he saw rising up before him the innumerable faces of the crowd; he saw them leaning towards him as the cart went by, those throats open to the sun of Thermidor. He saw the fury of these men's eyes, insensate with outrage, shouting at his crimson agony. He also saw the lure of those feminine charms that he himself had till then rejected. And, his eyelids half-shut, he dreamed of his destiny, this sacrifice of his person to his country, as if offered to those women's bodies. Climbing the already sticky steps of the guillotine, the man of Thermidor could feel in himself a consciousness and a bliss lofty enough to acquit his judges."

This poetic reconstruction of Robespierre's agony around a fantasy of life, mixing future glory, heroic vision, erotic sentiment, and epic narrative, seems to be, even today, the only Robespierrist discourse possible. In a certain sense, we can venture to say that if the aims of the Robespierrists are generally abandoned, there still survives this poetic force, this aesthetic intensity linked with the tale of agony.[47] The two most recent narratives, *Robespierre, derniers temps,* published by Jean-Philippe Domecq in 1984, adapted for the theater during the bicentennary of 1989, and then *Le Masque de Robespierre* by Gilles Aillaud, directed by Jean Jourdheuil in 1996, illustrate this poetic form.[48] Ailland's play is explicitly a "reverie on Robespierre," inventing situations, texts, and characters around the figure of the Incorruptible. Aillaud justifies his right to "poetic collage," associating Robespierre with David's work but also with Shakespeare, Sophocles, Bach, Wagner. The language is simple, timeless, or rather contemporary, eschewing any reconstitution of revolutionary rhetoric, but sometimes it recalls historical documents, such as certain speeches by Robespierre. Its language is also militant, with numerous allusions to the fractures of the French society at the end of the twentieth century—social, racial, and cultural fractures. At the end of the play, Robespierre sends a message to Toussaint-Louverture, like a flame transmitted by the white man to the black man, a link between two freed men, two leaders, but also an invitation to resist, to mistrust "Frenchmen of France as much as French colonists." Robespierre embodies the figure of a visionary prophet: he reveals man to himself by a kind of constant maieutic dialogue. He knows, though, that he remains misunderstood during his lifetime, and fated to death. But not to oblivion, since he carries in him, through his words given in the form of oracles, the future man, revealed, free, happy. There lies his tragedy: he returns to nothingness before seeing happiness with his own eyes. There also is his visionary greatness: he marked the path. During Robespierre's last night, Aillaud places in his mouth a final monologue in which poetry expresses this hope and this tragedy: "Perhaps Sophocles was right to write at the end of his life: 'It is best never to have been born; but once born, it is best to return as quickly as possible to nothingness.' I will add: Yes, but not before having, through one's splendor, given a glimpse of what man could be. But I feel in me a heavenly fatigue. Long and exhausting was my pilgrimage to the tomb. Today my gaze plunges, as into a new land, into the domain of night."

The last two pages of *Robespierre, derniers temps,* Domecq's book, form a poem written on the scaffold, of which this is the final stanza:

> They push him, against the plank, the straps beneath his chin
> soaked through, they wait to tip the plank forward,
> one of the executioners has slipped behind him and rips the bandage off with
> one stroke
> blood gushes forth
> he screams

The last cry, the scream, is not finished: the book, as well as the poem, ends without punctuation, without a final period. The vision of this agony is open, and the corpse—transformed into a poem—becomes a body screaming at us. It is the corpse of Robespierre that offers this phantasm of life to us, the "hideousness" of Thermidor turned into Robespierre, the poem.

Frontispiece from *Vues Philanthropiques sur l'abus des enterremens précipités* [Philanthropic Considerations on the Error of Premature Burials] by Marin Bunoust, 1826.

Madame Necker

OR, THE POETRY OF THE CORPSE

How does the swing from the scientific to the fantastic, from the language of reason to that of the imagination, come about? At the end of the eighteenth century in France a fundamental experiment is based precisely on that very change of course, the experiment of the corpse: contact with it, opening it up, its dissection by the medical establishments; its organization, its classification, its handling by the public health practices inherited from the century of the Enlightenment. Doctors, scholars, philosophers, artists, all have dealings with the corpse. By means of it they wish to understand, regulate, and purge human nature—not necessarily arrogantly to push back the limits of death, but, more humanly to grasp through reason its mechanisms, its organic functionings and malfunctionings. Yet in studying corpses too intimately, vision becomes clouded, imagination takes over, as if, in fine, only a semifictional shaping of the morbid were able to conjure up the terrible effects of the proximity of dead bodies, the dreaded putrefaction, that powerlessness before pain, those memories that escape. Madame Necker (Suzanne Curchod), newly arrived in Paris, "poor and beautiful," in the beginning of 1764 from Lausanne, wife of a businessman and future minister; in September 1764 mother of Germaine, the future Madame de Staël; in April 1766 hostess of one of the main philosophical salons of the time; in May 1794 dead in Beaulieu, between Geneva and Lausanne—Madame Necker alone embodies this double concern, paradoxical and ambiguous, reasonable and obsessive, addressed to the corpse by the end of the Age of Enlightenment.[1]

The hygiene that she imposes on her private life, her domestic rules, her charitable order—all these measures are on the side of reason. The testament that she leaves to her husband—as precise and ordered as her personal diaries, as minute and regulated as the charter of her hospice—is nonetheless inhabited by imagination, and depicts a morbid ceremony in which the vision of herself, of her dead self, cannot face the horrors, the pain, and the decomposition of the body except through an aesthetic handling of the corpse, and by following a poetic shaping of the narrative of remembering the body that no longer exists. It is by following the thread of this life, intimately wound around a tutelary passion for death, through reading private diaries, scientific treatises, philanthropic charters, family letters, testamentary dispositions, and moral precepts, that we can try to unravel this knot of contradictions, which turns scientific reason into a mind inhabited by madness. We read in Madame Necker's corpse the morbid impulse of a moment in history. Thanks to these disparate documents and these reconstituted narratives, each one set back in the context of being read in view of the others, it is as if history could again take on flesh by posing to this precise case, this particular intimacy, a question that haunted the morbid impulses of this moment poised between the Enlightenment and romanticism: how can one contrive to envisage a representation of oneself as a corpse? Madame Necker's entire life ends by being oriented toward a possible answer to this impossible question. The feeling of existing, minutely contained and revealed by strict rules of conduct, in the end passes into a representation of a nonexistent self, or rather one that no longer exists except as dead flesh, continuing to exist only by the beauty of the corpse. It is a matter of representation: the construction of an image of oneself as opposed to others, an endlessly revised, clarified, retouched construction, in the course of life. It is a construction, then, that must be by necessity offered to the exterior gaze, even one that is close, intimate: according to this spectacle, Madame Necker offers her corpse to be viewed by her family. But this exterior gaze stretches from family to society, since—and this is where the historian finds his subject—Madame Necker has not stopped taking into account "the public opinion of the corpse," the treatises, recommendations, and discussions that the century produced in quantity about the dead body, in order to fashion her representation as a future corpse. In a way, then, it is a question of rediscovering the threads of a representation of death that grows out of the strangeness of her morbid conduct contexted in the fabric of the diverse, but finally common, sources, which made this very strangeness possible.

THE RULES OF PRIVATE LIFE

Madame Necker's first field of experimentation was her own body, her *innermost being,* analyzed, listened to, scrutinized: "Let us fix our attention, then, on this secret labor that is made in us. How many things happen in this little universe," she writes in a chapter of her *Diary* entitled "On the Usefulness and Necessity of Examining Oneself Attentively."[2] All this literature of the self published as a collection at Madame Necker's death by her husband and relatives, organized into so many precepts, rules, conforming attitudes imposed on the "just development" of private life—all this prescriptive writing—is packed with formulas that reveal a mastery of the self pushed to an ideal at once enlightened and unsettling. The hygiene of the body and of thought is organized around these maxims—"Health has an immediate influence on the happiness and unhappiness of the soul"—and these certitudes—"For the mind to age less, one must form a series of well-defined ideas"—and takes up, once again, the praise of the science of the century, that of the body, the new medicine obstinately followed, courted, and tamed by Madame Necker, an amateur scholar indeed but erudite, hardworking, and introduced into the most famous medical milieus. "Medicine is the theology of the body," she asserts in one of her diaries, sure of being heard by her friends in promoting the observation and regimentation of the body as a new religion.

Daughter of a minister from Vaud, raised at the presbytery of Crassier, near Lausanne, Suzanne Curchod constructed a culture for herself with ever-punctilious attention. Orphaned when quite young, to survive she had to give lessons to the scions of the great Lausanne families, forging for herself through pedagogy and fear of being lowered in status a solid philosophical, literary, and practical knowledge. That is what characterizes her training as it manifests in her private diaries: no knowledge without practical usefulness, no learning without a field of experimentation. The pedagogical fiber is reinforced through this demand: her students, her relatives, her daughter, her invalids, and herself above all, always took the form of a venue of investigation, a substance to shape, a receptacle into which their learning could converge. Living in Geneva later, Suzanne Curchod, after having seduced and then rejected one of the most brilliant historians of the time, Edward Gibbon, gets close to the scholarly and medical circles sparked by the doctors Theodore Tronchin and Auguste Tissot, famous and widely recognized through all Europe. In this milieu she meets Madame Vermenoux, who decides, at the beginning of 1764, to bring this young, erudite girl to Paris as a lady's companion; she henceforth lives in a room in the Vermenoux town house, on Rue de la Grange-Batelière. There she conducts the salon of the mistress of the house. There, too, Suzanne Curchod shapes her destiny: she meets a regular visitor to the place, a young businessman from Geneva, Jacques Necker, whom she marries on September 30, 1764, at the age of twenty-seven (he is thirty-two). She learns there too about the social norms of the salon, made of "philosophers' dinners," readings, and enlightened conversation. From Necker she acquires a name, a situation, a fortune, and soon "a place in public opinion" when Necker enters into and then pursues a political career crowned by two posts as minister of finance for Louis XVI, the most popular man in the kingdom on the eve and at the beginning of the Revolution. From her second passion and occupation, that enlightened sociability, is born a salon, "her" salon, one of the most frequented and best reputed. In the Necker town house on Rue de Cléry, from 1770 onward one can meet Marmontel, Raynal, Duclos, Morellet, Suard, Thomas, as well as George Louis Leclere, Comte de Buffon and Tronchin, the two scientific minds won over by the friendship of Madame Necker. She will not write for the public, but leaves a significant correspondence and a no less abundant body of writing for private use. Sacrificing her literary pen, she decides to animate her salon and becomes passionate about natural and medical science. From this life of receptions, discussions, and readings, the mistress of the house intends to pursue her cultural enrichment. She will leave a number of summaries of books, maxims, *pensées,* commentaries about positions defended by the philosophers frequenting her table, letters at once mundane and literary, filled with commonplaces of the time and agitated by a feverish imagination, a literature that is in part published after her death in the form of several collections of *Mélanges* [Miscellanies].[3] There, the inquirer discovers her three main fields of experimentation: herself as a sick, suffering body, and as a rational mind troubled by passions; herself, again, through a daughter who must be perfectly brought up; herself, finally, as a great organism to be taken care of, embodied by the hospice for invalids that she takes charge of, orders, and regulates, beginning in the 1780s. These three interests—her body, her daughter, her hospital—scientific and egocentric, organize the entire life of Madame Necker, woman of the Age of Enlightenment, philanthropist, educator, before she became the architect of her own death.

Madame Necker always saw herself as ill. And, from all the testimony, all the letters and confidences, she was always known as an invalid. Beautiful, upright, even rigid—but ill. Writings of the time speak of an "inexorable nervous ailment," of fragility and anguish that ate away at her body to the point of paralyzing it, through sudden and terrible crises, before finally immobilizing her when she had barely turned fifty, then finishing her off in 1794 at the age of only fifty-four. From 1766, the time of her first crisis immediately following the birth of her daughter, Madame Necker herself speaks of a "languor that was like annihilation," a state of chronic physical depletion that, through its various manifestations, seems always to reveal itself by an identical symptom: as if the imagination were poured entire, alive, into a body that had become sick from having too much spirit. It is this constant state of sickness that leads Madame Necker to surround herself with doctors who, in turn, excite the imagination of the invalid. Similarly, since the imagination leads the passions that themselves govern the illnesses of the body, one has to know oneself, regulate oneself, describe oneself; it is a matter of giving precepts and maxims for one's own comportment. But this constant introspection is also a summons to imagination, and thus a vector of illness, a clinical symptom. It is a case of redoubling, where the cause and the remedies produce the same effects: starting the illness all over again through thinking of the illness, perpetuating the illnesses of the body by the very knowledge of the organism. It is not so much this assessment of a state of illness both feared and desired that should interest us here, as its effects on narrative, on autobiography: Madame Necker never stopped writing about herself, trying to understand and bring order to the troubles of her body and her mind. Literary and scientific applications of "Know Thyself" are not supposed to surprise the historians of the sensibility of the Age of Enlightenment, or those of Protestantism, but in this case they take an admirably obsessive turn: to leave nothing in her conduct to chance or to inspiration, and to submit her most insignificant actions, as well as her most serious decisions, to the control of the will. From year to year, the collections of personal precepts and of domestic resolutions follow each other, under various titles, but always explicit and minutely handwritten. *Maximes nécessaires à mon bonheur* [Maxims necessary to my happiness] outline rules of conduct invariably inspired by the same litany, "Always keep the mind fixed on. . . ," and which are solemnly written in a period from 1764, the date of her marriage, to 1766, the birth of Germaine. *Journal de mes défauts et de mes fautes, avec les meilleurs moyens de n'y pas retomber* [Journal of my failings and faults, with the best means not to relapse into them] records, humbly, precisely, on the model of the Christian book of contrition, the fits of passion and the daily deficiencies in the uses of "the right way to live [*savoir-vivre*]." *Journal de la dépense de mon temps* [Journal of how I spend my time] is a sort of agenda illuminated by a just and useful division of the hours of the day between the cares of the body and the labor of the mind, a private diary in which, every day, from waking up to going to sleep, each instant must absolutely find a use.

At the start of this collection, the mistress of the house placed a resolution that, under divine auspices, tells of the ambition of a completely regulated domestic life: "God gave me twenty-four hours to spend each day; here is the journal that must regulate its use, for I have only one single aim: that of pleasing all beings as perfectly as possible and of filling the task that He has given me. God will be the motive and the end of all my actions, the dominant thought toward which I will direct them all; but He does not demand over-long contemplations from me. I am a faithful servant endlessly busy in the interests of my Master, but who does not dare to converse with Him for long, feeling keenly that He is raised too high above me by His perfections not to be importuned by my verbiage. Thus I will employ ten minutes every evening to implore His protection, and twenty minutes every morning to represent to Him the use of my time of the previous day, and to renew my resolutions for the next one, in order that the idea of Him be present to me all throughout the day."[4]

Pushing this demarcation of useful hours even further, Madame Necker invents a system of life for herself in which "seven relationships" rule all her activity: with her husband, her child, her friends, her poor, her housework, her society, and her toilette. Determining the number of hours suitable to accord each day to each of her "relationships," she keeps, between 1777 and 1783, a book-journal divided into seven columns where she composes, like a scrupulous accountant, a representation of herself as an ordered and all-powerful woman. For it is indeed a matter of representation of self: to counter the illness that keeps attacking the body with sudden severe crises of paralysis and languor, to counter the anguishes that wrack her mind, to respond to these fits and these emotions by the rationality of number, of columns, of a balance that weighs faults and good actions, the arithmetic of virtue that puts into an equation the sagacity of conduct confronting the shameful disorder of impulses.

In her only daughter, Madame Necker finds another ideal to construct, another perfect representation of herself to build, with the same minute details and an identical moral arithmetic. Her daughter Germaine is thus raised with a luxury of precautions and an entirely scientific rigor. Her education is the opposite of Rousseau's *Émile* in many respects, since a similar pedagogical preoccupation ends up with opposite precepts: not to place the child in a natural space where the virgin mind will fill itself of its own accord but to transform it into a *living library,* a sort of Faustian challenge, that of creating a perfect little philosophical being. Germaine Necker is educated—with all that entails in terms of the sequence of role playing, forced detachment, privations—according to a model image derived from an ideal of corporeal and reasoned conduct dreamed up by her mother: a being with ordered deportment, studied toilette, supervised hygiene, but also a reading and writing being, soon to be the attraction of the maternal salon through her precocious conversations with expressly invited philosophers.

A WORK OF PUBLIC HYGIENE

Once Germaine has grown to be a young lady and her education finished, Madame Necker, in 1778, finds another passion, another field of experimentation in which to strengthen the public image of her husband by applying her precepts and her virtuous discipline. In the fall of 1777 she makes contact with the religious authorities of Paris, who control all the agencies and works of public health. She proposes founding a hospice that will welcome the indigent and sick of a *quartier.* The king provides funds as well as the Neckers, and the Church offers a place, the Benedictine convent of Notre-Dame de Liesse, which had just been closed down, in the parish of Saint-Sulpice, a building called the Necker Hospital from the beginning of the nineteenth century on. In 1778 Madame Necker conceives of the most precise and most enlightened ideas there, as she confides in a letter addressed to a friend from Nyon: "Our Hôtel-Dieu de Paris [the municipal hospital—TRANS.] is the theater of unhappiness and pain, the sick are as many as eight in the same bed. M. Necker occupies himself with reforming this disorder, but, to eliminate it, we must prove that the poor can be cared for in one single bed, with less expense than at the Hôtel-Dieu. This proof can be drawn only by example. I have taken charge of this, and the success depends henceforth on economy and caution."[5] Thus Madame Necker not only creates a hospice but pursues the issue of hospital reform that marks her time, as proved by the foundation of similar hospices in Paris in the years that follow—the Cochin hospital in 1780, the Santé in 1781, the Beaujon hospital in 1785. One rule of hygiene embodies this reform: one patient, one bed. Following the precepts of the two doctors who left their mark on her education and her Swiss sojourns, Tissot and Tronchin, the lady founder more generally arranges her hospice in accord with "the laws of humanity and decency": separation of the sexes, opening the rooms to outside air, sun, and light, heating in the winter, regular changing of bandages of the sick. . . . For ten years Madame Necker devotes herself to this ordering of bodies that, even more than a new science of medicine or revolutionary remedies, presides over hospital reform.[6]

She records all this, as always, in carefully kept registers, drawing up in 1780 a charter for her hospice, *Institutions, règles et usages de cette maison* [Institutions, rules and customs of this house], which, under the form of the first annual report, offers a precise description of the rooms, of the invalids accepted, and emphasizes the restoring of balance of admissions and dismissals in favor of the living. The hospice is comprised of eight vast rooms, with 128 beds, or 68 for men and 60 for women. Each room is well ventilated, each patient washed regularly, and the chart describes the daily schedules of the sick as well as the typical day of one of the twelve sisters of Charity who work at the hospital, a chronology that recalls the domestic precepts of Madame Necker for herself, since everything is regulated and timed, from rising at four in the morning to going to bed at nine at night. The principal innovation, to which the mistress of the site is particularly attached, consists of this "regular keeping of the book of invalids" that links to each patient admitted a personal record that will follow him for his entire stay. This is a great innovation of hospital procedure, pioneering for the time. It inscribes itself as a long-term evolution of the representation of illness and of the architecture that, at the same time, receives it, treats it, and banishes it through order and hygiene, a reasoned and medical confinement that is based on a transformation of the vision of the body, of the space that welcomes it, of the economy that takes charge of it. "We have undertaken, by order of His Majesty, to attempt the establishment of a small hospital of 128 patients," writes Madame Necker in 1780, "each with his own bed, cared for with the greatest cleanliness and with all the attention necessary to their recuperation; placed in well-ventilated rooms, odorless, noiseless; served by Sisters of Charity and by a doctor and a surgeon housed in the building and devoted to this single occupation; fed with the most salutary nourishment, and treated with the best-chosen drugs. We have filled all these conditions in a satisfactory way, and after a trial of more than a year, we are convinced that each patient costs a little less than seventeen sous a day."[7]

How can we fail to see here, even in the care for the domestic economy of the 128 beds of her hospice (but without any preoccupation with philosophical instruction, since it is here not a question of instructing minds but bodies) a collective application of the rules that Madame Necker had till then prescribed for the good health of her home? The organism formed by the 128 sick bodies of the charity hospice is a macrocosm corresponding, point by point, with the more intimate microcosm of the body of Madame Necker herself, and to be governed by identical "maxims necessary to my happiness," the same laws as those in the *Journal of My Failings and Faults, with the Best Means Not to Relapse into Them*. Madame Necker's philanthropy, her concepts of hygiene and health forged from contact with the enlightened doctors of Lausanne, Geneva, or Paris, fashion a representation of the sick body in which there is a complete similarity between private life and the collective organism, between the constructed image of her own body and the organic metaphor of a salubrious, well-ventilated, clean, ordered, regenerated whole.

When this ambition to regulate the use of every person's time turns away from life, it is projected onto a representation of death. The corpse is a state of the body, a state onto which Madame Necker maps a representation of time and space: it possesses its own rhythm "of life," as we shall see, and necessitates the construction of a particular space (in a project that the founder of the charitable hospice calls the "Waiting Chamber"), a room "that would serve as a place of deposit for those who would not want to keep their dead for more than twelve hours." This waiting chamber, a space for the dead and for the relatives who watch over them and take care of them, is conceived on a model reproducing, in the hospital, the adjacent space of life: an "accommodation divided between women on one side and men on the other," enclosed, well ventilated, and heated in the winter, "provided with individual beds and a guard." This idea, a funeral parlor before the name was used, open to the gathering of families as well as to the scientific discourse on death, and more precisely on the uncertainties of the signs of death, is not peculiar to the ordered mind of Madame Necker. Some months before, Dr. Thiery, from the Medical Faculty of Paris, had suggested in *La Vie de l'homme respectée et défendue* [Human life respected and protected] the construction of "special houses" maintained by civic functionaries, "houses of the state of death" where a "medical commissioner" would come officially to pronounce death, a place where each corpse would be visible, uncovered, lying in state, "palpable" by the public of friends and family. This first proposal is followed by many others, including what Madame Necker puts into service in her hospice. Note especially the "house of exhibition" of the Count Leopold de Berchtold, in 1790, where three spacious rooms are meant to receive newly deceased men and women, preserved for a few days until they have "actually turned into the condition of a corpse," while an "ingenious system of ventilation" dissipates the cadaverous smell.[8] We will also recall the "Necrodocium (*Nécrodoque*)" of Jean-Baptiste Davis, a "public building where bodies may be deposited until the obvious signs of putrefaction began to declare themselves," while, to preserve the humanity and hygiene of the room, "a mixture for the temporary preservation of the corpses would be spread on the bodies in order to avoid smell and pestilence."[9]

THE CRUSADES AGAINST APPARENT DEATH

These imagined rooms where death is accepted and tamed as well as controlled are representations of the scientific impulse of the time to banish a fear that doctors then placed regularly at the center of their debates, a terror that wound up assuming a conventional name: premature burial. We can indeed find an actual debate of opinion: more than twenty-five tractates, monographs, and pamphlets written by doctors, surgeons, scholars, and interested parties appear on the subject between 1740 and 1820, so much so that it becomes one of the divisions of scientific taxonomy proposed by the *Catalogue des sciences médicales* [Catalog of medical sciences] compiled in the middle of the nineteenth century.[10] Madame Necker takes a stand at the heart of this debate, since all her precepts, all her maxims, all her measures and precautions, aim for the most part at organizing the passage from the state of a living being to that of a corpse. The discussion is launched in fact by Jacques Bénigne Winslow, of Scottish origin, regent of the Faculty of Medicine of Paris and member of the Royal Academy of Sciences. In 1740 he defends a thesis called *Les Expériences de chirurgie les plus à même que toutes les autres à découvrir les marques d'une mort douteuse* [Experiments of surgery more appropriate than any others to discover the marks of a dubious death]. This thesis, in Latin, is translated and popularized in 1742 by Jacques-Jean Bruhier, zealous proselytizer for the cause of preventing premature burial. It is from this work of scientific popularization that the debate on "apparent death" will take shape, with a persistency not to be extinguished until the first third of the nineteenth century. Here then is the issue of the controversy, summarized in a phrase by Bruhier: "Death is certain, and it is not. It is certain since it is inevitable, it is not since it is sometimes uncertain that someone is dead." The force of the argument lies on the multiplication of examples of apparent death, and of premature burials, cited by Winslow and Bruhier, and then by their successors in this fight "for the public good." "Everyone knows that many people, thought to be dead, have come out of their shroud, their coffin, and even their tomb," writes Bruhier before enumerating 181 specific cases taken from the history of medicine, drawn from narratives, memories, and various correspondents, or from living testimony. Most often used is the example of Vesalius, the great pioneer anatomist, dissecting the chest of a corpse, perceiving that the heart is still beating, and putting this so-called corpse to death, only to be prosecuted as a murderer by the family of the victim before the tribunal of the Inquisition, then condemned to death but pardoned by the king of Spain, who commutes the punishment to a voyage to the Holy Land. This vision of terror is a nightmare that would haunt the history of medicine, a history hereafter composed of a multitude of cases of memorably "resuscitated" people, drowned men coming to in the middle of their own funeral, sudden fainting cases coming back to life a few seconds before being set in their coffins. This multiplicity of examples functions as a summons to the morbid imagination of the eighteenth century. Medical tracts proliferate: unbearable representations of being buried alive, of a living human "cadaverized" by mistake, finishing his life in the horrifying suffering, physical and psychological, of a prison of night and terror, his own coffin.

There is in all this a way of appealing to human sensibility mingled with a play on the evocative powers of the morbid imagination that is not without effect, as Bruhier summons it in the vigorous plea that opens his treatise: "It is a fact that some people buried too hurriedly found in the tomb the death of which they should not have been victims, and whose horrors greatly surpass those of the rope and the wheel. Fairy tales, you will tell me, pure fairy tales these stories are. You treat as a fable, then, the story of Scotus who gnawed his arms in the tomb? You do not believe that the same thing happened to the

Emperor Zeno after the repeated moans heard by those who were guarding him? All right, so be it, I agree. But what will you say to the testimonies of people who are above suspicion, who are of known probity, who will tell you only of what they have *seen,* and of whom there are some, still alive, who are able to tell what happened *before their eyes*?" The style of accreditation here called upon, through so many examples playing on the "effects of reality," thus of horror, of the narrative, through this confrontation between the appeal to the reader's imagination and the appeal to the truth of the witness, is close to the narrative system of fantastic literature, of the traditional tall tale (*conte*).[11]

The other thread of this representation, however, knotted inextricably with the narrative of numerous examples and the terrifying imagery of the fantastic, is scholarly discourse, the reasoned catalog of clinical hypotheses about apparent death. In this sense—and this is the new force in this discourse of persuasion—the treatise on premature burials makes the "living corpse" of myth, of fairy tale, even of religious narrative, pass into the scientific universe. The resurgence of the ancient terror of being buried alive, at the time of the Age of Enlightenment, clarifies this passage of the corpse from the terrifying representation of the fantastic tale to a fear that is certainly even more intense, since it is anchored henceforth in the discourse of reason and science. For, as Dr. H. Le Guern writes at the time, "It is definite that premature burials, sad to think of for anyone who reflects on them, could alone give birth to the vulgar superstition that believes in phantoms and lends faith to instantaneous resurrection. Formerly, people gave ear to these voices of the dead, astonished, terrified by these plaintive cries that came unexpectedly from the depths of caves. But today, it is science itself that tells us to lend our attention to these moans, not to see phantoms in them, but people presumed dead needing to be saved from a terrifying death."[12] Previously, as Philippe Ariès wrote, "death overlapped life," and the living dead, at certain times, according to certain circumstances, were able to leave their cemetery, their tomb, or their cave.[13] Now life sits astride death, the former sometimes extending itself into the appearance of the latter. If the limits between life and death, between living bodies and corpses, are porous in both cases, the confusion of previous times was expressed by priests, poets, or madmen; the confusion of the Age of Enlightenment can be untangled by scientists, and only by them, in the form of a series of precise symptoms adduced by doctors warning of premature interment. Apparent death hides itself here beneath clinical cases—mainly victims of suffocation, drowning, putrid exhalation, sudden faints, apoplexy, epilepsy, catalepsy, lethargy, fainting fits, or even "children pronounced dead when coming into the world," so many "fatal" reports in which the doctor recommends the relatives and family stay on guard.

To reassure public opinion, which is not a little alarmed by this debate, and to impose certainties on the uncertainties evoked by Bruhier, some doctors soon respond to the first treatises on premature burials, in fact relaunching the controversy. Antoine Louis, of the Académie royale de chirurgie [Royal Academy of Surgery], is one of them, and the most important one if one considers the fame that he enjoys. His *Lettre sur la certitude des signes de la mort. Où l'on rassure les citoyens de la crainte d'être enterrés vivants* [Letter on the certainty of the signs of death. In which we reassure citizens on the fear of being buried alive] answers point by point the arguments of his colleagues. "The truth of the facts that M. Bruhier reports can be contested," he writes directly, calling into question his method itself, since "the multiplication of examples proves nothing," and rejecting the appeal to the imagination made by the doctor: "The stories that you have read about apparent death have made the most lively impression on your minds," he ironically concedes to his adversary. "You continually suppose that one day you yourself could be the victim of such a cruel mistake. These ideas overwhelm you and put your mind in the most afflicted state. Then this fear is seized upon by the imagination, itself relayed by your science. And these affections find curious remedies." Dr. Louis reads afresh and with lucidity the technicalities of a representation of oneself as apparently dead; then stresses this passage from one universe to the other, from one discourse to the other, from fear to science, by the intermediation of the effects of imagination. To conclude, he wants to reassure by affirming to his readers that the "state of death has definite signs," and by enumerating them in order, he writes, "to prevent people from keeping their dead for too long at home and thus prevent an otherwise more definite danger: the effects of the putrefaction of the corpse on the atmosphere breathed in by a family stricken with mourning." Despite this vigorous and prestigious intervention, we must recognize that the "curious remedies" and the "affections of the imagination" continue to be developed by scholars and pseudoscholars at war with premature burial.

Motivated by her hospital experience, as well as by her taxonomic mind (that desire for order that keeps her from storing the knives with the forks, offers her a life classified into seven different domains, and prevents her from confusing a living body with a corpse), Madame Necker, whom we have not abandoned, makes an entrance onto the scene of this public debate. In 1790 she publishes a twenty-two-page pamphlet titled *Des inhumations précipitées* [On premature burials] in which she justifies herself by these words in the short foreword: "These reflections are fruit of long and attentive observations, made in a hospital for sick people, by a person who governed it for ten years, and who, despite all her efforts, could never obtain from the nuns, who were most compassionate toward the living, adequate care and respect for the dead. Let us hope that this work, in which feelings of humanity take precedence over the repugnance of the imagination, will seize the public's attention." Here Madame Necker offers like so many others her "considerations on the state of dying" in which she distinguishes different states, various *stages* rather, that punctuate the impinging of life on death. It is a representation of death that is outlined here, representation of a passage from life to death taking on a singular density, as if all science had to devote itself to it, taking back into account by rationalizing it the traditional role of religion, seeking to tame the passage by means of prescriptions, rites, penance, and the viaticum after Extreme Unction. Where the priest had officiated, henceforth the scholar must insinuate himself. For "when all the signs of life have disappeared, experience proves that *inner death* has not yet ended," writes Madame Necker. "The cessation of movement," she continues, "total impassivity, are only the signs of an *outer death*. And one is guilty of homicide if one buries the body before being assured that inner and complete death is absolutely consummated. Death begun is called *agony*. Apparent death, the second state, is a state of *hidden and insensitive life*. Death completely achieved is the state of *corpse*. But there is an interval between the death that one deems certain and the state of corpse. Death in the final hours is thus life reduced to the least possible degree, and if one could strike the senses by the spectacle of the ghastly effects of carelessness in these precious instants, one would shudder with horror." Madame Necker's entire aim is to draw attention to this "interval" that confers a strange density, temporal and clinical, almost an actual life, "hidden and insensitive," on death.

The main part of Madame Necker's pamphlet is devoted to describing these "curious remedies" aimed at avoiding premature burial. All these texts offer a kind of rereading of the funeral rites of history in the light of this image of the living-dead body. This historical rereading aims explicitly to condemn the Catholic treatment of the corpse for three principal failings: first, simple burning of incense in the deceased's room had replaced purging the body with boiling water, which might have been able to bring an apparently dead person back to life; second, the abandoning of loud lamentations, which also could awaken the dead; and third, the too-brief time preceding interment, since the Catholic Church allows rapid burial, even in the hours just after death, if the family so wishes. In contrast to this negligence, which, writes Dr. Pineau, "leads the priest to be interested in nothing but the soul of the dying person,"[14] treatises on apparent death cite examples of the Egyptian funeral rites that promote embalming— "that surgical proof which made evident the true condition of the body by beginning with the stomach, using incisions that are not lethal, thus permitting those apparently dead to be drawn out of their lethargy"[15]—as well as the Jewish tradition in which the corpse, washed and perfumed, is exposed for a few days in the entry of the house, submitted to the ordeal of "great lamentations" in which "the name of the dead person is called out, mixed with strident and lugubrious cries," then, finally, placed in "spacious caverns where it is impossible to suffocate in atrocious agonies."[16]

The example that is most often studied and praised, however, remains the Roman funerals: exemplary, for they are delayed—after washing the body with boiling water "so that heat might awaken the spirits if there were still any hidden in the body"; perfumed—the corpse, dressed, "all smells rubbed away," is kept for seven days on a bier. Above all, the funerals are loud, punctuated by the *conclamatio* in which the name of the dead person is solemnly called many times, then by the sounds of trumpets and horns, "so many musical instruments placed facing the corpse whose chest and head have been uncovered so that the sound of the instruments might make the greatest impression, thus more easily agitate the fibers to which the soul might still be attached, and enter wholly through the ears into all the sinuosities of the body."[17]

The medical prescriptions proposed by these treatises on apparent death try to actualize and systematize these historical considerations. They distrust, first of all, the uncertain signs of death that overhurried doctors, mourning relatives, or priests oriented only toward spiritual salvation rely on as proofs of the final transition to the cadaverous state. One of these treatises thus lists thirteen "uncertain signs" of death: suspension of breathing, stiffness of the limbs, cessation of movement, lack of heartbeats, spontaneous excretion of fecal matter, opacity of the eyes.... On the other hand, all the doctors strive to offer verification procedures for death that constitute, by themselves, a new representation reinforcing this density of life kept by the body in a state of death. These procedures consist of a series of proofs—the "proof of death"—that the corpse must undergo; rites of passage that these treatises on apparent death propose to establish as a legal requirement. We can group these proofs into four types: irritation, summons, scarification, and putrefaction.

Science, as we have seen, adopts as its own what historians (who are also for the most part doctors) thought they shed light on. The enemas, exterior and interior, of the Egyptians, Jews, or Romans, correspond to what, for example, Jacques-Jean Bruhier proposes in his treatise: to irritate the dead person's nostrils by inserting sneeze-inducing drops, brandy, or mustard; to rub the gums vigorously with the same things; to whip the organs of touch with stinging nettles; to irritate the intestines with enemas; to whip the body with a piece of cloth soaked in boiling water. In like manner, the Roman *conclamatio,* the lamentations of the Jews, propose for the doctors of the Enlightenment another model, modernized by the call at immediate proximity to the dead body: "It is essential to weary the ear with sounds, cries, noises, for the senses of hearing are the last to be extinguished."[18] As for scarification, it seems the true proof of death, and most of the doctors who denounce premature burials agree on this point: it is essential to "prick" the palms of the hands or the soles of the feet, to "scarify" the shoulder blades, the shoulders, the forearms, to "apply boiling wax" to the skin of the stomach "for the little fibrils of the extremities of the nerves, which constitute principally the organ of touch, pricked, separated, torn apart, burnt, by a violent impetus of needle, scalpel, flame, and stripped bare of the epidermis that covers them, transmit to the common seat of all sensations, by ways unknown until our time, and with extreme quickness, the feeling of the most penetrating pains."[19]

Combining contemporary exploration of the system of nervous irrigation that gives a sort of scientific foundation to the sensualist philosophy of the century with the researches on vitalism, equally contemporary, that recognize in man immense and sometimes hidden resources of life, it seems that these treatises on apparent death try to forge a new attitude about the corpse. Much more skeptical and willful, proceeding even with a certain violence, refusing death with more vehemence, demanding so many actions and proofs, they thus compose a ceremony for the dead body very different from the Christian rite of peaceful and submissive acceptance. In fact, the gratification offered by these funeral ceremonies is different. Acceptance is the condition of the blessed journey of the soul toward the beyond; proof by violence is a willful appeal to save some earthly lives. This violence, and sometimes the lack of understanding that greets it, are lucidly expressed by doctors, as well as the new proposed gratification: "What is your aim, they will ask me? What is the use of so much temerity, so much violence, so many attempts? What rage for cutting, piercing, burning, possesses you? This fortunate temerity was nonetheless one day recompensed when, after a long needle entered deeply beneath the nail of one of the fingers of an apoplectic woman who no longer showed any sign of life, the shock caused her instantly to come to herself in a start."[20]

Projects "to regulate corpses" are thus developed with such proofs as a basis, in which "current practices" are condemned (leaving the corpse in the cold on a pallet, sitting the body up for the wake, obstructing the natural outlets), and in which irritation, shouting, and scarification are advocated as the only means definitively to assure death, even if it means introducing some surprising innovations like those of the master in surgery Janin who, in 1772, passionately interested in recent researches, raises electricity to the role of "witness to actual death."[21] Electricity is in fact "the fluid that revives every animate being." "There is reason to presume," adds Janin, "that electrical fluid is the agent, or rather, the material soul of the Universe, and that it alone can distinguish bodies still living under the appearance of lethargy from actual corpses." This proof by electricity applied to the corpse, a discourse that analogically approaches the science of a belief, the medical discoveries of a pantheist system, is an example of the manner of accreditation of this pseudoscientific narrative in which reason seems incessantly reanimated by the imagination. And doctors, as well as poets—think of Mary Shelley's *Frankenstein*—are sensitive to this way of thinking that mingles material with spiritual lights.

But the decisive proof is time. Once again, and in a radical way, these treatises demand a modification of the sensibility about corpses and about the conception of the time of death. This demand is in part satisfied by the law of 19 Ventôse, Year XI, at the very beginning of the nineteenth century, that will make it obligatory to maintain a twenty-four-hour period of time before burial, and will charge a "doctor in medicine or surgery" with certifying all deaths. The treatises of the Enlightenment call for more: the more reasonable projects mention three days of delay, during which the body should be stretched out on a bed in the middle of a heated room, and the most obsessive of which go so far as to reconstruct the space and time of the cemetery around this fear of premature burial. The *Mémoire sur le danger d'être enterré vif, et sur les moyens de s'en garantir ou de s'en tirer* [Reflections on the danger of being buried alive, and on the means of protecting oneself or escaping from it] thus regulates the construction and placement of coffins: not nailed shut but closed by "a system of hinges opening from both sides," not cold but where the dead person is dressed in warm clothes, lying on wool pillows, not empty but "fed" since the family "places in the left hand of the dead person a piece of bread and a flask of good wine while still observing that the cork extends above the neck of the bottle far enough so that it can be easily uncorked," not buried deeply but "covered only with two or three inches of earth," not deprived of air but pierced with a "respirator," not silent but linked to life by sound. . . . In fact, this coffin, from a prison and a box turned into a door, then a hearth, signals the life that it might possibly conceal by means of an installation at once ingenious and logical (if we push this terror of being buried alive to its conclusion): "To the right fist of the body will be attached a bell cord that passes through its hand, and that leaves the coffin through a little hole. The bell, which will be responsive to this cord, is attached to a post embedded in the ground to the right of the coffin. If there are people who, to assure themselves of a more prompt aid, wish that instead of a hand-bell, one use stronger bells, one could procure them for them. So that the hand that will carry out this movement can more reliably obtain its effect, this hand should be raised up on a kind of pillow or small cushion narrow enough so that the smallest movement will cause the hand to fall into an empty space that will have been provided next to it; by this fall, the clapper in the middle of the bell will strike its side, and making it resound, this first noise should both give others warning, and also hearten the one buried alive to redouble his efforts and sound the sepulchral tocsin that will bring him help." Between the "sepulchral tocsin" and the "meal of corpses," this project does more than reform the cemetery as well as numerous plans of public hygiene the Enlightenment had suggested before it; it goes so far as to transform it into a space for life, semi-fantastic, by offering the dead the time and means to return to the living.

It is not so much by means of a delay, however long, that in most of these projects the false dead were separated from the actual dead, but a decisive wait for the first signs of putrefaction, the first miasma of "corpse smell." At this stage, the required reform of emotions roused by the corpse reaches its climax, and the abrupt transition not only divides scholars from people of religious persuasion but traverses the scientific community itself. How can an entire generation of enlightened doctors—formed by the hygienist principles that distanced cemeteries from urban centers, out of fear of contaminations from "pestilential effluvia"—how can they accept the preservation of bodies in the heart of a society of the living, as Berchtold recommends in his 1791 *Projet pour prévenir les dangers très fréquents des inhumations précipitées* [Project to prevent the very frequent dangers of premature burials], until the bodies are "stained all over with yellow, greenish, brown, blackish marks, mixed with blue, and at the same time accompanied by a strong corpse-like smell"? It is this final, radical precaution, violent to the point of imposing on man the image of his own decomposition, that decisively marks the members of this scientific movement of the second half of the eighteenth century. Militant against the dangers of apparent death, their precaution is inscribed in specific projects (the "waiting chambers" equipped and watched over to permit the putrefaction they allow people to await), and in the deathbed instructions of some militants, a precaution that, in practice, must generally, since it clashes with an almost universal reluctance, find another way, another representation of the self as corpse.

In her 1790 treatise Madame Necker deals point by point with the historical considerations and medical precautions previously mentioned: praise of Roman funeral rites, dissertations on the "corpse state," reforms of funerals and wakes, of burial, and of the placement of cemeteries. One finds in her writings every element of scientific revolt against premature burials, till the preservation of the corpse is pushed to the limits of the bearable. Finally, to conclude her treatise, Madame Necker aligns herself with the ultimate recommendations of the militants of the cause: the attitude toward the corpse can only be reformed if enlightened men, defying the superstitions and hasty rituals that the Catholic religion often imposes, explicitly insert these multiple and violent demands as the clauses in their wills. Madame Necker gives some examples of such "truly enlightened people," like Madame de Corbeville, who "will regulate by her will the time when she should be buried and the tests her body should undergo before enclosing it in a coffin," and judges this attitude "the wisest that has been thought of to date."[22]

TAMING THE HORROR OF THE CORPSE

If Madame Necker, so careful a guardian of the accounts of her virtues and failings, judges this conduct "the wisest," it is because she herself has put it into practice. In fact, if Madame Necker always saw herself as ill, she also often saw herself as dead, and in the course of her life drew up several completely explicit wills or testamentary drafts. In this sense, her first crisis of morbid anguish follows immediately upon the delivery of her child. She writes to a correspondent in 1766, when she is twenty-nine: "Death was at my bedside. They had so carefully hidden from me the revolting details of childbirth that I was as surprised as I was appalled. And I cannot prevent myself from thinking that they make most women take a reckless vow at the time of marriage: I doubt that they would go quite so willingly to the altar to swear to have themselves beaten up every nine months whatever happens."[23] This traumatic experience the body suffers, which is also a discovery for this Enlightenment woman who till then had had purely theoretical knowledge, is henceforth to be warded off: not only does Madame Necker refuse from then on any new pregnancy, but she has learned that death can come by surprise and that it must be prevented. The successive wills that she draws up are to serve this purpose. The first ones, mentioned in some letters, seem to be lost. But from 1777 on, a good number of testamentary texts remain to us, of which one bears as an epigraph this insistent supplication addressed to her husband: "Do not neglect these details, I beg you. Do exactly what I have said. Perhaps my soul will wander around you. Perhaps I may be able deliciously to enjoy your exactness in fulfilling the desires of the one who loves you so."[24] New crises of paralysis, anguish confronting death, occur repeatedly between 1783 and 1785. Each time, Madame Necker isolates herself, taking the waters and the air at Saint-Ouen, where her husband has for some time had a country property, at Marolles near Fontainebleau, at Spa, at Mont-Dore, at Montpellier, then at Coppet, in the château acquired by Necker near Geneva in 1783, where the couple spends part of the summer. In these secluded places, Madame Necker works on, revises, and corrects the most morbid clauses of her will.

The last wills are written at Rolle in the course of the summer of 1792, when, staying by the lake in the Château de Beaulieu, she feels that the gravity of paralytic crises leaves her with almost no respite. She uses the energy that remains to her to arrange the smallest details of her death, to specify the proofs her corpse must undergo, and to detail the plans for the construction of her tomb. Madame Necker dies on May 15, at the age of fifty-four, at the Château de Beaulieu. Five days later her daughter, Germaine de Staël, writes an alarmed letter to her lover, Comte Adolphe de Ribbing: "This wretched tomb for which [my mother] drew up plans will not be finished before August; and until then my father wants to keep the coffin. There are unheard-of details to tell you on the precautions my mother has taken so that one can be certain of her death, then to have her embalmed, preserved, exhibited, in short for this unfortunate man [Necker] to take care of her body as he had taken care of her."[25]

"Unheard-of details"? Rather, with a constant and obsessive logic of behavior and sensibility about the corpse, a continuation of her previous wills, which themselves intimately translated the attitudes of doctors militant for the recognition of the state of "apparent death." Madame Necker in fact demands that she be "left in [her] bed, head slightly elevated, without disturbing the body by any tying-up of the neck or elsewhere; the face uncovered and without any natural opening being closed."[26] Twelve hours after her death, her body can be carried into another bed, prepared "as is the custom," that is to say after having well ventilated the room and following the recommendations of a "certain warming of the covers." During this transfer to a prepared bed, they must "handle the body with the care one would use with a sick person, and keep it adequately covered, face bare, like that of people who are sleeping." Two doctors are invited to the ritual of verification, a "practicing surgeon" and the doctor who took care of the invalid in her last moments, Tissot. The former, under the watchful eye of the latter, follows the "detailed indications of all the means that must be used to guarantee that death is absolute," so many methods that Madame Necker herself inscribed them in her will: shouting at the top of the voice right next to the dead woman's face, rubbings "using a mixture of vinegar and boiling water," insufflation of the nostrils with a "spoonful of smelling salts mixed with ammonia spread on a feather," three scarifications on the shoulder blades, one burning on the stomach "using a hot iron," and, finally, the "leisure allotted to time to do its work." This final tactic takes the form of a delay necessary for the construction of the specified tomb, in the garden of the Coppet château acquired by the Neckers.

So it is not till September 8, 1794, that, after being embalmed—"One will not begin the dissection with the noble and vital parts"—Madame Necker can be placed in this sepulchral place, attended by her relatives and a portion of Lausanne and Geneva society. Between May 15 and September 8, Jacques Necker kept the iron coffin in which his wife lay in his bedroom at the Château de Beaulieu, watching over it continuously. He modified only one of his wife's final recommendations while still keeping the coffin near him: the cover is no longer of glass, transparent, but opaque. He "did not want to agree" to the glass cover "because the illness disfigured his wife and took away her beauty," reports *Le Sans-Culotte,* a Parisian paper, on August 2, 1794.

The next stage in this long process of Madame Necker's death begins with the embalming of her corpse when it is certain that it is a corpse. Embalming, thanks to hygienism and Egyptomania, is a practice whose adepts are more numerous at the end of the eighteenth century, as Philippe Ariès has shown.[27] Most of the treatises against premature burials recommend this procedure, which according to this logic is one more precaution: the opening up of the body, if—as is clearly stated—it begins with the extremities and the nonvital parts, is a supplementary form of proof by scarification and able to rouse a lethargic body from its torpor. Fervent hygienists that they are, these doctors agree with their enlightened colleagues to plead earnestly for internal and external purification of the corpse—washed, eviscerated, and embalmed. More than a funereal practice recommended by doctors and applied quite systematically to great statesmen or men of letters of the time—which, still today, has bequeathed to us a certain number of relics—embalming is part of an *aestheticized representation of the self as corpse.* This is representation in its main sense of spectacle: the corpse, embalmed, becomes literally presentable, since the process of internal and external putrefaction has been stopped. The corpse even becomes representable, an abstraction of the cadaverous presence now that preservation of it is possible. The embalmed corpse is also metonymically able to be delegated: the heart, for instance, is quite often kept in an urn by the relatives, but the viscera too can provide relics offered to the consideration of admirers. In this sense, representation of the embalmed corpse reaches its complete significance: purified, it is *presentable*; preserved, it is *re*-presentable; signified by an organic relic, it is *representable.*

In the case of militants attacking premature burials, the representational resources of embalming can be even more important: they make a poetic narrative of the corpse appear, its existence prolonged in imaginations that had till then been animated by an obsessive fear of apparent death and that are now inhabited by a possible aesthetization of the dead body. For if these treatises are the first to do violence to the corpse through multiple tests to make it confess its possible secret truth—"I am still alive"—they are also the first to embellish and adorn it once the certainty of death has been acquired. It is around putrefaction that this passage from violence to aesthetization takes place, in both cases representing a new consideration brought to the dead body in relation to the Christian concept of ashes. The doctor fighting against premature burial indeed wants to wait for putrefaction as absolute proof of death, but the only way to avert this unbearable representation consists in aestheticizing this wait, in embellishing or poetizing the preservation of the corpse. The decomposed, putrefied body is thus at the same time a proof *and* a refusal, the conclusion of a scientific logic *and* a taboo of representation. The certainty of death thus calls for the unrepresentable, the putrefied corpse. But this same certainty is also an appeasement, a reassurance, a form of well-being in death. It is in order to resolve this contradiction that the idea of embellishing the corpse intervenes, to make the certainty of death coincide with its beauty, sublimating by means of an aesthetic feeling—precisely the sublime—the forbidden and yet waited-for image of putrefied cadaverous flesh. This death, absolutely certain *and* absolutely beautiful, is finally representable only through this feeling of the sublime aestheticizing the corpse.

Madame Necker spent a part of her life foreseeing her death, defining this passage, representing herself to herself as an absolutely definite corpse. By this logic, it was necessary for her corpse to be also absolutely beautiful. So, by means of detailed and numerous prescriptions, she progressively refines a representation of herself as a "beautiful" corpse. This implies a morbid poetic construction, a physical postmortem embellishment, and a funeral ceremony that must assure the aestheticizing of her remains, preserved in an indefinitely visible earthly form. This companionship with the representation of the corpse is inscribed by her as a poetics that is little by little understood, and more and more necessary. As her intimate journals and letters progress, Madame Necker accepts "with composure [*douceur*]" the image of the corpse, mastering a first reaction of rejection. "One can only glimpse with horror the trace of this path of death that we are all obliged to follow. We think we feel the claws of a tiger that is in our heart. Our thoughts, faced with this corpse that we will become, flee from themselves and recoil with terror," she writes in 1771.[28] Madame Necker's thoughts then aim at overcoming this flight, this terror, this wild animal, by means of the creation of a different representation of the self. Here we are present, in a few years, at the formation of a radically funereal auto-representation, an experience that stems from a progressive and constant development beyond this previously impossible image of the self. This apprenticeship requires the acceptance of a certain number of morbid practices and reflections. Regular visits to places of death, first of all; this melancholy woman confesses a weakness for the poetry of tombstones: "I love sad thoughts. I often take walks in the refuges of death, since one must, through decency and wisdom, be coldly unhappy."[29] Then comes the period of visions of herself as a corpse, visions that perpetually haunt her mind: "I love to think," she writes for instance in 1777 to her friend the writer Thomas, "that they will raise a tomb for me among the beautiful trees of Saint-Ouen. You will make an inscription for it and, in your promenades, you will lend your ear to the sound of leaves rustled by the wind while pondering my remains. And at this sound that seems to imitate murmuring, a body will answer that manifests the look of life. Insensibly, then, my spirit will come to portray itself to your imagination, my faults will be erased by the sponge of death. You will say: 'She no longer exists for me. Nothing afflicts her now; but she cannot have changed her nature, and she still takes pleasure from my distress. Listen to her, look at her'. . . ."[30] This "look at her" reverberates like a revelation: it is a matter of looking the corpse in the face, and seeing in its beauty the image of a past life *and* a life that somehow seems to follow.

In this sense, the meeting and friendship with Buffon were for Madame Necker the occasion for a definitive realization, as she writes to Saussure in 1783: "No, it is not the corpse of the universe, as you forcefully said, that you saw stretched out beneath your feet; on the contrary, it is the noble and colossal body of sublime nature. What we think of as a corpse deserves another look: it is only a prolongation of life by death; and there is, says Buffon, a sort of courage of mind in being able to envisage, without being too frightened, and then with composure, the greatness of the bodies of the departed."[31] This companionship with the corpse is written about more and more intimately, more and more regularly, by Madame Necker, "with composure." Little by little, taming horror, the corpse becomes the focus for a true poetics, a sweet and morbid narrative composed by her with great transports of emotion about the death of her friend Buffon. This tale of agony, published in April 1788 after four days and four nights spent by the bedside of the dying scientist, *Derniers moments et agonie de M. le Comte de Buffon, décédé au Jardin du Roi dans la nuit du 15 au 16 avril 1788* [Final moments and death throes of M. the Count of Buffon, deceased at the Royal Garden on the night of 15–16 April 1788], is in fact more than a testimonial on the virtuous end and final words of a great man, a particularly prolific genre in the course of the last thirty years of the eighteenth century, when the philosophers of the Age of Enlightenment die, and then the statesmen of the Revolution. This narrative both presents a clinical case and attempts a poetic construction. Extremely detailed in its description of all the gestures, actions, and symptoms of the dying man's agony, it transforms the corpse into a poem once the "terrible spasm of death is calmed." Then, very quickly, "the imprint of the greatest beauty lay upon his mortal physiognomy. Death and immortality seemed to meet each other there and . . . that great living shade will wander around me endlessly." In the months that follow this death, Madame Necker continues her dialogue with the living-dead body of Buffon, substituting the death mask of her friend for the body now and hereafter hidden from her eyes. The death mask, kept at her house, is the closest representation of this corpse she so emotionally adored: "And I pour tears onto this living marble," she writes, trembling with emotion, to a friend. The continuation of life is not only linked to the spirit of the dead man and to the carefully nurtured memory of him; it is embodied in a corpse that she managed to face directly, almost with rapture.

It is this experience that Madame Necker wishes to have applied to her own body, and with that in mind she suggests it to those close to her. She writes to Thomas, "I desire nothing but a tomb where I precede Monsieur Necker. This refuge will be sweet to me, and I want them to enclose in it afterwards, with my remains, those of my husband; my remains will live in that expectation, waiting the way a young woman trembles in the hope of a letter. For death is a great idea: memory is expressed in this language that pierces through time, and the proof of existence seems to be able to present itself to everyone at the sight of these sublime ashes."[32] With Madame Necker, sublime beauty moves toward the corpse, that state in which the dead woman finds again the emotions and vitality of a "young woman." Here it is not a matter of some wholly spiritual beauty, but a physical one, "trembling" to use her expression, the most certain way of assuring memory, thus pursuing a life in the mind of the living. The corpse as physical beauty is the condition of memory, an obvious consequence that Madame Necker inscribed into her will.

A first part of this will, as we have explained, concerns the tests to which her body ought to be submitted. A second part suggests a ceremony aimed explicitly at aestheticizing her corpse and giving it over to public contemplation in reconstructed beauty. Through this "admirable" corpse, Madame Necker intends to preserve her youth. Further, she dies, as she writes to her husband in the epistolary preface to her final will, "before having passed the critical age of women," thus still fully a woman, self-willed, fertile; thus she can offer this treasure of youth, preserved, eternally arrested and presentable thanks to embalming, to her husband, as sign of a fidelity forever caught in the act, a prolongation of this virtuous life of love: "You cry, dear friend of my heart. You think that she no longer lives for you, the one who had joined her existence to yours in every respect. You are mistaken: this God who had joined our two hearts, this God who will overwhelm me with his favors, will not annihilate my being. When I write this letter, a secret emotion, an instinct that has never deceived me, spreads an unforeseen calm through my soul by preserving my remains from the attacks of death. I believe I see that this soul will still watch over your fate as you will always watch over my body, and, together, we will still enjoy tenderness. My friend, I speak to you at a time when all hearts are bared. Virgin and pure when I took the oath to be faithful to you, I have kept my oath in all its delicacy. It is a mild merit, that of having lived in innocence before marrying and of having remained perfectly chaste in the course of a long union. I die before having passed the critical age of women; I am happy about that since I spare you my old age.... I thought I should satisfy my heart and yours, by unreservedly abandoning all this to you, what will remain of me on earth, my mortal remains. These remains are still fertile; they must recall to you that in the flower of youth and beauty, you alone were master of the stainless person who was then an object of esteem and interest. Here then is a kind of separate last will, of a new genre; it is made up of the orders that I leave you about my remains. Since I am going to give you orders, counting on the empery of my love for you, I command you to follow them. These instructions about my remains and my burial are so close to my heart that fear of the least negligence painfully besets me. You must devote, to your friend who still lives in these remains, a part of the life that remains to you. I order you then to live to obey your God, and to live and take care of yourself to fulfill my intentions."[33] These injunctions represent, for Madame Necker, the conclusion of the aesthetic system fashioned around the vital, fecund presence of the corpse: "You must live for the beauty of my corpse."

All these recommendations are precise, as immediately after the death of her mother Germaine de Staël states in a letter to Henri Meister: "Perhaps you do not know that my mother gave orders so singular, so extraordinary, on the various ways of embalming her, preserving her, setting her in alcohol under glass, so that if, as she hoped, the features of her face had been perfectly preserved, my unfortunate father might spend his life contemplating her. That is not how I understand the need not to be forgotten."[34] And Necker, to the surprise and anger of his daughter, scrupulously carries out the funeral ritual: "My mother died," Madame de Staël writes, "and my father was not distraught or confused by the suffering that portrayed itself in him, and that would last as long as he lived; from the very first instant he executed my mother's last wishes for her remains and her burial, with a sensibility that concentrated all his force in accomplishing all these duties."[35] These "duties" were made scientifically precise by Madame Necker through long and patient researches. "Madame Necker," reports her direct descendant the Comte d'Haussonville, "had begun by wishing that the bed on which she died be carried into her tomb, hoping that, certain precautions being taken, and on condition that perfumes be burnt there day and night, the result that she wished for could be attained. She wanted the body of her husband to be brought there one day so that the two corpses could lie in the nuptial bed side by side. Then, when they succeeded in persuading her that what she wished for could not be executed, she had the various procedures of embalming explained to her, entering into all the details, even the most distressing, with incredible precision. On this point she requested consultations with many doctors, Swiss, English, French, as well as others at Vicq d'Azyr. Having been instructed in the various procedures for preservation of the body by injection or by immersion in an appropriate liquid, she made the choice of this latter procedure; her attention then turned to the enclosure where this immersion would take place. She decided on a substance which should be of black marble, as well as on the shape and exact dimensions."[36]

Presented like a fruit in her basket, preserved in the maturity of her body—this metaphor is ironically developed in the press of the time, as this quatrain shows:

> Here lies one who in her throes
> Conceived of nothing nobler
> Than being pickled in her tomb
> Like a plum in brandy—[37]

Madame Necker's remains are presented to be visited, to be seen: "She had prescribed, with the most extreme minuteness, the angle at which her body should be set so that her head, resting on a cushion, would always be above the edge of the enclosure, so that her husband, when he entered the monument, would be able to contemplate her features without revulsion."[38] Begun in the fall of 1793 in the woods of the Coppet château, the construction of this funeral monument takes a year: on September 8, 1794, Necker can place his wife's corpse there, embalmed, covered with a cloth of red silk, in the black marble enclosure filled with ethyl alcohol up to her face. Necker keeps the key. There is a guard charged with periodically renewing the liquid, as well as with another ritual: to place, each Thursday, on the edge of the vat, a letter written in Madame Necker's hand, addressed to her husband, letters being bequeathed by the deceased in order and abundance. Necker visits his wife daily for almost ten years, contemplating this speaking corpse.

Ten years later, in April 1804, when the former minister dies at Coppet, the wishes of his wife are finally accomplished: "You will have an iron door made in the wall for which you alone will have the key, a door that will serve to carry your body through when you no longer exist. You will observe the same precautions for your remains, the only difference being that you will order them to close the iron door one month after your death so that we can remain alone together." After having regulated her life, those of her relatives, and those of her invalids, after having prepared her death and the exhibition of her corpse, Madame Necker orders the funeral ceremony of her husband according to a ritual at once morbid and amorous, reinforcing the communion of dead souls by the scientific and poetic union of corpses: "They took Madame Necker perfectly preserved from the enclosure of spirits of wine; they placed her in the vat on one side, Monsieur Necker on the other. Both were covered with spirits of wine after they were draped in Madame Necker's dressing gown that her husband had kept, for ten years, under his pillow. Then they closed the iron door of the monument and walled it up."[39]

This sepulchral refuge will not be forced open until 1817, when, in death, Germaine de Staël joins her parents. Buried at the foot of the great marble basin in a grave previously prepared for this purpose, she disturbs the morbid intimacy of the two corpses in their thirteen-year tête-à-tête. Her son-in-law, the Duc de Broglie, master of the funeral ceremonies, recounts this fantastic vision: "I entered the sepulchral chamber alone. It was empty; in the middle was the black marble vat, still half filled with spirits of wine. The two bodies were stretched out next to each other and covered with a red cloak. Madame

Necker's head had sunk down. I did not see her face at all; Monsieur Necker's face was uncovered and perfectly preserved."[40]

The four porters follow, come to place Madame de Staël's coffin in the grave. It is at that moment that the *Gazette de Lausanne* offers a final detail, one last consideration: "One of the porters who was present at the procession said that when putting the coffin down he had brushed against Madame Necker's nose, which alone rose above the opaque liquid of the black marble vat. It had the dry touch of parchment."[41] The anecdote is no doubt invented—the funeral ceremonies at Coppet have inspired more than one legend—but it doesn't matter, since it expresses a representation of death, that of a new and obsessive, romantic eternity, conferred on the corpse as a poetic continuation of life. But the dryness of parchment, as well as the general submergence of the body, are also the sign of a limit, a failure of beauty with respect to the corpse, as if the actuality of organic anatomy had rebelled against the imagery of the romantic representation of the corpse.

AUTHOR'S ACKNOWLEDGMENTS

All my thanks to Keith M. Baker, Philippe Bordes, Christian-Marc Bosséno, Olivier Coquard, Andrew Curren, Laurent Gervereau, Jacques Guilhaumou, Valérie Hannin, Patrice Higonnet, Annie Jourdan, Colin Lucas, Jann Matlock, Dominique Poulot, Pascal Simonetti, and Myriam Tsikounas.

NOTES

INTRODUCTION
SUBLIME ABJECTION: THE ASCENDANCY OF CORPSES

1. Philippe Bordes, *La Mort de Brutus de Pierre-Narcisse Guérin,* (Vizille: Musée de la Révolution Française, 1996), work published on the occasion of the exhibition *Lucius Junius Brutus: L'Antiquité et la Révolution française.*
2. Robert L. Herbert, *David, Voltaire, Brutus and the French Revolution: an Essay in Art and Politics* (New York: Viking, 1973); Ian Donaldson, *The Rapes of Lucrecia. A Myth and its Transformations* (Oxford, 1982); Antoinette and Jean Ehrard, "Brutus et les lecteurs," *Revue européenne des sciences sociales* no. 85, (Claredon Press, 1989):102–13.
3. Pierre Baillot, *Récit de la Révolution de Rome, sous Tarquin le Superbe* [A Tale of the Roman Revolution, under Tarquinius Superbus], (Dijon, 1791), 20–21.
4. Philippe Bordes and Régis Michel, eds., *Aux armes et aux arts! Les arts de la Révolution, 1789–1977* (Paris: Adam Biro, 1988).
5. Philippe Ariès, *L'homme devant la mort* (Paris: Le Seuil, 1977); Michel Vovelle, *La Mort et l'Occident de 1300 à nos jours,* (Paris: Gallimard, 1983).
6. Thomas Crow, *Emulation: Making Artists for Revolutionary France* (New Haven, Yale University Press, 1995), especially the chapter on Drouais.
7. Udolpho van de Sandt, "Institutions et concours," in Bordes Michel, *Aux armes et aux arts!* 138–65.
8. "Procès-verbal des séances du Jury des arts, 17–19 pluviôse an II" (Minutes on the meetings of the Arts Panel, 17–19 Pluviôse Year II), cited in Bordes, *La Mort de Brutus,* 138–65.
9. *Lucius Junius Brutus: L'Antiquité et la Révolution française,* June 28–September 23, 1996, Musée de la Révolution Française, Vizille.
10. Régis Michel, *Le Beau idéal ou l'art du concept* (Paris: Réunion des Musées Nationaux, 1989).
11. See the three studies by Matthias Bleyl, "Marat: Du portrait à la peinture d'histoire," Jörg Traeger, "La Mort de Marat et la religion civile," and Klaus Herding, "La notion de temporalité chez David à partir du Marat," in the proceedings of the colloquium *David contre David,* ed. Régis Michel, vol. 1, 379–455 (La Documentation Française, 1993).

12. Bordes, *La Mort de Brutus,* 66.
13. Robert Simon, "Portrait de martyr: Le Peletier de Saint-Fargeau," in Michel, *David contre David,* vol. I, 349–77; Donna M. Hunter, "Swordplay: Jacques-Louis David's Painting of Le Peletier de Saint-Fargeau on His Deathbed," in *Representing the French Revolution: Literature, Historiography, and Art,* ed., James A. W. Heffernan, 169–210 (Hanover, N.H.: University Press of New England, 1992).
14. Jean-Claude Bonnet, ed., *La Mort de Marat* (Paris: Flammarion, 1986), particularly the article by Jacques Guilhaumou, "La mort de Marat à Paris (13 juillet–16 juillet 1793)," 39–80.
15. Antoine de Baecque, *Le Corps de l'Histoire: Métaphores et politique (1770–1800)* (Paris: Calmann-Lévy, 1993). Translated by Charlotte Mandell as *The Body Politic: Corporeal Metaphor in Revolutionary France, 1770–1800* (Stanford, Calif.: Stanford University Press, 1997). See especially the chapter "The Offertory of the Martyrs: The Wounded Body of the Revolution," 280–307.
16. Olivier Coquard, *Marat* (Paris: Fayard, 1994).
17. Louis-Sébastien Mercier, *Le Nouveau Paris* [The New Paris] (Paris, 1798), 175–76.
18. "Guérin ou l'allégorie de l'émigration," in Bordes and Michel, *Aux armes et aux arts!* 86–88.
19. *La Feuille du salut public* [The Paper of Public Safety], July 18, 1793.
20. *Le Thermomètre du jour* [The Daily Thermometer], July 17, 1793.
21. Keith M. Baker and Colin Lucas, eds., *The Terror,* vol. 4 of *The French Revolution and Modern Political Culture* (Oxford: Pergamon Press, 1994).
22. Jacques Guilhaumou, "Fragment d'une esthétique de l'événement révolutionnaire: Le cas de la mort de Marat," in *L'Art et le discours face à la Révolution* (Dijon: Presses de l'Université de Bourgogne, 1998); Jean-François Lyotard, *Leçons sur l'Analytique du sublime* (Paris: Galilée, 1991).
23. Daniel Arasse, *La Guillotine et l'imaginaire de la Terreur* (Paris: Flammarion, 1987).
24. Michel Vovelle, *Piété baroque et déchristianisation en Provence au XVIIIe siècle* (Paris: Le Seuil, 1973), 84: "One can measure the stages of a collective evolution, which progressively went from the semi-nudity of the shroud of the Baroque era to the custom of being buried fully clothed, then placed in a coffin."
25. Robert Favre, *La Mort dans la littérature et la pensée française au siècle des Lumières* (Lyon: PUL, 1978); Maurice Lévy, *Le Roman gothique anglais (1764–1824)* (Toulouse, Association des publications de la Faculté des lettres et sciences humaines, 1968); Jean-Marie Thomasseau, *Le Mélodrame sur les scènes parisiennes,* (Lille: Service de reproduction des thèses de l'université, 1974); proceedings of the colloquium *Mélodrames et romans noirs (1790–1870)* (Clermont-Ferrand: Association des publications de la Faculté des lettres et sciences humaines, 1994); Philippe Van Tieghem, *La Poésie de la nuit et des tombeaux* (Paris: F. Rieder, 1922).

26. Expression taken from the fine book by Myriam Revault d'Allonnes, *D'une mort à l'autre: Précipices de la Révolution* (Paris: Le Seuil, 1989), 195.
27. P. Hintermeyer, *Politiques de la mort: Le concours de l'Institut sur les funérailles convenant à un peuple libre, germinal an VIII* (Payot, 1981), as well as the *Rapport fait par les citoyens Hallé, Desessarts, Toulongeon, La Revellière-Lepeaux, Leblond et Camus, commissaires chargés par l'Institut National des Sciences et des Arts, de l'examen des mémoires envoyés au concours, sur les questions relatives aux cérémonies funéraires et aux lieux des sépultures* [Report made by the Citizens Hallé, Desessarts, Toulongeon, La Revellière-Lepeaux, Leblond and Camus, commissioners charged by the National Institute of Arts and Sciences, for the examination of the memoirs sent to the competition, on questions relative to funeral ceremonies and places of burial], (Paris, Year IX).
28. A. Mitchell, "The Paris Morgue as a Social Institution in the 19th Century," *Francia* (1976); Vanessa R. Schwartz, *The Public Taste for Reality: Early Mass Culture in Fin de Siècle Paris* (Berkeley: Univ. of California Press, 1993); Margaret and Patrice Higonnet, "Façades: Walter Benjamin's Paris," in *Critical Inquiry* 10 (March 1984), 391–419.
29. Alain Corbin, "Le Sang de Paris: Réflexions sur la généalogie de l'image de la capitale," in *Le Temps, le désir et l'horreur* (Paris: Aubier, 1991), 215–25.
30. Alain Monestier, *Le Fait divers* (Paris: Réunion des Musées Nationaux, 1982); Dominique Kalifa, *L'Encre et le Saint. Les récits de crime à la Belle Époque* (Paris: Fayard, 1995); Ruth Harris, *Murder and Madness: Medicine, Law, and Society in the Fin de Siècle Paris* (Oxford: Clarendon Press, 1989); Joëlle Guillais, *Le Chair de l'autre: Le Crime passionnel au XIXe siècle* (Paris: O. Orban, 1986); Robert Nye, *Crime, Madness, and Politics in Modern France: The Medical Concept of National Decline* (Princeton, N.J.: University Press, 1984. Jan Goldstein, *Console and Classify: The French Psychiatric Profession in the Nineteenth Century* (Cambridge: Cambridge Univ. Press, 1987); Jann Matlock, *Scenes of Seduction: Prostitution, Hysteria, and Reading Difference in Nineteenth-Century France* (New York: Columbia University Press, 1994).
31. Alain Corbin uses this expression in his essay published by Jean-Pierre Rioux and Jean-François Sirinelli, eds., *Pour une histoire culturelle* (Paris: Le Seuil, 1997), 103.
32. Ariès, *L'Homme devant la mort*, 114–15.

MIRABEAU; OR, THE SPECTACLE OF A PUBLIC CORPSE

1. Pierre Jean George Cabanis, *Journal de la maladie et de la mort d'Honoré-Gabriel-Victor Riquetti de Mirabeau* [Journal of the illness and death of Honoré-Gabriel-Victor Riquetti de Mirabeau], (Paris, 1791), 22.

2. François Furet, ed., *Mirabeau: Discours* (Paris: Gallimard, 1973); Guy Chaussinand-Nogaret, *Mirabeau* (Paris: Le Seuil, 1982); *Mirabeau entre le roi et la Révolution: Notes à la cour suivies de discours*, presentation and notes by Guy Chaussinand-Nogaret (Paris: Hachette, 1986).
3. Jean-Etienne-Marie Portalis, "Mes souvenirs politiques," *Séances et travaux de l'Académie des sciences morales et politiques* 48 365–66.
4. *Courrier de Provence,* no. 276.
5. *Mort de Mirabeau et ses dernières paroles, avec le détail de l'assassinat de son secrétaire* [Death of Mirabeau and his last words, with details of his secretary's assassination attempt], (n.p., 1791).
6. Cabanis, *Journal de la maladie,* 22–23.
7. Ibid., 54.
8. Ibid., 51.
9. These are the thoughts most reported by the press. We find them in Cabanis, *Journal de la maladie* (51–52); in the *Courrier de Provence,* no. 276; and in *Mort de Mirabeau.*
10. *Courrier de Provence,* no. 277.
11. Cabanis, *Journal de la maladie,* 44.
12. *Que fut Mirabeau?* [What was Mirabeau?], (n.p., 1791).
13. *Le Patriote français,* April 4, 1791.
14. *Le Patriote français,* April 3, 1791.
15. *Lettre du comte de Mirabeau au Comité des recherches* [Letter from the Comte de Mirabeau to the Comité des recherches], (n.p., 1789).
16. *Réponse à un écrit intitulé Lettre aux commettants du comte de Mirabeau* [Answer to a piece called "Letter to the supporters of the Comte de Mirabeau"] (Paris, n.d.).
17. E. Dumont, *Souvenirs sur Mirabeau* (Paris, 1832).
18. *Réflexions sur la délation et sur le Comité des recherches* [Reflections on accusation and on the Comité des recherches], (Paris, February 1790).
19. *Observations du comte de Lally-Tollendal sur la lettre écrite par M. le comte de Mirabeau au Comité des recherches contre M. le comte de Saint-Priest* [Observations of the Comte de Lally-Tollendal on the letter written by M. le Comte de Mirabeau to the Comité des recherches against M. le Comte de Saint-Priest], (Paris, 1789).
20. *Lettre aux commettants du comte de Mirabeau* [Letter to supporters of the Comte de Mirabeau], (n.p., n.d.).
21. Charles de Lameth, *Trahison découverte du comte de Mirabeau, par le rédacteur des Actes des capucins, en réponse aux Actes de apôtres* [The Comte de Mirabeau's treason discovered, by the editor of the *Actes des capucins,* in response to the *Actes des apôtres*], (n.p., n.d.).
22. Antoine de Baecque, "The Great Spectacle of Transparency: Public Denunciation and the Classification of Appearances," in de Baecque, *The Body Politic* 209–46;

Jacques Guilhaumou, "Fragments pour un discours de la dénonciation," in Baker and Lucas, *The Terror;* Colin Lucas, "The Theory and Practice of Denunciation in the French Revolution," *Journal of Modern History* 68, no. 4 (December 1996).

23. *Orgie et testament de Mirabeau* [Orgy and Testament of Mirabeau], (n.p., 1791).
24. *Les Actes des apôtres* often profited from Mirabeau's death, as well as the ceremony that surrounded it: "Funeral Oration for Honoré-Gabriel Riquetti de Mirabeau," no. 255, vol. 9; "On the Funeral Ceremony of Mirabeau," no. 256, vol. 9; "Political Oracle on the End of Great Men," no. 258, vol. 9.
25. *Actes des apôtres* 9, no. 255.
26. *Orgie et testament de Mirabeau.*
27. We can find a portrait of Mirabeau as "syphilitic but Herculean fucker" in the *Bordel national sous les auspices de la reine, à l'usage des confédérés provinciaux, dédié et présenté à Mlle. Théroigne, à Cythère et dans tous les bordels de Paris* [National bordello under the auspices of the queen, for the use of provincial confederates, dedicated and presented to Mlle. Théroigne, at Cythère and in all the bordellos of Paris], (1790).
28. *Orgie et testament de Mirabeau.*
29. *Journal de la vie et de la mort,* op.cit., p. 15.
30. *L'ordre et la marche de l'enterrement de M. de Mirabeau. La cause de sa maladie. Ses dernières paroles. Détail de l'assassinat de son secrétaire. Procès-verbal de l'ouverture de son cadavre. Grand bal donné par les aristocrates, le jour et à l'occasion de la mort de M. Mirabeau* [The order and procedure of the burial of M. de Mirabeau. The cause of his illness. His last words. Details on his secretary's assassination attempt. Report on the dissection of his corpse. Great ball given by the aristocrats, on the day and on the occasion of the death of M. Mirabeau], (n.p., n.d.).
31. *Détail exact de l'assassinat du secrétaire de M. Mirabeau* [Exact details of the assassination attempt made by the secretary of M. Mirabeau], (n.p., n.d.).
32. *Second avis aux bons patriotes sur les causes de la mort de Mirabeau* [Second opinion for the use of good Patriots on the causes of Mirabeau's death], (n.p., n.d.).
33. Cabanis, *Journal de la maladie,* 4.
34. Ibid., 14.
35. Ibid., 56.
36. Ibid., 64–65.
37. *Mort de Mirabeau.*
38. *Réquisitoire de l'accusateur public du tribunal du 1er arrondissement du département de Paris, et Procès-verbal de l'ouverture du cadavre de Honoré-Gabriel-Victor Riquetti l'aîné, ci-devant Mirabeau, décédé à neuf heures trois-quarts* [sic] *du matin, le 2 avril 1791* [Closing speech of the Public Prosecutor at the tribunal of the 1st Arrondissement of the Département of Paris, and Report on

the autopsy of the corpse of Honoré-Gabriel-Victor Riquetti the elder, formerly Mirabeau, deceased at nine and three-quarters [sic] o'clock in the morning, on April 2, 1791], (n.d.).

39. *Procès-verbaux de l'ouverture et de l'embaumement du corps de M. Mirabeau l'aîné* [Report on the autopsy and embalming of the body of M. Mirabeau the elder], (n.p., April 3, 1791).
40. *Réquisitoire de l'accusateur public.*
41. Ibid.
42. *Procès-verbaux de l'ouverture.*
43. *Réquisitoire de l'accusateur public.*
44. *Procès-verbaux de l'ouverture.*
45. Ibid.
46. *Archives parlementaires* 24 (April 2, 1791): 506.
47. Ibid., 510.
48. *Le Patriote français,* April 3, 1791.
49. *Le Patriote français,* April 4, 1791.
50. *Archives parlementaires* 24 (April 3, 1791): 536.
51. *Le Patriote français,* April 4, 1791.
52. *Archives parlementaires* (April 3, 1791): 536–37.
53. Ibid., 537–38.
54. *Détail exact des funérailles et enterrement de M. de Mirabeau, avec l'ordre de la marche et le procès-verbal de l'ouverture de son corps* [Exact details of the funeral and interment of M. de Mirabeau, with the order of the procession and the report on the autopsy of his body], (n.p., 1791).
55. Nicolas Ruault, *Gazette d'un Parisien sous la Révolution: Lettres à son frère, 1786–1796* (Paris: Perrin, 1975), 280, dated April 5, 1791. See also the description in *L'Ordre et la marche de l'enterrement de M. de Mirabeau* [The order and procession of the burial of M. de Mirabeau], (n.p., n.d.).
56. J. A. Cérutti, *Notice mortuaire sur M. Mirabeau* [Obituary of M. Mirabeau], (n.p., n.d.).
57. *L'Ami du peuple,* no. 419, (April 4, 1791).
58. *L'Ami du peuple,* no. 420, (April 5, 1791).
59. *L'Ami du peuple,* no. 424, (April 9, 1791).
60. *L'Ami du peuple,* no. 419, (April 4, 1791).
61. *Le Patriote français,* April 3, 1791.
62. Ibid.
63. *Le Patriote français,* April 4, 1791.
64. *Le Patriote français,* April 8, 1791.
65. *Opinion de Sieyès sur plusieurs articles du projet de constitution* [Opinion of Sieyès on many articles of the plan for a constitution], 2 Thermidor Year III, 7.
66. Roger Chartier, "Espace public et opinion publique," in *Les Origines culturelles de la Révolution française* (Paris: Le Seuil, 1990), 32–52; Mona Ozouf, "Le con-

cept d'opinion publique au XVIIIe siècle," in *L'Homme régénéré: Essais sur la Révolution française* (Paris: Gallimard, 1989); de Baecque, "Spectacle of Transparency," in *The Body Politic* 226–27.

VOLTAIRE; OR, THE BODY OF THE PHILOSOPHER KING

1. *La Chronique de Paris,* April 14, 1791.
2. *Les Révolutions de France et de Brabant,* April 18, 1791.
3. *La Chronique de Paris,* April 14, 1791.
4. See L.-J.-N. de Monmerqué, *Notice historique sur le marquis de Villette* (Paris, 1844); *Mémoires du marquis de Villette* (Paris: Société de l'Histoire de France, 1844).
5. Louis-Sébastien Mercier, *Parallèle de Paris et de Londres* [Parallels between Paris and London], (manuscript written in 1781; Bruneteau and B. Cottret, (Paris: Didier, 1982). Chapter 63, "Westminster and St. Denis," was in part reprinted by Mercier in his *Tableau de Paris,* vol. 6, 524. On the cult of great men in the eighteenth century: J.-C. Bonnet, "Naissance du Panthéon," *Poétique,* no. 33 (February 1978); M. Ozouf, "Le Panthéon: L'École normale des morts," in *Les Lieux de mémoire, vol. 1, La République,* ed. P. Nora (Paris: Gallimard, 1984), 139–66.
6. Mérard de Saint-Just, *Etrennes patriotiques, ou manuel du citoyen* [Patriotic New Year's gifts, or Manual of the citizen], (Paris, 1791); Marquis de Ximenès, "Les Grands Hommes n'ont rien à craindre de leurs rivaux," [Great men have nothing to fear from their rivals], in *Essai de quelques genres divers de poésie* [Essay on some diverse genres of poetry], (n.p., n.d.), and *Aux mânes de Voltaire* [To the shades of Voltaire], (Paris, 1779); Anarchasis Cloots, *Lettre d'un Prussien à un Anglais. Discours du 19 juin 1790* [Letter from a Prussian to an Englishman: Discourse of June 19, 1790], (n.p.), and *Voltaire triomphant, ou les prêtres déçus* [Voltaire triumphant, or priestcraft foiled], (n.p., n.d.); Villemure, *Sur l'apothéose de Voltaire et celle des grands hommes de la France* [On the apotheosis of Voltaire and that of the great men of France], (Paris, 1790).
7. *La Chronique de Paris,* January 14, 1791.
8. Maurice Dumolin, *Etudes de topographiç parisienne,* vol. I, (Paris: n.p., 1929) 304-8; J. de Sacy, "L'Hôtel de Villette," in *Le Faubourg Saint-Germain* (Paris, 1966), 106–9; P. Jarry, "L'Hôtel du marquis de Villette," *Bulletin de la Société d'histoire et d'archéologie du VIIe arrondissement* (1938): 309–11; B. Pons, "Hôtel de Villette," in *Le quai Voltaire,* studies offered to Colette Lamy-Lassalle, ed. M. Borjon and B. Pons (Paris, Délégation à l'action artistique de la ville de Paris, 1990).
9. *La Chronique de Paris,* January 14, 1791.
10. *La Chronique de Paris,* April 22, 1791.

11. The Comte de Ségur writes in his *Mémoires, ou souvenirs et anecdotes* (Paris, 1827), vol. 1, 166–87, "One has to have seen at that time the public joy, the impatient curiosity and the tumultuous eagerness of an admiring crowd to hear, envisage and even to glimpse this famous old man, witness to two centuries, who had inherited the brilliance of one and made the glory of the other; one must, I say, have been witness to it to form a fair idea of it. It was the apotheosis of a still living demi-god; he said to the people with as much reason as emotion: 'You want to make me die of pleasure, then.' In fact, the power of so numerous and such touching homages was beyond his strength; he succumbed to it, and the altar that was raised to him was promptly changed into a tomb."
12. Quoted by M. F. P. de Mairobert in *L'observateur anglais, on Correspondance secrète entre milord All'eye et milord AllE'ar* [*sic*] [Volumes 5–10 are also known as *L'Espion anglais*] (London: John Adamson, 1779–1786) 8: 311–12, who immediately adds: "Everything was not, however, rosy for Voltaire; if he was overwhelmed with a multitude of pieces of praising and insipid verses, there were people who sought to sharpen these sweetnesses with thornier writings; he received many anonymous letters that had the effect of preventing his self-love from becoming too exalted."
13. On this theatrical triumph, see J. A. Leith, "Les Trois Apothéoses de Voltaire," *Annales historiques de la Révolution française*, April–June 1979, 161–209.
14. Nevertheless the government ban, and thus the news of Voltaire's death, were related in letters and chronicles following the news: *L'Espion anglais* (1779–1786 9: 168–89); Grimm's *Correspondance littéraire* 7 (June 1778): 112; La Harpe's *Correspondance littéraire* 2: 248; the *Correspondance secrète inédite de Lescure* 1: 172; Bachaumont's *Mémoires secrets* 7 (June 14, 1778): 17. As for the *Gazette de France*, it announced the philosopher's death on June 8, 1778, while the *Journal encyclopédique* gave a detailed account of it on July 15, 1778. One might think that, after July 1778, the government ban had been lifted. The Comte de Ségur, in his *Mémoires* 1: 184–87, reports the atmosphere surrounding the death of the great man: "Those who did not have the power to oppose his triumph refused him a place in the midst of the tombs of the Parisian people. One of his relatives, council member of the Parlement, took away his body and carried it quickly to the abbey of Scellières [*sic*], where he was buried before the priest of the place had received the order to refuse him burial, a prohibition that came to him three hours too late. Without the zeal of this friend, the mortal remains of one of our greatest men, whose glory filled the world, would not have won a few feet of earth to cover them. Despite all the efforts of the clergy, the magistrates and the authorities, who for some time prohibited theaters from putting on Voltaire's plays and newspapers from speaking of his death, Paris was inundated with a flood of verses, pamphlets and epigrams, the only arms with which opinion could use to avenge this outrage made to the memory of a man who had made his country and his century illustrious."

15. *La Gazette de Cologne,* July 7, 1778; *La Gazette d'Utrecht,* July 12, 1778; and *Le Courrier de l'Europe,* no. 50, announced and commented on the death of Voltaire.
16. J. A. Leith ("Les Trois Apothéoses de Voltaire") counts, for instance, forty mentions of Voltaire during the year following his death in *Le Journal de Paris,* thirty-four the second year, thirty-five the third; similarly, in the *Annonces, Affiches et Avis divers,* nineteen the first year, twenty-eight the second, twenty-eight the third. The *Almanach littéraire* of 1779 was specially devoted to the philosopher and declared that "such a prodigy would forever raise the Eighteenth Century above any other age."
17. Leith, "Les Trois Apothéoses" 166-94.
18. Engraving by Fauvel after Macret, *Réception de Voltaire aux Champs-Élysées par Henri IV* [Reception of Voltaire at the Elysian Fields by Henri IV], in the Cabinet des Estampes of the Bibliothèque Nationale, reproduced by J. A. Leith, "Les Trois Apothéoses," plate IX.
19. *La Chronique de Paris,* November 25, 1790. See also the poem by Cubières-Palmézeaux, *Voltaire vengé* [Voltaire avenged] (n.p., n.d.); and the one by Ginguené, *La Satyre des satyres* [The Satire of Satires] (n.p., 1778), in which the poet writes, "It is difficult to portray the savagery with which the clergy of Paris refused burial to the greatest of the men of this century, although, in his final moments, he did no damage to the decency that the cult of the state in which one is born seems to require. It was nonetheless in the priests' interest to keep the religious flock that they still govern from believing that any man who has genius cannot have faith; but a spirit of vertigo had taken hold of the entire sacerdotal order, from the prelate, so famous for his *billets de confession,* down to the least curate at Saint-Sulpice. So much so that the philosopher's body was almost given to the street. This outrage, assuredly, will have to be, one day or another, avenged, and the ashes of genius honored as they deserve." Jules Michelet, *Histoire de la Révolution française,* chap. 11 of bk. IV (Paris: Robert Laffont, 1979), 1: 460, continued this tale of revenge into the nineteenth century: "Cruel death! Pursued on his death bed, even after death, banished, taken away at night by his relatives, on May 30, 1778, hidden in an obscure tomb, his return is decreed on May 30, 1791. He returns, but in daylight, in the broad sun of justice, carried triumphantly on the shoulders of the people, to the temple of the Panthéon. Above all, he saw the fall of those who banished him. Voltaire came: priests and kings are on their way out. His return is brought about, by a remarkable decree, while priests, surmounting the indecisions and scruples of Louis XVI, are about to push him to Varennes, to treason, to shame."
20. *Archives parlementaires,* meeting of May 30, 1791.
21. Ginguené, *Satyre,* 14.
22. In 1791 a pamphlet, *Observations sur M. de Voltaire* (n.p., n.d.), gives some details on the clandestine burial of the philosopher, committed to earth thanks to

a ruse of his nephew, the Abbé Mignot: "After having opened the corpse, they put it back together and decked it out with a wig and a dressing gown. M. l'Abbé Mignot returned to his abbey of Scellières [*sic*], and informed his monks that his uncle, although dying, by an invalid's fantasy, wished to come visit him. The carriage arrived some time afterwards, but the driver declared that his master had died on the way, and that he was even beginning to smell bad. Upon this declaration, confirmed by the doctors and surgeons of the house, they proceeded with the burial. This haste was indispensable and, when the news was made known, roused the wrath of the Church and the indignant reaction of the Bishop of Troyes."

23. *Sur l'apothéose de Voltaire* [On the apotheosis of Voltaire], (Paris, 1791).
24. If Rousseau's death was peaceful (see letter 10 of vol. 9 of *L'Espion anglais*), that of Diderot elicited some legends comparable to those surrounding Voltaire's remains. A. M. Wilson, in his *Diderot* (New York: Oxford University Press, 1972), reports thus that: "The Jansenist review *Les Nouvelles ecclésiastiques*, very hostile to Diderot and to the Abbé Marduel, abbot of Saint-Roch, published a long exposé in which they claimed that Diderot had died in the countryside and that the corpse had been transported to Paris (November 26, 1784). This story was spread all through Catholic Christendom." In the *Revue d'histoire de l'Église de France* 10, (1925): 41, Louis Marcel refutes these rumors: "The Death of Diderot, according to unpublished documents."
25. *Testament de M. de Voltaire, trouvé parmi ses papiers après sa mort* [Last Will of M. de Voltaire, found among his papers after his death], (n.p., 1762).
26. *Voltaire aux Champs-Elysiens, oraison funèbre, histoire, satyre, le tout à volonté* [Voltaire at the Elysian Fields: funeral oration, history, satire, all as you like it], (n.p., 1773).
27. *Voltaire de retour des Ombres, et sur le point d'y retourner pour n'en plus revenir* [Voltaire back from the Shades, and on the point of returning there never to come back again], (n.p., 1776).
28. Nicolas Sélis, *La Relation de la maladie, confession et mort de M. de Voltaire* [Description of the illness, confession, and death of M. de Voltaire], (n.p., 1761; republished in 1778, with significant "additions").
29. *Lettre d'un philosophe chinois sur la mort supposée de M. de Voltaire* [Letter from a Chinese philosopher on the supposed death of M. de Voltaire], (n.p., n.d.); see also *Le codicille de M. de Voltaire, trouvé dans ses papiers après son décès* [The codicil of M. de Voltaire, found in his papers after his decease], (n.p., n.d.). Epistle to Urania was Voltaire's early and most violent attack on Christianity, published in 1722 as *Le Pour et le Contre.*
30. *La Gazette de Cologne,* July 7, 1778.
31. *Actes des séances du Club des Jacobins* [Minutes of the meetings of the Jacobin Club], meeting of November 10, 1790.
32. *La Chronique de Paris,* November 25, 1790.
33. *Le Patriote français,* April 8, 1791.

34. *Archives parlementaires,* meeting of May 30, 1791.
35. *La Chronique de Paris,* May 14, 1791.
36. Taken from the registers of the deliberations of the Clerk's Office of Romilly-sur-Seine, May 9, 1791, f. 9.
37. On the "dispersion of relics," see the G. Desnoireterres, *Le Retour et la mort de Voltaire à Paris* (Paris, 1876).
38. A. F. Lemaire, *Le Citoyen français,* no. 1, dated 24 Brumaire Year VIII, reports this anecdote.
39. Nicolas Ruault, *Gazette d'un Parisien sous la Révolution: Lettres à son frère (1786–1796)* [Gazette of a Parisian under the Revolution: letters to his brother (1786-1796)], op.cit., May 17, 1791, 238–39.
40. *La Chronique de Paris,* May 14, 1791.
41. Ibid.
42. *La Feuille du jour,* Paris, BN: Lc2 488, July 18, 1791.
43. Ibid. The journalist Parisau asks ironically, "I wonder if it was indeed the skeleton of Voltaire that was so ceremoniously transported on a chariot harnessed with twelve white horses. Honest people have doubts on this point. I will explain them to you. Have patience, it is a disquisition—but Voltaire wrote a few himself, and even a few merry ones on certain relics. It seems to me that his remains are scarcely more definite than the two legs of Saint Ovid, or the five heads of Saint John the Baptist, or the tips of the Virgin's sleeve, that can be seen at Prague with the apron of the butcher who killed the Fatted Calf upon the return of the Prodigal Son."
44. *Le Journal de la cour et de la ville* [Paper of the town and court], (Paris), July 6, 1791.
45. G. Desnoireterres, *Le Retour et la mort* 485–86.
46. A. Barbeau, *L'Exhumation de Voltaire* (Troyes, 1847).
47. "Lettre de l'abbé Mignot à M. Patris," in *Oeuvres inédites,* ed. Grosley (Paris, 1856), vol. 2, 456.
48. *La Feuille du jour,* July 18, 1791.
49. The mayor of Romilly, Favreau, responds to these rumors in the *Chronique de Paris* dated July 31, 1791: "I am mayor of Romilly; I was born there; I know all the inhabitants. I saw Voltaire's body arrive at Scellières [*sic*]; I undressed it; I saw it put into a coffin; I saw the casket being sealed. There was never a question of its being kidnapped. And when M. Charron, in the presence of four to five thousand people, identified the body of Voltaire, we recognized it, embalmed it and preserved it through the attentions of his beloved disciple, Charles Villette." The village priest, Bouillerot, also refutes these rumors: "I was witness to the exhumation of Voltaire. We found an emaciated, dried-up but intact corpse, whose members were attached. It was removed from the ditch with many precautions, and only the calcaneum became detached, which someone carried. The body was exhibited for two days to the public gaze in the Romilly church, then enclosed in a sarcophagus, placed for a time in the sacristy, then removed

to the chancel, under a tent, until the day of transferal to Paris" ("Lettre de M. Bouillerot à M. Patris," in *Oeuvres complètes de Voltaire,* ed. Beuchot, Paris: Garnier Frères, 1877–85, vol. 1, 441–42). As for Villette, he responds to the collection of accusations, especially about the cost of the ceremony that Quatremère de Quincy, leader along with Lanjuinais and Fauchet of the anti-Voltairean Patriots, estimated at "more than 100,000 *écus,*" in the *Chronique de Paris* of July 9, 1791.

50. *La Feuille du jour,* July 31, 1791.
51. G. Desnoireterres, *Le Retour et la mort,* 485–86.
52. *La Chronique de Paris,* July 11, 1791.
53. *La Chronique de Paris* published a narrative of the transfer from which we drew our descriptions: *Détail exact et circonstancé de tous les objects relatifs à la fête de Voltaire* [Exact and detailed description of all the subjects connected with the festival of Voltaire], n.p., n.d.
54. Bibliothèque de l'Arsenal, RA, IV, 727; quoted by Marie-Louise Biver, *Fêtes révolutionnaires à Paris* (Paris: PUF, 1979).
55. Biver, *Fêtes révolutionnaires,* 39–42.
56. *Ordre du cortège pour la translation des mânes de Voltaire, le lundi 11 juillet 1791* [Order of the procession for the transferal of the remains of Voltaire, on Monday, July 11, 1791], captioned engraving from the Hennin collection, Cabinet des Estampes, Bibliothèque Nationale.
57. Ibid.
58. *Le Courrier des 83 départements,* July 5, 1791. Gorsas describes with precision the preparations for the transfer (the chariot, the installation of the body, the ceremony itself) in the numbers of his *Courrier* dated July 6, 11, and 13, 1791. Similarly, the *Annales patriotiques et littéraires* by Carra and Mercier repeat them in the numbers of June 26, July 11, July 15, July 18, and August 14, 1791.
59. R. Pomeau and R. Vaillot, eds., *Voltaire en son temps* (Oxford: Voltaire Foundation, 1988), 321.
60. *Le Courrier des 83 départements,* July 11, 1791.
61. Ibid.
62. Ruault, *Gazette,* July 15, 1791, 251–52.
63. "Détail exact"; *Ordre et marche de la translation de Voltaire* (n.p., n.d.).
64. "Détail exact."
65. Ibid.
66. Ibid.
67. Ibid.
68. Marie-Joseph Chénier, *Hymne sur la translation du corps de Voltaire* [Hymn on the transfer of Voltaire's body], published in July 1791.
69. Ibid.
70. "Détail exact."
71. *Le Mariage de Figaro,* seventh couplet of the vaudeville finale (*Oeuvres de Beaumarchais* [Paris: Gallimard, Pléiade ed., 1988], 488). This stanza is dis-

played on the façade of Villette's town house during the ceremony of transfer ("Détail exact," 7).

72. *Journal de Prudhomme* (Paris, n.d.), 1:334.
73. *Le Courrier des 83 départements,* July 13, 1791.
74. *Lettre apologétique à Messieurs les administrateurs du département de Paris* [Apologetic letter to the Administrators of the Département of Paris], (n.p., n.d.). This letter is replicated as a *Pétition à l'Assemblée nationale* [Petition to the National Assembly], signed by 160 names, protesting against the "corruption of customs" commended by Voltaire (n.p., n.d.).
75. *Archives parlementaires,* meeting of May 8, 1791. The opposition of the Jansenists to the Voltaire ceremony unleashed an intense polemic. See the *Réponse à la pétition des 160 jansénistes relative à la translation de Voltaire* [Response to the petition of 160 Jansenists concerning the transfer of Voltaire], (n.p., n.d.), treating this text as a "Capuchinade," and suggesting that "the Jansenists be dressed like ancient sacrificial priests, holding in their hand burning thuribles; thus decked out, they should precede the triumph of Voltaire, singing the hymn to his glory and themselves burning their petition in their censers." See also *Réponse d'un ami des grands hommes aux envieux de la gloire de Voltaire* [Response of a friend of great men to those envious of the glory of Voltaire], (n.p., n.d.); *Voltaire vengé* [Voltaire avenged], followed by an *Observation sur la Pétition des prêtres et des maîtres d'école* [Observation on the Petition of Priests and Schoolmasters], (n.p., n.d.); and, in the other, counterrevolutionary and anti-Jansenist, camp: *La Feuille du jour* [Paper of the Day] dated July 31, 1791, which recalls "the Fauchets and other convulsionaries that the jubilee of the author of *Zaïre* suffocated."
76. *La Chronique de Paris,* July 13, 1791.
77. *L'Apothéose de Voltaire, ou le triomphe de la religion et des moeurs* [The Apotheosis of Voltaire, or the triumph of religion and custom], (n.p., n.d.). We find numerous attacks seeking to discredit Villette for his homosexual tastes in *Les Actes des apôtres* 5, no. 131: 16; 7, no. 181: 3 and 9; 7, no. 184: 15; 7, no. 185: 13–15; 7, no. 200: 20; 10, no. 277: 13. The "ci-derrière" Marquis de Villette figures prominently in the satiric gallery of the degenerate Jacobins, as a pornographic libel of 1791 perpetuates him: *Vie privée et publique du ci-derrière marquis de Villette, citoyen rétroactif et membre du club jacobin* [Private and public life of the *ci-derrière* Marquis de Villette, retroactive citizen and member of the Jacobin Club], (Paris, 1791).

THE PRINCESSE DE LAMBALLE; OR, SEX SLAUGHTERED

1. Jules Michelet, *La Révolution française,* (Paris: Robert Laffont, 1979) vol. 4, 181.
2. Ibid., 180.

3. Pierre Caron, *Les Massacres de septembre* (Paris, En vente à la Maison du livre français, 1935); Frédéric Bluche, *Septembre 1792: Logiques d'un massacre,* (Paris: Robert Laffont, 1986).
4. Lucien Lambeau, *Essais sur la mort de madame la princesse de Lamballe* (Lille, 1902); Paul Fassy, *La Princesse de Lamballe et la prison de la Force* (Paris, 1868); Georges Bertin, *Madame de Lamballe d'après des documents inédits* (Paris, 1888), 309–56; Alain Vircondelet, *La Princesse de Lamballe* (Paris: Flammarion, 1995), 13–15 and 244–52.
5. *Souvenirs d'un vieillard sur des faits restés ignorés: Journées des 10 août, 3,4, 5, 9 et 12 septembre 1792* [An old man's memories of deeds mostly unknown: Days of August 10 and September 3,4,5, 9 and 12, 1792], (Brussels, 1843).
6. *La famille royale préservée au Temple par la garde nationale de Paris et surtout par la conduite énergique d'un officier municipal, secondé par les commissaires de service, le 3 septembre 1792* [The royal family kept at the Temple by the National Guard of Paris and above all by the energetic conduct of a municipal officer, aided by military commissioners, on September 3, 1792], manuscript quoted in Bertin, *Madame de Lamballe,* 323–26.
7. A. de Beauchêne, *Louis XVII, sa vie, son agonie, sa mort* (Paris, 1851), vol. I, 364.
8. Lambeau, *Essais sur le mort,* 22–33.
9. Michel Foucault, *Surveiller et punir* (Paris: Gallimard, 1975); translated by Alan Sheridan as *Discipline and Punish: The Birth of the Prison* (New York: Pantheon, 1977), 47–48.
10. On violence and massacres during the Revolution: Georges Lefebvre, *La Grande Peur de 1789* (1932; reprint, Paris: Armand Colin, 1988); Michel Vovelle, *La Mentalité révolutionnaire: Société et mentalités sous la Révolution* (Paris: Messidor, 1985); Colin Lucas, "The Violence and the Terror," in Keith M. Baker, ed., *The Terror,* vol. IV of the collection *The French Revolution and the Modern Political Culture,* Keith M. Baker and Colin Lucas, eds. (Oxford: Pergamon Press, 1994).
11. Quoted by Bertin, *Madame de Lamballe,* 332–34.
12. Ibid., 334.
13. Quoted by Louis Mortimer Ternaux, *Histoire de la Terreur, 1792–1794* (Paris, 1862–1881), vol. 3, 245–46.
14. Ferdinand Brunot, *Histoire de la langue française des origines à nos jours* (Paris: A. Colin, 1905; reprint 1972), vol. 9, 883.
15. *La Juste Vengeance du peuple. Détail exact. La tête de la ci-devant princesse de Lamballe promenée et son corps traîné par les rues* [The Just Vengeance of the people. Exact details. The head of the former Princesse de Lamballe paraded and her body dragged through the streets], (n.p., n.d.).
16. *Justice du peuple ou Grand détail de ce qui s'est passé hier concernant les traîtres de la nation* [Justice of the people, or Great detail of what happened yesterday concerning the traitors of the nation], (n.p., n.d.).

17. J. J. Regnault-Warin, *Le Cimetière de la Madeleine* (Paris, n.d.).
18. *La Chronique de Paris,* August 21, 1792.
19. Quoted by M. de Lescure, *La Princesse de Lamballe* (Paris, 1864), 351.
20. *Grand Détail exact de la réception de Madame de Lamballe à la Cour, et l'agréable accueil qu'elle reçut du roi et de la reine* [Great exact details of the reception of Madame de Lamballe at the Court, and the cordial welcome she received from the king and queen], (n.p., n.d.).
21. Gabriel Brizard, "Dédicace à la liberté," in *Les Imitateurs de Charles IX ou les conspirateurs foudroyés, drame en cinq actes et en prose* [The Imitators of Charles IX, or the conspirators struck down, drama in five acts and in prose], (Paris, 1791).
22. *Désespoir de Marie-Antoinette sur la mort de son frère Léopold II, empereur des Romains, et sur la maladie désespérée de Monsieur, frère du roi de France* [Despair of Marie-Antoinette at the death of her brother Leopold II, Emperor of the Romans, and at the desperate illness of Monsieur, brother of the king of France], (n.p., n.d.).
23. *Essais historiques sur la vie de Marie-Antoinette, reine de France, pour servir à l'histoire de cette princesse* [Historical essays on the life of Marie-Antoinette, Queen of France, to serve as the history of this princess], (n.p., 1791), 102.
24. Quoted by Edmond and Jules de Goncourt, *Histoire de Marie-Antoinette* (Paris, 1862), 221.
25. *Moniteur universel,* August 20, 1792.
26. Quoted by Abbé Augustin Lambeau, *Essais sur le mort,* 25–26.
27. Barruel, *Histoire du clergé pendant la Révolution française* [History of the clergy during the French Revolution], (London, 1797), vol. 2, 126.
28. *Idées des horreurs commises à Paris, dans les journées à jamais exécrables des 10 août, 2, 3, 4 et 5 septembre 1792 ou Nouveau Martyrologe de la Révolution française* [Ideas of the horrors committed in Paris, on the forever execrable days of August 10, September 2, 3, 4 and 5 1792, or New martyrology of the French revolution], (Paris, 1793).
29. *Gazette de France,* May 19, 1770.
30. *Marie-Antoinette: Correspondance secrète entre Marie-Thérèse et le comte de Mercy-Argenteau* [Marie-Antoinette: Secret correspondence between Marie-Thérèse and the Comte de Mercy-Argenteau], (Paris, 1975), vol. 1, 223.
31. Quoted by A. E. Sorel, *La Princesse de Lamballe* (Paris: Hachette, 1933), 145.
32. Louis de Bachaumont, *Mémoires secrets pour servir à l'histoire de la république des lettres en France depuis 1762 jusqu'à nos jours* [Secret memoirs to serve as the history of the republic of letters in France from 1762 to the present], (n.p., 1777–89), May 28, 1774.
33. Ibid., September 20, 1775.
34. Mme de Genlis, *Mémoires inédits sur le XVIIII siècle et sur la Révolution française* [Unpublished memoirs on the eighteenth Century and on the French Revolution], (Paris, 1825), vol. 2, 285.

35. *Marie-Antoinette: Correspondance secrète,* letter from Mercy, on February 28, 1777.
36. Bertin, *Madame de Lamballe,* chapters 9 and 10, 143—73.
37. *Bulletin du comte de Fersen au Prince régent de Suède, de ce qui se passe en France* [Bulletin from Count Fersen to the Prince Regent of Sweden, on what is happening in France], Brussels, September 9, 1792.
38. *La Juste vengeance du peuple.*
39. Ibid.
40. Rétif de la Bretonne, *Vingt nuits à Paris,* 11th night (Paris, 1794).
41. Quoted by M. de Lescure, *Princesse de Lamballe,* 421.
42. Rétif de la Bretonne, *Vingt nuits à Paris.*
43. Beauchêne, Louis XVII, 364–65.
44. *Souvenirs de Mme Vigée-Lebrun* [Memoirs of Mme Vigée-Lebrun], (Paris, 1835–37), vol. 2, 214.
45. Harmand de la Meuse, *Anecdotes relatives à quelques personnes et à plusieurs événements remarquables de la Révolution* [Anecdotes involving some people and many remarkable events of the Revolution], (Paris, 1814), 52.
46. Bachaumont, *Mémoires secrets,* November 5, 1767.
47. Ibid., February 8, 1775.
48. Ibid., April 24, 1784. Quoted by Bertin, *Madame de Lamballe,* 171–72.
49. Ibid., May 2, 1785.
50. *Krankheitsgeschichte der Prinzessin von Lamballe* [History of the Illness of the Princess of Lamballe], (Paris: Leipzig, 1786); French translation in J. E. Dezeimeris, *Dictionnaire historique de la médecine ancienne et moderne* (1839).
51. *Bulletin du comte de Fersen,* September 19, 1792.
52. Antoine Sérieys, *Anecdotes inédites de la fin du XVIIIe siècle* [Unpublished anecdotes on the end of the eighteenth century], (Paris, 1801), chap. 15.
53. Bachaumont, *Memoires secrets,* 69.
54. Quoted by G. Bertin, *Madame de Lambelle,* 69.
55. Ibid., 161.
56. *Les Crimes des reines de France depuis le commencement de la monarchie jusqu'à Marie-Antoinette* [Crimes of the queens of France from the beginning of the monarchy to Marie-Antoinette], (Paris, 1791), 438. On the subject of this "lesbian conspiracy" and on the lewd fantasies surrounding the person of Marie-Antoinette, see the fine book by Chantal Thomas, *La Reine scélérate: Marie-Antoinette dans les pamphlets* (Paris: Le Seuil, 1989), 123–29.
57. *Fureurs utérines de Marie-Antoinette, femme de Louis XVI* [Uterine furies of Marie-Antoinette, wife of Louis XVI], (n.p., n.d.).
58. Ibid.
59. *Vie de Marie-Antoinette d'Autriche, reine de France, femme de Louis XVI, roi des Français* [Life of Marie-Antoinette of Austria, queen of France, wife of Louis XVI, king of the French], (Paris, 1791).

60. *Les Bordels de Lesbos, ou le Génie de Sapho* [The brothels of Lesbos, or the genius of Sappho], (Saint Petersburg, 1790).
61. *Idées des horreurs commises à Paris.*
62. E. Roch Mercandier, *Histoire des hommes de proie* [History of men of prey], (Paris, 1798), 34.
63. Sérieys, *Anecdotes,* chap. 15.

LOUIS XVI; OR, THE SACRED REMAINS

1. *Archives parlementaires,* meeting of September 21, 1792.
2. *Les Révolutions de Paris,* no. 185, 194.
3. On the execution of King Louis XVI, see especially, from among a profusion of texts: Daniel Arasse, *La Guillotine et l'imaginaire de la Terreur* (Paris: Flammarion, 1987); P. and P. Girault de Coursac, *Enqête sur le procès du roi* (Paris: Ed. de Guibert, 1992).
4. Marcel Reinhardt, *La Chute de la royauté, 10 août 1792* (Paris: Gallimard, 1969).
5. Antoine de Baecque, "La sévérité républicaine face à la majesté royale," in *Révolution et République: l'exception française,* ed. M. Vovelle (Paris: Ed. Kimé, 1994).
6. *Archives parlementaires,* meeting of August 10, 1792.
7. Marquis de Beaucourt, ed., *Captivité et derniers moments de Louis XVI. Récits originaux et documents officiels* [Captivity and final moments of Louis XVI: Original narratives and official documents], collected and published by the Marquis de Beacourt, 2 vols. (Paris, 1892).
8. Albert Soboul, *Le Procès de Louis XVI* (Paris: Gallimard, 1973); Michael Walzer, *Régicide et Révolution: le procès de Louis XVI* (Paris: Payot, 1989).
9. *Détails intéressants relatifs à la captivité de Louis XVI et à sa comparution à la barre* [Interesting details concerning the captivity of Louis XVI and his appearance at the bar], (n.p., n.d.).
10. *Grand détail exact de l'interrogatoire de Louis Capet à la barre de la Convention nationale* [Great exact detail on the interrogation of Louis Capet at the bar of the National Convention], (n.p., n.d.).
11. Alain Boureau, *Le Simple Corps du roi: L'Impossible Sacralité des souverains français* (Paris: Ed. de Paris, 1988).
12. François Furet and Ran Halévi, *La Monarchie républicaine: La Constitution de 1791* (Paris: Fayard, 1996).
13. Daniel Arasse, *La Guillotine,* 67.
14. Ibid., 71.
15. Marquis de Beaucourt, *Captivité,* vol. 1, 309–39.
16. Cléry, *Journal de ce qui s'est passé à la Tour du Temple, par Cléry* (Paris: Editions Jean de Bonnot, 1968), 143.

17. *Arrêté de la section des Gravilliers, comme quoi tout homme qui criera grâce ou qui s'agitera sans considération sera arrêté et conduit en prison*... [Decree of the Gravilliers *section*, on how any man who cries "mercy" or who acts without consideration will be arrested and led to prison . . .], (n.p., n.d.).
18. C. Maugras, ed. *Journal d'un étudiant pendant la Révolution* (Paris, 1910), 316.
19. Arasse, *La Guillotine,* 71–74.
20. *Archives parlementaires,* meeting of January 20, 1793.
21. Ibid.
22. Beaucourt, *Captivité,* vol. 2, 313–14.
23. *Journal des hommes libres de tous les pays* [Newspaper for free men of all countries], January 22, 1793.
24. *Le Journal de Perlet,* January 22, 1793.
25. *Le Républicain,* January 22, 1793.
26. *La Gazette nationale,* January 23, 1793.
27. *Les Révolutions de Paris,* no. 185 (January 19–26, 1793).
28. Beaucourt, *Captivité,* vol. 2, 274–75.
29. Marat, *Journal de la République française,* January 23, 1793.
30. Arasse, *La Guillotine,* 72.
31. *Le Républicain,* January 22, 1793.
32. *Les Révolutions de Paris,* no. 185 (January 19—26, 1793).
33. *Journal de Perlet,* January 22, 1793.
34. *Le Guillotine dans la Révolution,* exhibition catalog. Institut Français de Florence, 1986.
35. *La Guillotine dans la Révolution,* 42.
36. Ibid., 45.
37. Antoine de Baecque, "The Defeat of the Body of the King: Essay on the Impotence of Louis XVI," in *The Body Politic: Corporeal Metaphor in Revolutionary France, 1770—1800,* trans. Charlotte Mandell (Stanford, Calif.: Stanford University Press, 1997).
38. *Sermon civique aux soldats de la République par le citoyen Dorfeuille* [Civic sermon to the soldiers of the Republic by Citizen Dorfeuille], published in the *Archives parlementaires,* meeting of January 23, 1793.
39. *Archives parlementaires,* meeting of 28 Floréal, Year II.
40. Citizen Guirault, *Oraison funèbre de la section du Contrat social* [Funeral oration of the "Contrat social" *section*], published in the *Archives parlementaires,* meeting of January 23, 1793.
41. *Archives parlementaires,* December 25, 1792.
42. Beaucourt, *Captivité,* 317–18.
43. *Le Thermomètre du jour,* February 21, 1793.
44. Louis-Sébastien Mercier, "De la race détrônée" [On race dethroned], in *Le Nouveau Paris* vol. 3 (Paris, 1795), 3–4.
45. *Les Révolutions de Paris,* no. 185 (January 19–26, 1793).

46. François Riou, *Conseil des Cinq-Cents: Discours sur la juste punition du dernier roi des Français* [Council of the Five Hundred: Speech on the just punishment of the last king of the French], 1st Pluviôse, Year V.
47. *Conseil des Cinq-Cents: Discours prononcé par J. Ch. Bailleul avant la prestation du serment de haine à la royauté et à l'anarchie* [Council of the Five Hundred: Speech uttered by J. Ch. Bailleul before the taking of the oath of hatred against royalty and anarchy], meeting of 2 Pluviôse, Year VI.
48. *Le 22 janvier ou la queue du 21* [January 22 or the tail of the 21st], (n.p., Year VII).
49. *Conseil des Anciens: Motion d'ordre prononcée par Pierre Guyomar sur la chute du Trône* [Council of Elders: Motion for order uttered by Pierre Guyomar on the fall of the Throne], 17 Nivôse, Year V.
50. J. F. N. Dusaulchoy, *Hymne pour l'anniversaire de la juste punition du dernier roi des Français* [Hymn for the anniversary of the just punishment of the last king of the French], (Paris, Year V).
51. *Lettre-circulaire de M. François de Neufchâteau à l'occasion de la prestation du serment de haine à la royauté et à l'anarchie* [Circular letter by M. François de Neufchâteau on the occasion of the taking of the oath of hatred against royalty and anarchy], (n.p., n.d.).
52. *Appel à l'honneur français: Sur la fête du 21 janvier* [Call to French honor: On the festival of January 21], (Paris, Year V).
53. Citizen Emmanuel, *Projet de fête pour célébrer dignement la mort de Louis XVI* [Project for a festival to celebrate properly the death of Louis XVI], (n.p., Year V).
54. Antoine de Baecque, "Les Restes Sacrés de Louis XVI, un patrimoine d'expiation," papers from the colloquium *L'Esprit des lieux. Le Patrimoine et la cité*, under the direction of D. Grange and D. Poulot (Grenoble: Presses Universitaires de Grenoble, 1997).
55. Aside from the classic works by Ernst Kantorowicz and by Ralph Giesey, translated into French, the best synthesis on the values of the body of the king of France seems to me the essay by Robert Descimon and Alain Guéry, "La 'monarchie royale,'" *Histoire de la France*, ed. A. Burguière and J. Revel (Paris: Le Seuil, 1989).
56. Antoine de Baecque, "Le Dernier Jour de Louis XVI," *L'Histoire*, January 1995; J. M. Darnis, *Les Monuments expiatoires du supplice de Louis XVI et de Marie-Antoinette sous l'Empire et la Restauration* (Paris, 1981).
57. Chateaubriand, *Mémoires d'outre-tombe*, pt. 1, bk. 5, chap. 8. (Paris: Garnier Frères, 1899–1900).
58. Beaucourt, *Captivité*, 353–69.
59. P. and P. Girault de Coursac, *Louis XVI, un visage retrouvé* (Paris: Ed. de l'oeil, 1990).
60. *Un Episode sous la Terreur* (Paris, 1831); a story collected in the series "Scènes de la vie politique."

61. *La Guillotine dans la Révolution,* catalog of the exhibition at the Institut Français de Florence, 1986.
62. Susan Dunn, *The Deaths of Louis XVI: Regicide and the French Political Imagination* (Princeton, N.J.: Princeton University Press, 1994).
63. See the study by A. Vacquier, *Le Cimetière de la Madeleine et le Sieur Descloseaux* (Paris: Fédération des Sociétés Historiques et Archéologiques de Paris et d'Ile-de-France, 1961).
64. *Liste des personnes qui ont péri par jugement du Tribunal révolutionnaire, depuis le 26 août 1792 jusqu'au 13 juin 1794 (25 prairial an II), et dont les corps ont été inhumés dans le terrain de l'ancien cimetière de la Madeleine, situé rue d'Anjou, Faubourg Saint-Honoré, appartenant à présent à M. Descloseaux, comme on le verra par son certificat ci-joint* [List of the people who have perished under sentence of the Revolutionary Tribunal, from August 26, 1792, to June 13, 1794 (25 Prairial, Year II), and whose bodies were buried in the land of the former Madeleine cemetery, situated on the Rue d'Anjou, Faubourg Saint-Honoré, belonging at present to M. Descloseaux, as one can see from his certificate included here], (n.p., n.d.).
65. The two most well known are the work by Jean-Joseph Regnault-Warin, *Le Cimetière de la Madeleine* (n.p., 1801), and by Willemain d'Abancourt, *Le Cimetière de la Madeleine* (Paris, 1802).
66. Jean-Marie Darnis, op.cit.
67. "Le vingt et un janvier mil huit cent quinze," in *Le Journal des débats,* January 19, 1815.
68. E. L. Barbier, *Notice sur l'exhumation de Leurs Majestés Louis XVI et Marie-Antoinette* (Paris, 1815), 23. See also Chateaubriand, *Mémoires,* pt. 3, bk. 5, chap. 10.
69. *Journal royal,* January 23, 1815, 67.
70. *Eloge funèbre de leurs Majesté Louis XVI et Marie-Antoinette, prononcé en la basilique de Saint-Denis par Monseigneur l'évêque de Troyes* [Funeral oration in praise of Their Majesties Louis XVI and Marie-Antoinette, spoken in the Basilica of Saint-Denis by Monseigneur the Bishop of Troyes], January 21, 1815.
71. A. P. M. Gilbert, *Description historique de l'Église royale de Saint-Denys* [Historical description of the Royal Church of Saint-Denys], at (Saint-Denis, 1815).

GEFFROY; OR, THE FEAR OF OTHERS

1. *Archives Nationales,* W 389, no. 904, item 9.
2. *Archive Nationales,* F(7) 4577.
3. *Archive Nationales,* W 389, no. 904, item 9.
4. Ibid.
5. Daage-Menonval, *Le Crime et la Vertu, ou L'Admiral et Geffroy* [Crime and

Virtue, or L'Admiral and Geffroy], (Rouen, n.d.). The playwright came to give a presentation copy of his play to the Convention on 27 Prairial, Year II.

6. *Archives parlementaires: Recueil complet des débats législatifs et politiques des chambres françaises* [Parliamentary archives: Complete collection of the legislative and political debates of the French chambers], Editions du CNRS, meeting of 15 Prairial, Year II, vol. 9, 287.
7. For a methodological exploration of this, see de Baecque, *The Body Politic,* 1–25.
8. *Archives parlementaires,* meeting of 4 Prairial, Year II, vol. 90, 571–72.
9. *La Feuille de la République* [The Paper of the Republic], no. 325 (6 Prairial, Year II). See also the *Annales de la République française* [Annals of the French Republic], no. 176 (6 Prairial, Year II).
10. *Archives parlementaires,* meeting of 4 Prairial, Year II, vol. 90, 577—83.
11. On this ceremony of the public reading of the bulletin concerning the health of Louis XVI in 1791, see de Baecque, in "The Defeat of the Body of the King: Essay on the Impotence of Louis XVI," *The Body Politic,* 29–75.
12. Mona Ozouf, "La Révolution française et la formation de l'homme nouveau," in *L'Homme régénéré. Essais sur la Révolution française,* 116–57; Bronislaw Baczko, "L'Utopie et l'idée de l'histoire progrès," *Revue des sciences humaines,* no. 155 (1974) 473–91; M. Baridon, "Les Concepts de nature humaine et de perfectibilité dans l'historiographie des Lumières," in the papers of the colloquium *L'Histoire au XVIIIe siècle* (Aix-en-Provence: Publications de l'Université de Provence, 1980), 353–75; A. de Baecque, "Regeneration: The Marvelous Body, or, The Body Raised Upright of the New Revolutionary Man," in *The Body Politic,* 131–56.
13. *Encyclopédie,* article on "Régénération," vol. 13, (1765), 912–13.
14. K. F. Reinhardt, *Le Néologiste français, ou Vocabulaire portatif des mots les plus nouveaux* [The French Neologist, or Portable Vocabulary of the newest words], (Paris, 1796).
15. *Archives parlementaires,* meeting of 18 Floréal, Year II, vol. 90, 132–43.
16. *Archives parlementaires,* meeting of 7 Prairial, Year II, vol. 91, 32–41.
17. O. Blanc, *La Corruption sous la Terreur, 1792–1794* (Paris: Robert Laffont, 1992).
18. Charles-Louis Corbet, *Apostrophe au peuple anglais* [Address to the English people], (n.p., Year II).
19. *Archives parlementaires,* meeting of 7 Prairial, vol. 91, 41–43. It is interesting to compare this speech with the report presented by Saint-Just on 23 Ventôse, Year II, on "The factions from abroad, and on the conspiracy hatched by those factions in the French Republic to destroy the Republic government through corruption and to starve Paris." On the subject of the discourse on foreigners, see S. Wahnich, *L'Impossible citoyen: l'étranger dans le discours de la révolution française* (Paris: Albin Michel, 1997).

20. On Republican martyrs, see Antoine de Baecque, "The Offertory of the Martyrs: The Wounded Body of the Revolution," in *The Body Politic*, 280–307.
21. *Archives parlementaires,* meeting of 5 Prairial, Year II, vol. 90, 583–84.
22. Concerning the justification of the Terror by the struggle against corruption, see especially Albert Mathiez, *La Corruption parlementaire sous la Terreur* (Paris, 1912), and also, by the same author, *Le Bolchevisme et le Jacobinisme* (Paris, 1920).
23. *Archives parlementaires,* meeting of 16 Prairial, Year II, vol. 91, 296 (Surveillance committee of the commune of Givet).
24. *Détail de la véritable marche des cérémonies et de l'ordre à observer dans la fête de l'Être Suprême* [Details on the actual procedure of the ceremonies and on the order to be observed during the festival of the Supreme Being], (Paris, Year II).
25. *Véritable détail de la cérémonie qui doit être célébrée Décadi 20 prairial* [True detail on the ceremony that should be celebrated on Décadi, 20 Prairial], (n.p., n.d.).
26. *Archives parlementaires,* meeting of 27 Messidor, Year II, vol. 93, 212.
27. *Archives parlementaires,* vol. 93, 258.
28. *Archives parlementaires,* vol. 92, 494.
29. *Archives parlementaires,* meeting of 29 Messidor, Year II, 230–32.
30. *Archives parlementaires,* meeting of 27 Prairial, Year II, vol. 91, 663.
31. *Archives parlementaires,* meeting of 13 Prairial, Year II, vol. 91, 201.
32. *Archives parlementaires,* meeting of 22 Prairial, Year II, vol. 91, 476.
33. *Archives parlementaires,* meeting of 18 Prairial, Year II, vol. 91, 375.
34. *Archives parlementaires,* meeting of 25 Prairial, Year II, vol. 91, 577.
35. *Archives parlementaires,* meeting of 19 Prairial, Year II, vol. 91, 413.
36. *Archives parlementaires,* meeting of 17 Prairial, Year II, vol. 91, 321.
37. *Archives Nationales,* F(7) 4577.
38. The documentation of the trial of the fifty-four condemned on 29 Prairial, Year II, has been collected by A. Tuetey in his *Répertoire général des sources manuscrites de l'histoire de Paris pendant la Révolution française* (Paris, 1914), vol. 11, 594–679. A fine study is waiting to be undertaken here on the "fabrication" of the guilty from the detailed and profuse "proofs of guilt."
39. *Archives parlementaires,* meeting of 5 Prairial, Year II, vol. 90, 608.
40. *Archives parlementaires,* meeting of 11 Prairial, Year II, vol. 91, 133.
41. *Archives parlementaires,* meeting of 12 Prairial, Year II, vol. 91, 163.
42. *Archives parlementaires,* meeting of 14 Prairial, Year II, vol. 91, 232.
43. *Archives parlementaires,* meeting of 21 Prairial, Year II, vol. 91, 440.
44. *Archives parlementaires,* meeting of 6 Prairial, Year II, vol. 90, 635.
45. *Archives parlementaires,* meeting of 6 Prairial, Year II, vol. 90, 628.
46. *Archives parlementaires,* meeting of 29 Prairial, Year II, vol. 91, 685.
47. *Archives parlementaires,* meeting of 10 Messidor, Year II, vol. 92, 247–248.
48. *Le Journal de la Montagne,* no. 65, dated 13 Messidor, Year II, gives a detailed account of the reception ceremony for Geffroy into the Club des Jacobins.

ROBESPIERRE; OR, THE TERRIBLE TABLEAU

1. Gérard Walter, *La Conjuration du neuf thermidor* (Paris: Gallimard, 1974), recalls the essential facts and leaves the rest to the reference books. For the immediate political interpretation of the event, see Françoise Brunel, *Thermidor: La Chute de Robespierre* (Brussels: Complexe, 1989).
2. This is the thesis that Jean Thorel supports in *La Fin de Robespierre* (n.p., 1975): the bullet from the gendarme Merda's pistol may have struck Robespierre at the instant that Robespierre was attempting suicide with his own pistol.
3. On the body as "political form," see de Baecque, *The Body Politic*.
4. Merlin de Thionville, *Capet et Robespierre* (n.p., n.d.). Some attribute this portrait to Roederer. See also the book by Louis Jacob, *Robespierre vu par ses contemporains* (Paris, 1938).
5. The most recent work on the Terror (stemming from a colloquium held at Stanford in December 1992) advances a good number of these complementary and contradictory interpretations: Keith Baker and Colin Lucas, eds. *The Terror,* vol. 4 of the collection *The French Revolution and Modern Political Culture* (Oxford: Pergamon Press, 1994).
6. *Le Cri de la vengeance* [The Cry for revenge], (n.p., n.d.).
7. *Le Tombeau des vivants* [The Tomb of the living], (n.p., n.d.).
8. *Robespierre aux enfers. Pour faire suite au dialogue entre Marat et Robespierre* [Robespierre in Hell. As a continuation of the dialogue between Marat and Robespierre], (n.p., n.d.).
9. Edme Bonaventure Courtois, *Rapport fait au nom des comités de salut public et de sûreté générale, sur les événements du 9 thermidor an II* [Report made in the name of the Committees of Public Safety and of General Security, on the events of 9 Thermidor, Year II], National Convention, on 8 Thermidor, Year III.
10. See the edition formed under the direction of Jean-Claude Bonnet, *Tableau de Paris* (Paris: Mercure de France, 1994).
11. A. C. Thibaudeau, *Le 9 thermidor* (n.p., n.d.).
12. Portiez de l'Oise, *Le 9 thermidor* (n.p., n.d.).
13. *Nouveaux et intérressants détails de l'horrible conspiration de Robespierre* [New and interesting details of the horrible conspiracy of Robespierre] (Paris, n.d.).
14. Quoted by Hector Fleischmann, *Le Masque mortuaire de Robespierre* (Paris, 1911).
15. *Histoire de la conjuration de Maximilien Robespierre* [History of the conspiracy of Maximilien Robespierre], by Galart de Montjoye, (n.p., n.d.).
16. *Faits recueillis aux derniers instants de Robespierre et de sa faction* [Facts collected at the final instants of Robespierre and his faction], (n.p., n.d.).
17. *Nouveaux et intéressants détails.*
18. Edme Bonaventure Courtois, *Rapport fait au nom de la commission chargée de l'examen des papiers trouvés chez Robespierre* [Report made in the name of the

commission appointed to examine the papers found at Robespierre's house], by Courtois, National Convention, 16 Nivôse, Year III.

19. Roux, *Relation de l'événement du 10 thermidor* [Account of the event on 10 Thermidor], (n.p., n.d.).
20. *Faits recueillis.*
21. L. Duperron, *Vie secrète, politique et curieuse de M.J. Maximillien Robespierre* [Secret, political and curious life of M.J. Maximillien Robespierre], (Paris, Year II).
22. *Faits recueillis,* see also the *Rapport des médecins Vergez et Marrigues, médecins et chirurgiens militaires, sur l'état des blessures de Robespierre* [Report of Doctors Vergez and Marrigues, military doctors and surgeons, on the state of Robespierre's wounds], text included in the edition of the first report by Courtois.
23. *La Journée du 9 thermidor* [The Day 9 Thermidor], (n.p., n.d.).
24. *Robespierre peint par lui-même et condamné par ses propres principes* [Robespierre portrayed by himself and condemned by his own principles], (n.p., n.d.).
25. *Portraits exécrables du traître Robespierre et de ses complices, tenus par les furies, avec leurs crimes et forfaits que l'on découvre* [Execrable portrayals of the traitor Robespierre and his accomplices, held by the Furies, with their crimes and infamies discovered], (n.p., n.d.).
26. Germaine de Staël, *Considérations sur les principaux événements de la Révolution française* [Considerations on the principal events of the French Revolution], (Paris: Delunay, 1818) vol.2, 133.
27. Quoted in Jacob, *Robespierre vu par ses contemporains.*
28. Hippolyte Taine, *Les Origines de la France contemporaine* (Paris: Robert Laffont, Coll. Bouquins, 1988), vol. 2, 125.
29. P. J. F. N. de Barras, *Mémoires de Barras* (1831), vol. 1, 147–51.
30. Courtois, *Rapport fait au nom de la commission.*
31. On the analysis of these images of Thermidor, see the innovative work by Ewa Lajer-Burcharth, "The Aesthetics of Male Crisis: The Terror in the Republican Imagery and in David's Work from Prison," in *Femininity and Masculinity in Eighteenth Century Art and Culture,* ed. Gill Perry and Michael Rossington (Manchester: Manchester University Press, 1994), 219–43.
32. Jean-Joseph Dussault, *Les Nouvelles Politiques,* 13 Thermidor, Year II; quoted in Jacob, *Robespierre vu par ses contemporains.*
33. Three authoritative works on the "question of the Terror" in political Thermidorian thinking are: the work by Mona Ozouf, "De thermidor à brumaire: Le Discours de la Révolution sur elle-même," *Revue historique*, 1970, 31–66; Ozouf, "Thermidor ou le travail de l'oubli," in *L'École de la France* (Paris: Gallimard, 1984); Ozouf, "The Terror after the Terror: An Immediate History," in Baker and Lucas, *The Terror,* 3–18; Bronislaw Baczko, *Comment sortir de la Terreur. Thermidor et la Révolution* (Paris: Gallimard, 1989); Françoise Brunel, "Bridging the Gulf of the Terror," in Baker and Lucas, *The Terror.*

34. *Testament de Maximilien Robespierre*... (n.p., n.d.).
35. Bronislaw Baczko, "Robespierre Roi ... ," in *Comment sortir de la Terreur.*
36. Bronislaw Baczko, "La Fin de l'an II," and "L'Horreur à l'ordre du jour," in *Comment sortir de la Terreur.*
37. Méhée de la Touche, *La Queue de Robespierre, ou les dangers de la liberté de la presse* [The Tail of Robespierre, or the dangers of freedom of the press], (Paris, 9 Fructidor, Year II). On this text, read M. Biard, "Après la tête, la queue! La rhétorique antijacobine en fructidor an II-Vendémiaire an III," in *Actes du 120th congrès national des sociétés savantes* (Aix-en-Provence, 1995), devoted to *L'an III*, published in 1997 by the CTHS, 201–13.
38. Ange Pitou, *La Queue, la tête et le front de Robespierre* [The Tail, the head and the forehead of Robespierre], (n.p., n.d.).
39. Quoted by Walter, *La Conjuration,* 428.
40. *Réponse à la Queue de Robespierre* [Answer to the Tail of Robespierre], (n.p., n.d.).
41. *Plan de conduite pour tous les anneaux de la queue* [Plan of conduct for all the rings of the tail], (n.p., n.d.).
42. Godineau, *La Mort de Robespierre* [The Death of Robespierre], (n.p., Year II).
43. Antoine Sérieys, *La Mort de Robespierre* (n.p., n.d.).
44. The most detailed study on the death masks of Robespierre is Fleischmann, *Le Masque mortuaire de Robespierrre.*
45. Quoted by Hippolyte Buffenoir, *Portraits de Robespierre* (Paris, 1882).
46. Ernest Hamel, *Histoire de Robespierre* vol. 3 (Paris, 1867).
47. Two contemporary French writers are working to this day on Robespierre, the playwright Gilles Aillaud and the novelist Pierre Michon.
48. Jean-Philippe Domecq, *Robespierre, derniers temps* (Paris: Le Seuil, 1984), adapted to dramatic form by Pierre Béziers, *Un Robespierre de papier* (Lyon: Éditions de l'Aube, 1989); Gilles Aillaud, *Le Masque de Robespierre* (Chrisian Bourgois, 1996), play directed by Jean Jourdheuil, premiered at the Théâtre National de Strasbourg on January 9, 1996.

MADAME NECKER; OR, THE POETRY OF THE CORPSE

1. M. Gambier-Parry, *Madame Necker* (London: Blackwood, 1913); A. Corbaz, *Madame Necker* (Paris: Payot, 1945); P. Kohler, *Madame de Staël et ses amis; Au château de Coppet* (Lausanne: spes, 1929).
2. *Mélanges des manuscrits de Madame Necker* (Paris, 1798).
3. *Mélanges des manuscrits*; *Nouveaux mélanges de Madame Necker* (Paris, 1801); *Esprit de Madame Necker,* (Paris: M. Barère, 1808).
4. *Mélanges des manuscrits.*
5. Quoted by P. Deschambre, *Dictionnaire encyclopédique des sciences médicales* (Paris, 1876), 337.

6. M. Foucault, *Naissance de la clinique, une archéologie du regard médical* (Paris: PUF, 1972).
7. Madame Necker, *Hospice de charité* (Paris, 1780).
8. Leopold de Berchtold, *Projet pour prévenir les dangers très fréquents des inhumations précipitées. Distribué gratis pour le bien de l'humanité* [Project to prevent the very frequent dangers of premature burials. Distributed gratis for the good of humanity], (Paris, 1791).
9. J. B. Davis, *Projet de règlement concernant les décès, précédé de réflexions sur l'abus des enterrements précipités et sur l'incertitude des signes de la mort* [Project for regulating decease, preceded by reflections on the malpractice of premature burials and on the uncertainty of signs of death], (Verdun, 1806).
10. *Catalogue des sciences médicales* (Paris, 1857), vol. 1, 522–25.
11. T. Todorov, *Introduction à la littérature fantastique* (Paris: Le Seuil, 1970); F. Flahault, *L'Interprétation des contes* (Paris: Denoël, 1988).
12. H. Le Guern, *Rosaline, ou les mystères de la tombe: Recueil historique d'événements nécessitant qu'on prenne des précautions pour bien constater l'intervalle qui peut s'écouler entre la mort imparfaite et la mort absolue* [Rosaline, or the mysteries of the tomb: Historical collection of events that necessitate precautions to make certain of the interval that can occur between incomplete death and absolute death], (Paris, n.d.).
13. Philippe Ariès, *L'Homme devant la mort* (Paris: Le Seuil, 1985), vol. 2, 113.
14. M. Pineau, *Mémoire sur le danger des inhumations précipités, et sur la nécessité d'un règlement pour mettre les citoyens à l'abri du malheur d'être enterrés vivants* [Essay on the danger of premature burials, and on the necessity of a regulation to protect citizens from the misfortune of being buried alive], (Niort, n.d.).
15. M. B. Durande, *Mémoire sur l'abus de l'ensevelissement des morts* [Essay on abuses in the burial of the dead], (Strasbourg, 1789).
16. Theiry, *La vie de l'homme respectée et défendue dans ses derniers moments, ou instructions sur les soins qu'on doit faire aux morts et à ceux qui paraissent l'être, sur les funérailles et les sépultures* [The life of man respected and defended in his final moments, or instructions on the precautions that must be taken with the dead and those who seem to be so, on funerals and burials], (Paris, 1787).
17. Marin Bunoust, *Vues philanthropiques sur l'abus des enterrements précipités. Précautions à prendre pour que les vivants ne soient pas confondus avec les morts* [Philanthropic views on the abuses of premature burials. Precautions to be taken so that the living not be confused with the dead], (Arras, n.d.).
18. M. Janin, *Réflexions sur le triste sort des personnes qui sous une apparence de mort ont été enterrées vivantes, et sur les moyens qu'on doit mettre en usage pour prévenir une telle méprise* [Reflections on the sad fate of people who under the appearance of death have been buried alive, and on the means that should be put into effect to prevent such a mistake], (The Hague, 1772).

19. *Mémoire sur le danger d'être enterré vif, et sur les moyens de s'en garantir ou de s'en tirer* [Reflections on the danger of being buried alive, and on the means of protecting oneself or escaping from it], (n.p. 1787).
20. H. G. du Faÿ, *Des vols d'enfants et des inhumations d'individus vivants. Suivi d'un aperçu pour l'établissement des salles mortuaires* [On the abductions of children and on burials of living individuals. Followed by an argument for the establishment of mortuary rooms], (Paris, n.d.).
21. Janin, *Terrible supplice et cruel désespoir des personnes enterrés vivantes et qui sont présumées mortes* [Terrible torture and cruel despair of people buried alive and who are presumed dead], (Paris, 1782).
22. *Des inhumations précipitées* [On premature burials], (Paris, 1790), 19.
23. Quoted by the Comte d'Haussonville, *Le Salon de Madame Necker* (Paris, 1882), 132.
24. Quoted by d'Haussonville, *Salon,* 290.
25. Germaine de Staël, *Correspondance générale de Madame de Staël,* (Paris: J. J. Pauvert, 1979), vol. 3, pt. 1, 2.
26. Quoted by Corbaz, *Madame Necker,* 183.
27. Ariès, *L'Homme,* 115–18.
28. *Esprit de Madame Necker,* 205.
29. Ibid., 296–97.
30. Ibid., 322–23.
31. Ibid., 297–98.
32. Ibid., 320–21.
33. Madame Necker's will was published in part in Germaine de Staël, notes to the *Notice sur M. Necker,* (n.p., 1804), 228–32.
34. De Staël, *Correspondance générale,* 1-2.
35. De Staël, *Notice sur M. Necker,* 227.
36. D'Haussonville, *Salon,* 288.
37. Quoted in *Le Mercure de France,* March 15, 1927.
38. Quoted in *L'Intermédiaire des chercheurs et des curieux,* no. 1662 (April 10, 1927).
39. D'Haussonville, *Salon,* 299.
40. Quoted by Corbaz, *Madame Necker,* 218.
41. *Gazette de Lausanne,* August 6, 1817, quoted by Kohler, *Au Château,* 94.

INDEX

Acadmy of Painting competition (1793), 1–4
  death of Brutus subject, 2
Actes des apôtres, 22
Aillaud, Gilles, 171
Albion, as source of foreign money, 130
d'Alembert, 40
  critique of Voltaire's statue, 51
Annales de la République français, 106
Anticlericalism in Paris (1791), 38
Arasse, Daniel, 100
Ariès, Philippe, 12, 186, 196
d'Artois, Comte, 89
  green livery as Royalist emblem, 7
"Austrian committee" idea, 74, 75

Babeuf, François Noël, 169
Bachaumont, L. P. de, 81
Bailleul, 108
Balzac, Honoré de, 114
Barère, Bertrand, 28, 90, 124–125
  and concept of the "corrupt," 129, 130
  use of Geffroy's "martyrdom," 139
Barnave, Antoine, 15, 30
  representative to Mirabeau, 18
de Barras, Paul Vicomte, 159
Barruel, Abbé, 75
Barry, Mme du, 76
Basire, Claude, 66
Beaujon hospital, 181
de Berchtold, Count Leopold, 184, 193
Bernard, Jean, 166
Berther, 65
Billaud-Varenne, Jean-Nicolas, as accomplice of the tyrant, 161, 162, 165
Blanzy, 79
Blood
  as good-luck charm, 106
  symbolism in death of Louis XVI, 111–112
Boiston, Philippe, bust of Brutus, 2
Bretonne, Rétif de la, 79
Brissot, 19, 29
  response to Mirabeau's funeral, 32–33
Brizard, Gabriel, 38, 39, 73
de Broglie, Duc, 202
Brugnon, 45
Bruhier, Jacques-Jean, 185, 190
Brutus, Lucius Junius
  law above all, 1
  as Lepeletier symbol, 3
  tutelary figure for Republicans, 2
Buffenoir, Hippolyte, 166, 168
de Buffon, Comte, 178, 198–199
Burke, Edmund, 69

Cabanis, Pierre Jean George, 15, 18
  description of Mirabeau's condition, 23, 33
  idea of pathology of political engagement, 24–25
Calas, Jean, daughters in Voltaire ceremony, 53
Capet, Louis
  burial debate, 97
  as common name of Louis XVI, 89

not a "monument," 98
Capucins/Capucines, 38
Carmelites/Discalced Carmelites, 38
Carra, 74
Cellerier, Jacques, 50
Chabot, 97
Chabroud, 45
Chambon, 94
Champ de la Fédération, patriotic catacombs, 29, 45
Charlat, 62
Charles X, 119
Charlier, 124, 156
Charron
and transfer of Voltaire's body, 46, 49
and Voltaire "relic," 46
Chateaubriand, and political sense of Louis XVI's exhumation, 118
Chénier, Marie-Joseph, hymn of Voltaire, 54
Chronique de Paris, 38, 44, 49, 52, 72
Cistercians, 38, 41
Citoyen français, 46
Clermont, Mademoiselle de, 77
Cléry, 92, 94, 95
relics of Louis XVI, 113
Cloots, Anarchasis, 38
Cochin hospital, 181
Collot d'Herbois, Jean-Marie
as accomplice of the tyrant, 161, 162, 165, 169
assassination attempt, 121–122
and Geffroy at Convention, 141
temporary closure, 142
testimony, 126–127
Combet, Louis, 168, 169
de Comps, 23
Condorcet, 40
Constituent Assembly, importance of Mirabeau, 16
de Corbeville, Madame, 193
Corbin, Alain, 11
Corday, Charlotte
green hat, 7
Marat's assassin, 6
Cordeliers, 38
Corpse; *see also* Funeral parlor concept
apparent death/fear of premature burial, 184–187, 191–192
of Brutus portrait as interpretation of the Terror, 9–10
central role of in rituals of the French Revolution, 8
corpses as sacrificial rites, 66–67
symbolism of, 8–9
dissection and study of, 175
and embalming, 196–197
of Princesse de Lamballe
a *cosa mentale*, 64
procession to declare guilt, 63
as royal denaturation substitute, 70
symbolism of decapitation, 75–76
of Louis XVI
and history of nineteenth century, 119
inflated narratives, 104–106
influence on Royalists, 112–113
made commonplace, 96
Royalist concerns for, 115
as metaphor for conspiracy, 69
Mirabeau's (interpretations of), 22
of Madame Necker, her focus on, 176, 197
of Robespierre; *see also* Robespierrist poetics
apocryphal will, 160–162
cadaverization prior to his death, 154–155, 159
emblematic and metonymic qualities, 153
rapid disappearance of, 151, 164
"spectacle of horror," 151–152
tableau of the Terror, 149–150
"tail"/obscene pamphlets, 161–165
savage inner life and mastery conflict, 12
of September massacre victims, 67
symbolic and political functions, 68–69
as a state of the body, 183–184
taboo in public sphere from Directory onward, 11

"visions" of corpses/curiosities, 11–12
of Voltaire
as bodily proof of his values' glory, 47
as physical sign of new vs. Ancien Régime, 41
symbolism of in reburial ceremony, 50
Courtois, 159
Courtois, Edme Bonaventure, 148
Couthon, Georges, 125, 127, 139, 145
Curchod, Suzanne; *see* Necker, Madame
Curtius, 167

Damoureau, Vicar, 97
Danjou, 115, 116
Danton, 90, 125, 130, 148
mastiff's head, 158
David, Jacques-Louis
admiration for Brutus, 1, 2
decoration of Voltaire's reburial chariot, 50
influence in painting competition, 4
Lepeletier, 5, 7
Lepeletier's funeral ceremony, 6
Marat, 5, 7
Marat's funeral ceremony, 5–6
students and "dying athlete genre," 3
Davis, Jean-Baptiste, 184
Dayot, Armand, 167
Delorme, 80
Descartes, R., consideration for "Temple of great men," 37, 45
Descaves, Lucien, 166
Descloseaux, 115
and Louis XVI's remains, 115–116
Desmeunier, 28
Desmoulins, Camille
in imagery of "cage of Robespierre," 148
praise of de Villette, 37
response to Mirabeau's funeral/death, 32, 33
Despréménil, Jean-Jacques, 30
Détournelle, Athanase, defender of Guérin, 5
Diderot, Denis, 149
Dietrich, August, 168
Dillon, Comtesse de, 77, 78
Directory, and commemoration of Louis XVI's execution, 109–110
Domecq, Jean-Philippe, 170–172
Dominicans, 38
Don Juan, defiant death, 42
Dorfeuille, Citizen, 103
Dreux-Brézé, and Mirabeau, 15
Dubois-Crancé, Edmond, 28
Duc d'Orléans, witness to dismembered Princesse de Lamballe, 63
Duclos, 178
Dumas, 137
Dusaulchoy, 109
Dussault, 160
Duval, Amaury, 1
"Dying athlete" genre, 3
Dying philosopher myth, 42

d'Eglantines, Fabre, 125
Elisabeth, Mme, 92
Executions
guillotine as device of the Enlightenment, 63–64
public massacres during Revolution, 64

Fère, 65
Fermont, 30
de Fersen, Count Axel von, 70
Feuillants, 15, 38
Feuille du jour, 48, 49
de Firmont, Abbé Edgeworth, 92, 95, 113
First (1st) Pluviôse celebration, 107–108
Fleischmann, Hector, 166, 168, 170
Foucault, Michel, 63
Foulon, Joseph-François, 65
Fouquier-Tinville, Antoine, 139
Fourcroy, 27
Franciscans, 38
François, Henri, 93
French Republic
fable of origins/oath over a corpse, 3

archetype of Louis XVI's bloody head, 100–101
foundational sacrifice of Louis XVI, 91, 96, 99
baptismal value, 100
"hatred of kings" emotion, 98
no public proclamation, 87
Frochot, Nicolas, 18
Funeral parlor concept
"house of exhibition" (Count de Berchtold), 184
"Necrodocium" (Davis), 184
"special house" (Dr. Thiery), 183–184
vs. fear of "premature burial," 184–186
"Waiting Chamber" (Mme Necker), 183
Funeral practices
embalming, 196
of the Enlightenment
and distancing from the dead, 10
and guillotine, 63
and macabre in literature, 10
resumption after the Directory, 11
of the revolutionary community, 29–31
Roman, 189

Gamain, François, 103
Gance, Abel, 169
Garat, 92
Gautier, stories of Voltaire's corpse, 48
Gazette nationale, 98
Geffroy-*effroi*, 140
Convention speech, 140–141
cult of, 122, 132–133
examples, 133–135
main function, 136
"martyrdom" to "family values" transition, 142
shooting, 121
political use of, 123–126
symbolism
martyr's body and national body, 135–136
regeneration vs. corruption struggle, 130
wound importance, 126, 129
as miracle, 127
physical regeneration, 127, 137–138
and "regeneration" of society, 127–128
Genlis, Mme de, 77
Gibbon, Edward, 177
Gillray, James, 69
Godineau, 166
Gorsas, Antoine Joseph, 51
Gossec, François-Joseph, 54
Gossin, 40
Goupil, 29
Green color, as Royalist emblem, 7
Griepenkerl, Robert, 168
Grimm, 40
Grison, 62
Grouvelle, 92
Guérin, Pierre-Narcisse, 4
politics, 7
runner up in painting competition
Brutus' corpse as echo of Marat's, 5
corpse depiction vs. rules of decorum, 7
nightmare goal, 8
vs. Harriet's depiction of corpse, 4–5
Guillotin, Dr., 63
Guillotine
and equality of executions, 91, 96
vs. living death of Robespierre, 156
Guyomar, Pierre, 108, 109

Hamel, Ernest, 166, 167
Hamerling, Robert, 168
Hanriot, 145
Harriet
painting competition winner, 4
depiction of corpse, 4
d'Haussonville, Comte, 201
Hébert, 92, 99, 126, 130
Hervelin, Jacques-Charles, 65, 75
Histoire romaine, 2
Houdon, Jean-Antoine
statue of Voltaire, 50, 51
use as body double, 54

Hydra, as symbol of royalist resurgency, 162, 170

Isnard, Maximin, 108–109

Jacob, Jean, 48
Jacobins, 38
  and "regeneration," 129
Janin, 191
Jansenists, and Voltaire's death, 42, 58
Jourdheuil, Jean, 171
Journal de la maladie et de la mort d'Honoré-Gabriel-Victor Riquetti de Mirabeau, 24–25
Journal de la République française, 96
Journal de la société républicaine des arts, 5
Journal de Perlet, 98, 100, 152
Journal des hommes libres de tous les pays, 98
Le Journal français, 104

Keravenant, Abbé de, 93

La Harpe, 40
Lacoste, Elie, 137, 141
Lajuinais, 58
Lally-Tollendal, Marquis de, 20–21
Lamarck, Cheralies de, 18
Lamballe, Princesse de
  career as courtier, 71, 72–73, 76–77
  death/dismemberment of, 9, 12, 61
    as a *cosa mentale*, 64
    differing descriptions, 65–66, 76
    final toilette, 79
    heart references, 75
    political justifications, 67–68
    procession to declare guilt, 63
    procession to Marie-Antoinette, 61, 62, 63, 79–80
    radical symbolism, 68–69, 75–76
    and Royalist narrative, 69–70
    and sexuality, 83–84
  feminine pathology, 81
  friendship with Marie-Antoinette, 71, 72–73, 76–77
    lesbian conspiracy rumors, 82–83
    "slave" of queen, 78
    superintendent of the Petit Trianon, 7–78
  pallor, 80
  paper war, 73–74
  representation as a conspirator, 72
  trial of, 61–62
  vapors, 80–81
    and charlatan cures, 81
Lameth, Alexandre de, 23–24
Lameth, Charles de, 21, 23
L'Amiral, 121, 137, 139–140
Lanjuinais, 45
L'Apothéose de Voltaire, 58
Le Chepelier, 30
Le Guern, Dr. H., 186
Lebas, 145
Lebrun, 92
Leclere, George Louis, 178
Legras, 137
Legros, 93, 95
Lejay, 20
Lemaire, A.F., "relic" of Voltaire, 46
Lenoir, 115
Lepeletier de St. Fargeau, Louis-Michel, 3
  assassination, 93, 102
  depiction by David, 5
  funeral ceremony, 6
Lettre aux commettants, 21
Louis, Antoine, 187
Louis XV, friend of Princesse de Lamballe, 76
Louis XVI
  death, 9, 95–96
    archetype for Republic, 100–101
    burial debate, 97
    celebration day of, 107–108
    counter-ritual, 92, 93
    equality of execution, 91–91
    as founding rite of first Republic, 87
    inflated narratives of, 104–106
    preparations for execution, 94–95
    as a radical "non-event," 98
    support for by Montagnards, 90–91
    symbolic importance of, 110

exhumation, 116–117
reburial, 118–119
leaving the Tuileries, 88
"Louis the last," 87
metamorphosis of public image, 103
pamphlet/cartoon attacks, 57
pig's head symbolism, 110–111
relics, 113
and reconstitution of royal identity, 114
ritual of humiliation, 89–90
secret correspondence with Mirabeau, 30
trial, 90
visit to Champ-de-Mars, 29
Louis XVIII, 116

Mably, 45
Marat, Jean-Paul, 3
depiction by David, 5
depiction by Guérin, 4–5
depiction by Harriet, 4
eagle's head, 158
funeral/arrangement of corpse, 6
glory and terror juxtaposition, 7–8
leprosy, 6
on Louis XVI's execution, 96, 99
response to Mirabeau's funeral/death, 32, 33
Marie-Antoinette
exhumation of, 116
narratives of her anti-French sentiments, 73–74
Petit Trianon, and position of Princesse de Lamballe, 77
rumors of lesbian conspiracy, 82–83
witness to dismembered Princesse de Lamballe, 63, 74–75
Marie-Thérèse, Empresse, 77, 78
Marmontel, 178
Martyrology as History, 123
Masuyer, 103
Mathiez, Albert, 166
Meister, Henri, 200
Mélingue, Lucien, 166
Mercandier, E. Roch, 84
Mercier, Louis-Sébastien, 6, 105, 149
writings on Westminster Abbey, 38
de Mercy-Argenteau, Comte, 77, 78
Merda, Charles-André, 145, 147
Mesmer, Franz, 81
Meudon, human skin tanning, 12
Michelet, Jules, 61
view of massacre of Princesse de Lamballe, 64
Mignot, Abbé, 41
Mirabeau, Honoré-Gabriel-Victor Riquetti de
charisma, 15
corpse interpretations, 22
as pathology of conspiracy, 23–24
as Patriot martyr, 24–25
as scandal of the flesh, 22–23
correspondence with Louis XVI, 30
criticism of private vs. public life, 21–22
as first "Great Man" of the Revolution, 9, 15
funeral ceremony, 28, 31–32
pantheonization, 30
"Letter on public denunciation," 20
lion's head, 158
political aspect of death of, 33
as a politician, 16
public autopsy, 25–26
ceremony, 26–27
report distribution, 27–28
public death, 9, 17
his participation in, 18
and paper war, 16–17
and revolutionary transparency, 19
public vs. private domain, 33–34
and the Terror, 66
Monarchy
and death of Louis XVI, 91
restoration of corpse, 118–119
tales of martyrdom, 93, 113, 114–115
and ideas about the royal person, 90, 96
properties of royal blood, 102
The Montagnard, 90–91

Montesquieu, 45
Montlausier, 30
Morellet, 178
The Morgue, 11
Mort de Robespierre, 166

Necker Hospital, 181
Necker, Jacques, 178, 195–196, 201–202, 203
Necker, Madame, 175
  the body (observation/regulation)
    corpse as state of the body, 183
    as new religion, 177
  and Buffon's death, 198–199
  domestic rules, 176–177
    as examples reason, 175
    "seven relationships," 180
  focus on her own death, 9, 193–194
    as "beautiful" corpse, 197–198, 200
    detailed steps, 195–196, 201–202
    as examples of imagination, 176
  interest in her body, self-perception as invalid, 178–180
  interest in her daughter, 180–181
  interest in public hygiene, 181–183
    innovation of medical record, 182
  on premature burials, 188–189, 193
    inner vs. *outer* death, 188
  reason vs. imagination, 175
  salon, 178
  "Waiting Chamber" (funeral parlor), 184
Le Néologiste français, 128

l'Oise, Bourdon de, 103
l'Oise, Portiez de, 149
Orgie et testament de Mirabeau, 22

Palloy, 39
Paré, Ambroise, 128
Parisau, story of Voltaire's death/corpse, 48–49
Patoret, 29–30
Patriote français, 19, 32–33
"Patriotic Catacombs," 29, 45
Pelletier, Jean-Baptiste, 121
de Penthièvre, Duc, 62, 76
Petit-Manin, 80
Philippeaux, 103
Picpus, 38
Pigalle, Jean-Baptiste, hyperrealistic statue of Voltaire, 51
Pineau, Dr., 189
Pitou, Ange, 163
Pitt, and assassination fears in France, 122, 133
Pointal, Citizen, 65
Polignac, Comtesse, 77, 78
Pope Pius VI, 56
Portalis, Jean Étienne Marie, 15
Pouget, 65
Prudhomme, Louis Marie, 57, 106

Quai de Voltaire
  corpse return, 55
  creation of, 38–39

Raynal, 178
Réception de Louis Capet aux enfers, 101
Récit de la Révolution de Rome, 2
Récollets, 38
Réflexions sur la fête du 21 janvier, 108–109
Regeneration concept, 127–128
  in political vocabulary, 128–129
  and symbolic use of Geffroy's wound, 130
  vs. "corrupt," 129
Regnault, Cécile, 137, 139
Regnault, Jean-Baptiste, 4
Relation des derniers instats de Louis Capet, 105
Le Républicain, 98, 100
Reubell, Jean-François, 110
Révolutions de Paris, 71, 99, 100, 106–107
de Ribbing, Comte Adolphe, 194
Riou, François, 107
Rituals of the French Revolution
  corpse in central role, 8

relics from Voltaire/sanctification phenomenon, 46
Robespierre, Maximilien, 30
apocryphal will, 160–161
association with royalty rumors, 162
cadaverization, 153–154
"cage of" image, 148
call for Louis XVI's death, 91
cat's head, 158
and the "corrupt," 129–131, 142
death
accounts of, 146–147, 151
the agony of the Incorruptible, 145–146, 150
"divine justice" of, 157
double interpretation, 152–153
execution, 146
mask, 150, 167
preparations, 150–151
suicide or murder victim, 145
tyrant turned corpse, 9, 147
written vs. visual images, 147–148
description of Louis XVI's execution, 101
and Geffroy's wounds, 139
and Montagnards, 90
plots against him, 122
premonitions of his death, 159
psychopathological portrait of, 157–159
"tail of," 161–165
Robespierrist poetics, 167, 170–172
academic networks, 166–167
theater, 165–166, 167–169
La Rochefoucauld, 29
Roederer, 88
Rolland, Romain, 168–169
Rollin, Charles, 2
Rousseau, Jean-Jacques
consideration for "Temple of great men," 37, 45
Émile, 180
Roussel, 65
Royale, Mme, 92
Royalist narrative
of Louis XVI's death, 114–115
and conservation of royal heritage, 116
of Princesse de Lamballe's death, 70
Ruault, Nicolas, 31, 46, 52
Ruffin, 137
Rumsard, 168

"Saint Guillotine," 8
Saint-Just, Mérard de, 38, 145
Saint-Priest, Comte de, 20
Sainte-Genevieve, 30
Sanson, Henri, 93, 105
Santé hospital, 181
Santerre, General, 90, 95
Sardou, Victorien, 167
Saussure, 198
Savoie-Carignan, Marie-Thérèse-Louise de; *see* Lamballe (Princesse de)
Seiffert, 81
Sélis, Nicolas, 42
September massacres, and language, 66–67, 80
Sérieys, Antoine, 166
Servan, 21
Sèze, Raymond de, 90
Shelley, Mary, 191
Society of Friends of the Constitution, and Mirabeau's death, 18
Sombreuil, Mlle de, blood-drinking, 12
de Staël, Germaine, 157, 175
burial, 202–203
education, 180–181
on her mother's burial plans, 194–195, 200
Suard, 178

Taine, Hippolyte, 69, 158
Talleyrand, Charles-Maurice de, 18, 28–29
in scandalous tale of Mirabeau, 22
Tallien, Jean Lambert, 149
"Temple of French Genius," 45
"Temple of great men," considerations, 37
The Terror
decapitation symbolism, 75–76

documentary archives of proofs and wounds, 123–124
and idea of "the mass," 66
narrative of martyrdom, 123
and portraits of corpses, 9–10
and the "Republican monster" image, 69
as revolutionary sacrifices, 67
and struggle against "corruption," 131–132
tableau of and corpse of Robespierre, 149–150
and wounding of Geffroy, 122, 132, 136
reparation demands, 138–139
Tertullian, 102
La Tête ou l'oreille de cochon, 110
Thermomètre du jour, 105
Thibaudeau, Comte Antoine-Claire, 149
Thiery, Dr., 183–184
Thionville, Merlin de, 146, 150, 157–158
Thomas, 178
Thuriot, as accomplice of the tyrant, 161, 162
Tirceux, 65
Tissot, Auguste, 177, 182, 195
de la Touche, Méhée, 162, 163
Trahison découverte, 21
Transparency
Mirabeau and talent, 19, 33–34
dreamed transparency of corpse, 24–25
public vs. private life, 20–21
shameful transparency of corpse, 22–24
Tronchin, Dr. Theodore, 42, 43, 177, 178, 182
Tussaud, Madame, 167

Vadier, Marc-Guillaume, as accomplice of the tyrant, 161, 162
Varicourt, Mlle de, 39
Vergniaud, Pierre Victurnien, 88
Vermenoux, Madame, 177
Vermond, Abbé de, 77
Vesalius, 185
Vieuzac, Bertrand Barère de, 123
Villeneuve, famous engraving, 101, 102
Villette, Marquis Charles de la
disciple of Voltaire, 39, 58
homages to Voltaire, 37–38, 40, 47
and plan to transfer his remains, 44
rejection of Voltaire's physical double, 51
in scandalous tale of Mirabeau, 22
and Voltaire's embalming, 46
Voltaire, Marie-François Arouet
admiration for Brutus, 1, 2
Brutus, 44, 50
death, 9, 40
and concealed burial, 41
in fictional pamphlets, 42
"fine" vs. "horrible," 41–42, 43
exhumation, 9, 40–41, 45
campaign to transfer remains, 44–45
procession, 53–54
public display of body, 46–47, 49–50
as sign of rupture between Ancien Régime and new, 41
Irène, 39, 53
opponents, 58
posthumous triumph, 40
push for honors for by Villette, 38
"rebirth," 55

Westminster Abbey, influence of honoring remains of national heros, 38, 44
Winslow, Jacques Bénigne, 184

Ximènes, Marquis de, 38